The Fine Line

The Fine Line

*Making Distinctions
in Everyday Life*

—

EVIATAR ZERUBAVEL

THE FREE PRESS
A Division of Macmillan, Inc.
NEW YORK

Maxwell Macmillan Canada
TORONTO

Maxwell Macmillan International
NEW YORK   OXFORD   SINGAPORE   SYDNEY

The Free Press
A Division of Macmillan, Inc.
866 Third Avenue, New York, N.Y. 10022

Maxwell Macmillan Canada, Inc.
1200 Eglinton Avenue East
Suite 200
Don Mills, Ontario M3C 3N1

Macmillan, Inc. is part of the Maxwell Communication
Group of Companies.

Printed in the United States of America

printing number
1 2 3 4 5 6 7 8 9 10

Library of Congress Cataloging-in-Publication Data

Zerubavel, Eviatar.
    The fine line: making distinctions in everyday life / Eviatar
Zerubavel.
        p.   cm.
    Includes bibliographical references and index.
    ISBN 0-02-934420-4
    1. Perception.   2. Social perception.   I. Title.
BF311.Z37   1991
302'.12—dc20   91-21867
                                                                          CIP

To Noam,
  who taught me that socks can also be mittens.

There are not many differences in mental habit more significant than that between the habit of thinking in discrete, well-defined class-concepts and that of thinking in terms of continuity, of infinitely delicate shadings-off of everything into something else, of the overlapping of essences.

Arthur O. Lovejoy, The Great Chain of Being

Contents

Preface

My interest in lines and distinctions goes back to 1950, when, as a two-year-old separated for seven months from my mother, I missed the opportunity to go through the normal process of developing a well-articulated self. The inordinate preoccupation with boundaries I consequently developed was further intensified by growing up in Israel in the 1950s, which entailed a most pervasive experience of geographical and political closure.[1] I recall my shock during the Six-Day War as I so casually crossed for the first time the Israel-Egypt border, which until then had seemed to me virtually uncrossable.

This early interest in boundaries later evolved into an intellectual obsession in college, when I discovered Gestalt psychology and began to appreciate the intimate relation between differentiation and perception, lines and meaning. Then, in graduate school, I was fortunate enough to study with Erving Goffman, who was just completing *Frame Analysis,* a masterful study of our experiential partitioning of reality. The process of drawing lines soon became a major focus of my work on time, as I began to explore the structure of social cycles,[2] the delineation of both sacred and private time,[3] and the differentiation of weekends from weekdays.[4] I slowly realized that I was becoming increasingly interested in the general phenomenon of making distinctions, and by late 1984 began work on the present book.

Before I began writing I had some very fruitful discussions about boundaries with Don Handelman and Lynn Collins. Judith Thomas, Karen Cerulo, Richard Williams, Deborah Wolfe, and Liora Gvion-Rosenberg then read an early draft of the book and gave me some useful preliminary leads. Zali Gurevitch, Barry Schwartz, and Viviana Zelizer read a second draft and provided me with further indispensable feedback. Kai Erikson, Paul DiMaggio, Susan Gal, Christena Nippert-Eng, George Shulman, Robert Zussman, Lee

Clarke, Mark Granovetter, Julie Gricar, Carolyn Williams, Naomi Gerstel, Myron Aronoff, Michele Lamont, Louise Mirrer, Allan Horwitz, and David Halle also read various portions of the manuscript and made many additional invaluable suggestions. I also wish to thank Joyce Seltzer for her considerable editorial help and Mila Sklar and John Kocon for the graphic illustrations. A small grant from Rutgers University's Center for the Critical Analysis of Contemporary Culture helped in obtaining the necessary permission to reproduce the works of art.

I am particularly grateful to Nira Farber and Murray Davis, whose extremely dedicated reading of the manuscript provided me with extensive feedback that I still regard as an author's dream. I also owe special thanks to Susan Spieler for helping sensitize me to the psychological dimension of the process of drawing lines and making distinctions.

My family has been most supportive of the book during the six years it took me to write it. It was the constant encouragement and great enthusiasm about the project of my wife, Yael, throughout this period that gave me much of the moral strength I needed to complete it. My daughter Noga gave me many substantive insights as well as a rare glimpse into our social world as seen by a child. I am also grateful to my son Noam, to whom I dedicate the book, for having taught me some critical lessons about mental flexibility.

Cheltenham, Pennsylvania
March 1991

The Fine Line

Introduction: In the Beginning

In the beginning . . . the earth was unformed and void . . . and God divided the light from the darkness. And God called the light Day, and the darkness He called Night.[1]

The very first act of the Creation was one of dividing. It was through being separated from one another that entities began to emerge. The first day was thus spent on dividing the light from the darkness while the next two were dedicated to separating the waters under the heaven from those above it as well as from the dry land.[2] Indeed, according to Genesis, the first three days of the Creation were devoted exclusively to making distinctions.

Like most cosmogonies, the biblical story of the Creation is an allegorical account of the process through which we normally create order out of chaos. These theories of the origin of the universe almost invariably describe the formation of essences (the heavens, the earth, life) out of a boundless, undifferentiated void.[3] Distinctions, they all tell us, are at the basis of any orderliness.

Separating entities from their surroundings is what allows us to perceive them in the first place. In order to discern any "thing," we must distinguish that which we attend from that which we ignore. Such an inevitable link between differentiation and perception is most apparent in color-blindness tests or camouflage, whereby entities that are not clearly differentiated from their surroundings are practically invisible.[4] It is the fact that it is differentiated from other entities that provides an entity with a distinctive meaning[5] as well as with a distinctive identity that sets it apart from everything else.

The way we cut up the world clearly affects the way we organize our everyday life. The way we divide our surroundings, for example, determines what we notice and what we ignore, what we eat and what we avoid eating. By the same token, the way we classify people determines whom we trust and whom we fear, whom we marry and whom we consider sexually off limits. The way we partition time

1

and space likewise determines when we work and when we rest, where we live and where we never set foot.

Indeed, our entire social order is a product of the ways in which we separate kin from nonkin, moral from immoral, serious from merely playful, and what is ours from what is not. Every class system presupposes a fundamental distinction between personal features that are relevant for placing one in a particular social stratum (for example, occupation, color of skin, amount of formal education) and those that are not (for example, sexual attractiveness, height, intelligence), and any society that wishes to implement a welfare or retirement policy must first distinguish the well-to-do from the needy and those who are fully competent to work from those who are "too old." By the same token, membership in particular social categories qualifies us for, or disqualifies us from, various benefits, exemptions, and jobs.[6] It is the need to distinguish "us" from "them" that likewise generates laws against intermarriage, and the wish to separate mentally the "masculine" from the "feminine" that leads to the genderization of professions and sports.

It is boundaries that help us separate one entity from another: "To classify things is to arrange them in groups . . . separated by clearly determined lines of demarcation. . . . At the bottom of our conception of class there is the idea of a circumscription with fixed and definite outlines."[7] Indeed, the word *define* derives from the Latin word for *boundary,* which is *finis*. To define something is to mark its boundaries,[8] to surround it with a mental fence that separates it from everything else. As evidenced by our failure to notice objects that are not clearly differentiated from their surroundings, it is their boundaries that allow us to perceive "things" at all. These lines play a critical role in the construction of social reality, since only with them do meaningful social entities (families, social classes, nations) emerge out of the flux of human existence. Examining how we draw them is therefore critical to any effort to understand our social order. It also offers us a rare glimpse into the not-so-orderly world that underlies our social world, the proverbial chaos that preceded the Creation.

Boundaries are normally taken for granted[9] and, as such, usually manage to escape our attention. After all, "Nothing evades our attention so persistently as that which is taken for granted. . . . Obvious facts tend to remain invisible."[10] In order to make them more "visible," we must suspend our usual concern with what they separate and focus instead on the process by which we cut up the world and create meaningful entities. In short, we must examine how we actually separate entities from one another, whether it be humans from animals, work from hobby, official from unofficial, or vulgar from refined.

The way we cut up the world in our mind manifests itself in how we construct age, gender, and ethnicity as well as in how we arrange food in supermarkets and books and movies in bookstores and video stores. It is manifested as well in how we divide our homes into separate rooms, and in our sexual taboos. Conventional metaphors such as *closed, detached,* and *clear-cut* similarly reveal how we experience reality as made up of insular entities, while our need to keep such discrete islands of meaning neatly separate from one another is evident from our gut response to ambiguous creatures.

The way we draw lines varies considerably from one society to another as well as across historical periods within the same society. Moreover, their precise location, not to mention their very existence, is often disputed and contested within any given society. Nonetheless, like the child who believes the equator is a real line[11] or the racist who perceives an actual divide separating blacks from whites, we very often experience boundaries as if they were part of nature. Not until he smashes the nurse station's glass do McMurphy's fellow inmates in *One Flew over the Cuckoo's Nest* realize that the wall dividing the sane from the insane is not as inevitable as it seemed.[12]

Several years ago I had a dream in which everything around me was noticeably cracked. After a while, however, as I took off my glasses, all the cracks suddenly disappeared and everything seemed to flow smoothly into everything else. I then looked at my glasses and realized that the cracks were on them! As the dream seems to imply, boundaries are mere artifacts that have little basis in reality. It is we ourselves who create them, and the entities they delineate are, therefore, figments of our own mind. Nonetheless, our entire social order rests on the fact that we regard these fine lines as if they were real.

Things assume a distinctive identity only through being differentiated from other things, and their meaning is always a function of the particular mental compartment in which we place them. Examining how we draw lines will therefore reveal how we give meaning to our environment as well as to ourselves. By throwing light on the way in which we distinguish entities from one another and thereby give them an identity, we can explore the very foundations of our social world, which we normally take for granted.

At a time when political and moral distinctions are constantly blurred—when the international order we have regarded for nearly half a century as a given is virtually collapsing and our definitions of work, art, and gender are in flux—the very notion of a social order is being questioned. At such a point it is therefore critical for us to understand the actual process by which we establish boundaries and make distinctions. How we draw these fine lines will certainly determine the kind of social order we shall have.

1

Islands of Meaning

The first man who, having enclosed a piece of ground, bethought himself of saying "This is mine," and found people simple enough to believe him, was the real founder of civil society.[1]

We transform the natural world into a social one by carving out of it mental chunks we then treat as if they were discrete, totally detached from their surroundings. The way we mark off islands of property is but one example of the general process by which we create meaningful social entities.

In order to endow the things we perceive with meaning, we normally ignore their uniqueness and regard them as typical members of a particular class of objects (a relative, a present), acts (an apology, a crime), or events (a game, a conference).[2] After all, "If each of the many things in the world were taken as distinct, unique, a thing in itself unrelated to any other thing, perception of the world would disintegrate into complete meaninglessness."[3] Indeed, things become meaningful only when placed in some category.[4] A clinical symptom, for instance, is quite meaningless until we find some diagnostic niche (a cold, an allergic reaction) within which to situate and thus make sense of it.[5] Our need to arrange the world around us in categories is so great that, even when we encounter mental odds

5

and ends that do not seem to belong in any conventional category, we nonetheless "bend" them so as to fit them into one anyway,[6] as we usually do with the sexually ambiguous[7] or the truly novel work of art.[8] When such adjustment does not suffice, we even create special categories (avant-garde, others, miscellaneous) for these mental pariahs.

The process of placing the various things we perceive in categories, however, is usually accompanied by a complementary process of separating them from other things. That entails isolating mental entities from the context in which they are experienced and treating them as if they were totally detached from their surroundings.[9] Such discontinuous experience of reality presupposes a fundamental distinction between "figures" and the "ground" within which they are perceptually embedded.[10]

The images of figure and ground, of course, are visual, and vision "is our intellectual sense par excellence. It discriminates and defines. . . . When we open our eyes, a diffuse ambience of sounds and smells yields to a sharply delineated world of objects. . . . Sight gives us a world of discrete objects. . . ."[11] Nonetheless, as evident from any attempt to follow one of the many simultaneous conversations one hears at a party, the inevitable connection between differentiating figures from grounds and the ability to "focus" is not confined to vision alone. Separating things from the context in which they are embedded (decontextualization) is the basic model for mental differentiation in general. Like their visual prototype, all mental entities are experienced as insular "figures" that are sharply differentiated from the ocean surrounding them. To capture fully our phenomenology of the social world, we must first examine, therefore, the way we carve such supposedly discrete islands of meaning out of our experience.

Chunks of Space

The perception of supposedly insular chunks of space is probably the most fundamental manifestation of how we divide reality into islands of meaning. Examining how we partition space, therefore, is an ideal way to start exploring how we partition our social world.

The way we carve out of ecological continuums such as continents and urban settlements supposedly insular countries and neighborhoods is a classic case in point.[12] Despite the fact that Egypt and

Libya or Chinatown and Little Italy are actually contiguous, we nevertheless treat them as if they were discrete. Such discontinuous perception of space is nicely captured by the map shown here, which almost literally lifts Montana out of its actual context. Not only does it represent that state as a discrete three-dimensional chunk jutting out of a flat backdrop, it also portrays both the Missouri River and the Rocky Mountains as if they indeed broke off at its borders.

Spatial partitions clearly divide more than just space. The lines that mark off supposedly insular chunks of space often represent the invisible lines that separate purely mental entities such as nations or ethnic groups from one another, and crossing them serves to articulate passage through such mental partitions. That is why we attribute such great symbolic significance to acts such as trespassing[13] or crossing a picket line and regard the crossing of the Red Sea by the ancient Israelites coming out of Egypt as an act of liberation. That is also why the Berlin Wall could represent the mental separation of democracy from communism and why opening the border between Austria and Hungary in 1989 could serve as a symbolic display of the spirit of glasnost.

Often abstract and highly elusive, mental distinctions need to be concretized. Wearing different sets of clothes, for example, helps substantiate the mental distinction between business and casual or ordinary and festive, just as color coding helps us mentally separate different types of information we put in our notebooks, calendars, or files. Choosing among different variants of a language (such as the one used for speeches and the one used for intimate conversations) likewise helps express the mental contrast between the formal and the informal.[14] In a similar manner, we often use differentiation in space to reinforce mental differentiation. Partitioning our home into separate rooms, for example, helps us compartmentalize our daily activity into separate clusters of functions (eating, resting, playing, cleaning) as well as mentally separate culture (study) from nature (bathroom)[15] or the formal (living room) from the informal (family room). Along similar lines, separate aisles in music stores help reinforce the mental separation of classical and popular music, just as separate floors of department stores help us keep the worlds of men and women separate in our mind. In a similar manner, we express discontinuities among supposedly separate bodies of information by relegating them to separate drawers, newspaper sections, and library floors; and keep different categories of food separate in our mind by assigning them to separate pages of restaurant menus, chapters of-

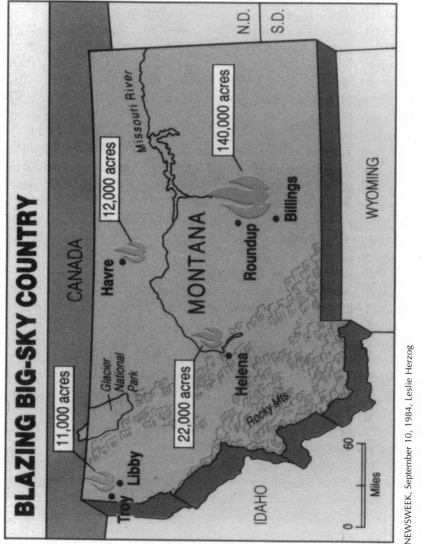

BLAZING BIG-SKY COUNTRY

NEWSWEEK, September 10, 1984, Leslie Herzog

Carving discrete chunks of space out of ecological continuums: a visual representation of the social construction of islands of meaning

cookbooks, aisles of supermarkets, and sections of the refrigerator. Similar forms of zoning help give substance to the mental contrasts between even more abstract entities such as the sacred and the profane,[16] the permitted and the forbidden,[17] the dangerous and the safe, and the good and the evil.[18]

The mental role of spatial partitions is also evident from the way neighborhood boundaries graphically outline rather elusive social class differences.[19] Even more revealing is the way separate bathrooms in the army help articulate status differences between officers and soldiers. The conspicuous absence of doors from rooms we define as public likewise highlights the role of spatial partitions in keeping the private and public spheres separate.[20] "A lock on the door," notes Virginia Woolf in her aptly titled study of privacy and selfhood, *A Room of One's Own,* "means the power to think for oneself."[21] It is the realization that the definition of our selfhood is at stake that makes us so sensitive to the symbolism of having the license to close the door to our room or office.

Blocks of Time

The way we divide time is evocative of the manner in which we partition space. Just as we cut supposedly discrete chunks like countries and school districts off from ecological continuums, we also carve seemingly insular segments such as "the Renaissance" or "adolescence" out of historical continuums. Such discontinuous experience of time is quite evident from the way we isolate from the flow of occurrences supposedly freestanding events such as meetings, classes, and shows, some of which we further subdivide into smaller though still discrete particles—meals into courses, baseball games into innings.[22] It is also manifested in our ability to create stories with beginnings and ends as well as in the way we break down novels, sonatas, and plays into chapters, movements, and acts.

In a similar manner, we isolate in our mind supposedly discrete blocks of time such as centuries, decades, years, months, weeks, and days, thus perceiving actual breaks between "last week" and "this week"[23] or "the fifties" and "the sixties." That is why many of us may not carry over sick days from one year to the next and why officials try to use up their entire budget before the end of the fiscal year. A similar discontinuity between successive tax years also leads some couples to plan the births of their offspring for December, even to the point of inducing those that would naturally have occurred in January.

Central to such discontinuous perception of time is our experience of beginnings, endings, and "turning points." Most revealing in this regard is the sense of conclusion we experience as a performance, picnic, or season is coming to an end,[24] the radical change we expect at the turn of a century or a millennium or even between two contiguous decades, and the experience of a "fresh" start (or "turning over a new leaf") often associated with the beginning of a "new" year. Even in services that operate around the clock, night staff are often expected to allow the day ("first") shift a fresh start with a "clean desk."[25] A pregnant friend of mine who came back to the same clinic that had handled her previous pregnancy within the same year was asked to provide her entire medical history all over again, as she would now be considered a "new" case.

Temporal differentiation helps substantiate elusive mental distinctions. Like their spatial counterparts, temporal boundaries often represent mental partitions and thus serve to divide more than just time. For example, when we create special "holy days," we clearly use time to concretize the mental contrast between the sacred and the profane.[26] In a similar manner, we use it to give substance to the equally elusive contrast between the private and the public domains, using, for example, the boundary of the workday to represent the mental partition between being "on" and "off" duty.[27] Groups likewise use the way they periodize their own history to highlight certain ideological distinctions, as evident, for example, in the Zionist use of "the Exile"[28] or the American use of "the Great Depression" or "Vietnam" as discrete historical eras. The boundaries of the Sabbath, the workday, and "the Vietnam era" clearly represent major mental discontinuities. Like neighborhoods, drawers, and wings of museums, what they define are clearly more than mere chunks of time.

Frames

Temporal differentiation often entails an experience of discontinuity among different sorts of reality as well. Transitions from televised news to commercials or from live coverage to replay, for example, obviously involve more than just breaks in time. Along similar lines, warmup and "real" jumps in long-jump competitions are clearly anchored not only within two distinct blocks of time but also within two separate realms of experience, as are comments made before meetings begin and those included in the official minutes.[29]

Spatial differentiation often entails similar experiential discontinuity. The knight on the chessboard and the glass of water on the table are obviously situated not only within two distinct chunks of space but also within two separate "realities." That is also true of what occurs on and off the stage or inside and outside the picture frame.

Crossing the fine lines separating such experiential realms from one another involves a considerable mental switch from one "style" or mode of experiencing to another, as each realm has a distinctive "accent of reality."[30] At the sound of the bell that signals the end of a boxing match, as brutal punches are instantly transformed into friendly hugs, our entire sense of what is real is dramatically altered. That also happens, of course, when actors enter the stage and are immediately transformed into fictional characters. Picture frames similarly remind viewers that they cannot smell the flowers or eat the apples they see in pictures,[31] as pictorial space is "a structure altogether different from the real space we experience. Within actual space an object can be touched, whereas in a painting it can only be looked at; each portion of real space is experienced as part of an infinite expanse, but the space of a picture is experienced as a self-enclosed world. . . . [The work of art] builds a sovereign realm."[32]

It is precisely that quality that makes frames the ideal prototype of all boundaries delineating the various realms of our experience,[33] those mental lines that separate ordinary reality from the "worlds" of art, dream, play, and symbolism as well as off-the-record from official statements, parenthetical from ordinary remarks,[34] the metaphoric from the literal, satire from sheer slander, commentary from pure coverage, parody from plagiarism, and maneuvers from actual war. Framing is the act of surrounding situations, acts, or objects with mental brackets[35] that basically transform their meaning by defining them as a game, a joke, a symbol, or a fantasy. Play, for example, is actually "a name for contexts in which the constituent acts have a different sort of relevance . . . from that which they would have had in non-play. . . . The essence of play lies in a partial denial of the meanings that the actions would have had in other situations."[36]

A frame is characterized not by its contents but rather by the distinctive way in which it transforms the contents' meaning. The way framing helps de-eroticize what we normally consider sexual is quite suggestive of the remarkable transformational capacity of frames. The party frame, for example, allows even perfect strangers to hold one another while moving together in a pronounced rhythmic fashion (though only while the music is playing).[37] In a similar manner, in the context of art, respectability is granted to otherwise obscene literary passages and poetic metaphors as well as to nude modeling and photography,[38] just as the play frame helps de-eroticize games such as "house" and "doctor." Ordinary sexual meanings are likewise antisepticized by science, which allows genital display in anatomy books, and medicine, which de-eroticizes mouth-to-mouth resuscitation and gynecological examinations.[39]

In cutting chunks of experience off from their surroundings, frames obviously define not only different but also separate realms of experience. In delineating a space which the viewer cannot enter, picture frames, for example, "[cut] the artist's statement off from the room in which it is hung,"[40] thus visually articulating an experiential cleavage between ordinary reality and the artistic realm.[41] Supposedly bounded, experiential realms do not spill over into one another,[42] and the "reality" of any object is therefore always confined to the boundaries of the particular frame within which it is situated. That is why it is so difficult to prolong a dream after waking up or to sustain an erotic experience when someone knocks on the door, as well as why we normally do not hold others responsible for any harm they may have caused us in our fantasies. Along similar lines, terrified as we are by Captain Hook, Darth Vader, or the Wicked Witch of the West when we read about them or watch them on the screen, we nonetheless know that they can never step out of the fictional frames in which they belong and therefore cannot really hurt us.

Picture frames also make us disregard the wall surrounding the picture.[43] Like them, all frames basically define parts of our perceptual environment as irrelevant, thus separating that which we attend in a focused manner from all the out-of-frame experience[44] that we leave "in the background" and ignore. Thus, for example, when we play checkers, the material of which the pieces are made is considered totally irrelevant to the game and, therefore, out of frame. In fact, when a piece is missing, we often replace it with a coin, totally disregarding the latter's ordinary monetary value. Likewise, within an erotic context, we normally perceive others as attractive or not, ignoring ordinary distinctions based on social class, status, or ethnic origin.[45]

Moreover, frames make us ignore entire acts or objects despite their obvious physical presence in the situation. At concerts, for example, we usually disregard such acts as replacing a mouthpiece or wiping spittle off one's horn, which are clearly not part of the framed performance in which they are visually embedded. We likewise ignore "background" activity such as nail biting or doodling at meetings and routinely skip page numbers and translators' notes when reading books.[46] And just as we exclude from the game frame such accidents as unintentionally knocking a piece off the chessboard (in sharp contrast to removing deliberately a captured piece), we also instruct jurors to ignore "unacceptable" evidence presented to them.

The experiential discontinuity between what is situated "inside" and "outside" frames also applies to human objects, as mere presence at a social situation may not always guarantee inclusion in the frame surrounding it.[47] In social gatherings, full-fledged participants are often surrounded by a mental partition[48] that keeps mere bystanders practically "out of focus." (Such discontinuity becomes apparent when we poke fun at those who laugh at jokes that were not addressed to them or when cardplayers scold kibitzers who offer unsolicited advice: "Who asked you, anyway?")[49] Cabdrivers, waiters, stenographers, and children are often assigned such out-of-frame status. So are technicians installing equipment at rock concerts, attendants who clean after the animals at circuses, food vendors at sports events, and photographers at weddings, all of whom are clearly situated outside the entertainment frame that surrounds everyone else. Despite their obvious physical presence at these situations, they are considered "non-persons"[50] and thus relegated to the out-of-frame "background." That is also why we sometimes fail to notice the very presence of those we assume do not understand the language we speak or the topic we discuss.[51]

Chunks of Identity

The manner in which we isolate supposedly discrete "figures" from their surrounding "ground" is also manifested in the way we come to experience ourselves.[52] It involves a form of mental differentiation that entails a fundamental distinction between us and the rest of the world. It is known as our sense of identity.

The most obvious form of identity is the experience of an insular self that is clearly cut off from one's surrounding environment,[53] a

self with "clear and sharp lines of demarcation" that we experience as
autonomous and "marked off distinctly from everything else."[54]
Such self presupposes the experience of some "ego boundary"[55] that
marks the "edge" of our personhood,[56] the point where we end and
the rest of the world begins. Such boundary is at the heart of the
fundamental experiential separation of what is "inside" the self from
what lies "outside" it.[57]

The experience of a self presupposes some "psychological division from the rest of the world."[58] It is a product of a long process
that begins when, as infants, we psychologically disengage ("hatch")
from our initial "symbiotic" relationship with our most immediate
other, usually our mother.[59] As a result of such process of individuation, we withdraw from a somewhat fluid reality into one where
the self as well as other individuals with sharp and firm contours
seem to emerge as discrete entities that are clearly separate from their
environment.[60]

The self is but one particular focus of identity. There are many
other answers to the existential question of where we end and the rest
of the world begins, and they all involve supposedly bounded clusters of individuals (a family, a profession, a political party, a nation)
who experience themselves collectively—and are usually perceived
by others—as insular entities[61] clearly separate from everyone else.
In short, we experience ourselves not only as "I" but also collectively
as "we," that is, as liberals, baseball fans, Muslims, women, humans. It is such perceptions of social clusters as discrete entities that
lead us to regard a marriage between a Christian and a Jew or an
Armenian and a Pole as "mixed."

The experience of such discrete entities presupposes a perception of some boundaries surrounding them.[62] Even a couple going
steady experiences some clear partition separating them from others around them.[63] Such fine mental lines help us perceive a fundamental discontinuity between insiders and outsiders, those
included in a social cluster and those who are left outside its confines. Only in relation to those lines do sentiments such as fidelity,
loyalty, or patriotism, for example, evolve, and only in relation to
them do we learn whom we can trust and of whom we should
beware, who is available to us as a sexual partner and whom we
must avoid. These are the boundaries that basically define the mental entities we come to experience as "us" and "them." They constitute the basis of our sense of identity and determine much of the
scope of our social relations.

Mental Fields

Early in life space is the only mode available for organizing a self.[64] Indeed, our individuation begins with the development of locomotor functions such as crawling, which allow us to literally withdraw from others.[65] Later we establish some nonspatial sense of selfhood,[66] actualizing our separateness by acts such as saying no[67] and experiences such as ownership of toys, yet the basic way in which we experience the self and its relations with others remains spatial nonetheless. We thus associate selfhood with a psychological "distance" from others[68] and experience privacy (including its nonspatial aspects, such as secrecy) as having some "space" for ourselves or as a "territory" of inaccessibility surrounding us.[69] We experience others as being "close" to or "distant" from us and portray our willingness or unwillingness to make contact with them using topological images such as "opening up" (or "reaching out") and being "closed" (or "removed").[70] We also use the image of "penetration" to depict the essence of the process of becoming intimate.[71]

Similar spatial imagery captures our experience of groups as bounded, "closed"[72] entities that one almost literally "enters" and "exits."[73] We thus "*in*corporate" members into, "*ex*pel" them from, and assign them "central" or "marginal" places in groups. We also use images such as "*extra*marital" (or "*out of* wedlock"), "mobility,"[74] and "knows his place"; perceive actual social "distance"[75] between blacks and whites or senior and junior executives; and mentally locate "distant" relatives in terms of the number of "steps" they are "removed" from us.[76] Such mental geography has no physical basis but we experience it as if it did.

We likewise use spatial images to depict supposedly discrete chunks of professional jurisdiction (boundary, turf, territory, arena)[77] as well as knowledge. We thus perceive academic disciplines as surrounded by mental "walls"[78] and works as lying on the "fringes" of sociology or outside our "area" of expertise, and regard those whose interest does not transcend the confines of their "field" as "limited" or "narrow minded." Similar spatial imagery seems to underlie our perception of the *extra*curricular, *extra*judicial, and *eso*teric as well as of insular "domains" such as work, religion, or art.

Somewhat similar is our experience of the fine mental lines that separate acceptable from unacceptable behavior—the assertive from the rude, the funny from the crude. We basically "confine [ourselves]

to a particular radius of activity and . . . regard any conduct which
drifts outside that radius as somehow inappropriate or immoral. . . .
Human behavior can vary over an enormous range, but each community draws a symbolic set of parentheses around a certain segment
of that range and limits its own activities within that narrower
zone."[79] Our quasi-spatial experience of such "normative outlines"
of society[80] is quite evident from our use of verbs such as "*transgress*" or "*ex*ceed" (which literally mean to step or go beyond),
prefixes such as "over-" (as in "*over*ambitious"), "out-" (as in "*out-
law*"), or "extra-" (as in "*extra*vagant"), and metaphors such as "line
of decency"[81] or "limits of authority."

In a somewhat similar manner, we also "enter" conversations,
go "out of" business, portray breakthroughs as the crossing of a
Rubicon[82] or a forbidden frontier,[83] and can appreciate a cartoon
depicting someone reaching a line demarcated by the sign "Boundary of Self Respect."[84] Similar spatial imagery also underlies such
concepts as "*extra*ordinary," "*out*standing," or "*ex*otic."

Spatial metaphors pervade much of our thinking.[85] In a wide
variety of contexts, we use them to depict purely mental relations
among entities. In fact, we basically experience reality as a "space"[86]
made up of discrete mental fields delineated by mental "fences"[87]
that define[88] and separate them from one another. Given the significance of proximity in perceptual grouping (the closer things are to
one another, the more we tend to perceive them as a single entity[89]),
we use closeness as a metaphor for conceptual similarity,[90] essentially seeing difference in terms of mental distance.[91] We thus consider similar mental items as belonging "together"[92] and different
ones as being "worlds apart," and we may even try to locate an item
"exactly halfway" between two others.[93]

A foremost prerequisite for differentiating any entity from its
surrounding environment are exceptionally strong intra-entity
relations.[94] A mental field is basically a cluster of items that are more
similar to one another than to any other item. Generating such fields,
therefore, usually involves some lumping. As we group items in our
mind (that is, categorize the world), we let their similarity outweigh
any differences among them. As a result we perceive mental fields as
relatively homogeneous lumps and regard their constituent items as
functionally interchangeable variants ("allo-" variants) of a single
unit of meaning.[95] Even when we notice differences among them,
we dismiss them as totally irrelevant[96]—"making no difference"—
and consequently ignore them.

Thus, despite the obvious differences among them, we regard the prefixes of the adjectives "*in*accurate," "*im*proper," "*dis*honest," and "*un*usual" as functionally equivalent variants of a single morpheme.[97] We regard them as basically "the same" because no confusion of meaning is likely to occur if one of them is substituted for another (that is, if we say "disaccurate" or "unproper"). Nor do we normally attribute much significance to the difference between right-eye and left-eye winks, which we perceive as functionally interchangeable variants of a single gesture,[98] or between a kiss and an affectionate look, which we often substitute for each other as tokens of intimacy.[99] Along similar lines, we usually ignore the obvious difference between 490- and 540-millimicron-long light waves, regarding both as variants of the color "green,"[100] and casually substitute pretzels for potato chips as party snacks. And though clearly aware of the difference between thirty-one- and twenty-eight-day blocks of time, we nonetheless regard both as structurally equivalent variants of the unit "month"[101] and expect identical monthly paychecks for January and February. Along similar lines, we usually perceive conventional historical periods as relatively homogeneous stretches, often lumping together events that occurred centuries apart from one another yet within the same "period" (as in "the Middle Ages").[102]

In a similar manner, we establish social clusters in our mind by regarding all cluster members as similar and ignoring all differences among them, as when we lump together all those whose income falls below a certain "poverty line" as an undifferentiated lot—"the poor." We generally tend to downplay differences within our own group as well as among others,[103] as evident from the extremely broad categories ("Orientals") in which we lump those who came to America[104] or from various catchall categories for outsiders, such as the ancient Greek "barbarian," the Armenian *odar*,[105] the Gypsy *gadjo*, or the Jewish *goy*.

Ignoring intracluster differences and regarding all cluster members as basically "the same" often results in stereotypes, as when racists claim that all blacks are lazy or that all Orientals look alike. Nonetheless, without some lumping, it would be impossible ever to experience any collectivity, or mental entity for that matter. The ability to ignore the uniqueness of items and regard them as typical members of categories is a prerequisite for classifying any group of phenomena. Such ability to "typify"[106] our experience is therefore one of the cornerstones of social reality.

Ritual Transitions

Most of the fine lines that separate mental entities from one another are drawn only in our own head and, therefore, totally invisible. And yet, by playing up the act of "crossing" them, we can make mental discontinuities more "tangible." Many rituals, indeed, are designed specifically to substantiate the mental segmentation of reality into discrete chunks. In articulating our "passage" through the mental partitions separating these chunks from one another, such rituals, originally identified by Arnold Van Gennep as "rites of passage,"[107] certainly enhance our experience of discontinuity.

The various rites we perform when we cross the equator, tropic of Cancer, or arctic circle[108] are perfect cases in point. In dramatizing our passage through these imaginary lines that exist only on maps, they certainly make them more "tangible" (somewhat like the road sign Welcome to Massachusetts). In a similar manner, we also dramatize the mental discontinuity between the public and private domains by knocking on the door before entering a room as well as by altering our appearance, as in the following caricature of a stereotypical return home, "from 'a hard day at the office': a banal scene in which the social passage is signified by the man successively removing his hat . . . taking off his jacket, stripping away his tie (exaggerated gesture), opening his shirt collar. . . . A whole set of statements about the contrast between [home] and the 'larger world' is going on."[109] Along similar lines, soldiers coming home even for a few hours often change into civilian clothes just to actualize their "exit" from the military world. Lowering their voices on entering church similarly helps congregants substantiate the mental separation of the sacred from the profane, whereas the ritual apology ("I beg your pardon") we offer on entering each other's "personal space" likewise promotes our experience of an insular self.

In a similar manner, weddings substantiate the boundaries of the family, whose crossing transforms people into spouses and in-laws. They also signal, of course, the crossing of the mental partition that separates marriage from singlehood, just like puberty rites[110] (or modern equivalents such as obtaining a driver's license or going for the first time to an R-rated film), which dramatize the transition from childhood to adulthood. (The fact that we rarely celebrate divorces and usually articulate second weddings considerably less than first ones suggests that entering marriage entails a much greater break in identity than exiting or reentering it.) In dramatizing the moments of entering and exiting it, birth and death rituals[111] like-wise substantiate the experience of life as a discrete block of time (as well as the mental contrast between life and nonlife). The need to substantiate the way we segment time into discrete blocks also ac-counts for the holidays we create to commemorate critical transition points between historical epochs[112] as well as for the rituals we de-sign to articulate significant changes in our relative access to one another—greetings, first kisses, farewell parties, bedtime stories.[113] Changes of lighting or background music likewise signal transitions among successive segments of theatrical performances, films,[114] rock concerts, and circus shows, whereas ritual switches from sitting to standing help to "punctuate" religious services[115] and demarcate fea-tured solos in jazz.

The ritual of raising the curtain before the beginning of a show[116] and the almost obligatory "once upon a time" or "and they lived happily ever after"[117] that signal crossings of the line separating fairy tales from "real" life similarly serve to substantiate the boundaries of frames.[118] So do the ritual glove touch or kickoff that prefaces sports events, the suspension of meter that signals the dissolution of the poetic frame,[119] and the caption "The End" that used to announce the conclusion of films. (Within films, conventional cues such as soft focus, overexposure, change from color to black and white, and suspension of background music often signal transitions from char-acters' here and now into their memories, fantasies, or dreams.) Along similar lines, organ preludes are often used to announce a religious frame,[120] "soft" music (and candlelight) a romantic frame, and dance music (and hors d'oeuvres) a party.

By switching from one language to another or even from stan-dard to colloquial speech, we often articulate transitions from for-mality to informality or from just talking to quoting.[121] In a similar manner, speakers often clear their throats to announce the conclusion of their informal introductory remarks (just as chairpersons use gav-els to announce the formal parts of meetings), change their tone to signal diversions from the general thrust of their talk to "parenthet-ical" remarks, and sit down to announce the beginning of the more informal question-and-answer part.[122] Children likewise use a change of voice to "enter" the make-believe frame[123] and the ritual call "Time" to exit from a game in order to tie a loose shoelace or get a drink.

Along similar lines, by punishing deviants who transgress its moral boundaries, society not only forces us to see that such lines do indeed exist but also demarcates their precise "location." Like weddings, funerals, and bedtime stories, punishment is a ritual that dramatizes the act of crossing some mental partition. In substantiating the mental segmentation of human behavior into acceptable and unacceptable, it serves to "locate and publicize"[124] moral edges:

> The deviant is a person whose activities have moved outside the margins of the group, and when the community calls him to account for that vagrancy it is making a statement about the nature and placement of its boundaries. . . . Members of a community inform one another about the placement of their boundaries by participating in the confrontations which occur when persons who venture out to the edges of the group are met by policing agents. . . . Whether these confrontations take the form of criminal trials, excommunication hearings, courts-martial, or even psychiatric case conferences, they [demonstrate] where the line is drawn. . . . Morality and immorality meet at the public scaffold, and it is during this meeting that the line between them is drawn. . . . Each time the community moves to censure some act of deviation, then, and convenes a formal ceremony to deal with the responsible offender, it . . . restates where the boundaries of the group are located.[125]

Moral boundaries remain a meaningful point of reference, of course, only as long as society indeed curbs all attempts to transgress them.[126] When society fails to punish deviants who venture beyond the limit of what it defines as acceptable, members will wonder whether such a line really exists.

Only the need to announce crossings of frame boundaries prompts us to indent quotations like the one above on a page of text[127] and only the need to substantiate an insular self compels us to say grace before we ingest parts of the environment into our body through the act of eating. Substantiating the insularity of conventional chunks of space, time, and identity is likewise the only reason for the rites we perform around doorsills,[128] the birthday cards[129] and New Year midnight kisses with which we "punctuate" life as well as history, and the various initiation rites (such as baptism, adoption, and naturalization) by which we dramatize the incorporation of new members into religious communities, families, or nations. Such rituals of "passage" are all products of some basic need to substantiate in our acts the mental discontinuities we perceive in our mind. As such, they play a major role in our ability to think analytically.

2

—

The Great Divide

That's one small step for man, one giant leap for mankind.[1]

Mental Gaps

Creating islands of meaning entails two rather different mental processes—lumping and splitting. On the other hand, it involves grouping "similar" items together in a single mental cluster—sculptors and filmmakers ("artists"), murder and arson ("felonies"), foxes and camels ("animals"). At the same time, it also involves separating in our mind "different" mental clusters from one another—artists from scientists, felonies from misdemeanors, animals from humans. In order to carve out of the flux surrounding us meaningful entities with distinctive identities, we must experience them as separate from one another.

Separating one island of meaning from another entails the introduction of some mental void between them. As we carve discrete mental chunks out of continuous streams of experience, we normally visualize substantial gaps separating them from one another.[2] Such mental versions of the great divides that split continuous stretches of land following geological upheavals underlie our basic experience of mental entities as situated amid blank stretches of emptiness. It is our perception of the void among these islands of meaning that makes

21

them separate in our mind, and its magnitude reflects the degree of separateness we perceive among them.[3]

Gaps are critical to our ability to experience insular entities. The experiential separateness of the self, for example, is clearly enhanced by the actual gap of "personal space"[4] that normally envelops it.[5] By literally insulating the self from contact with others, such a gap certainly promotes its experience as an insular entity. A similar experience of an island situated in a vacuum often leads us to confine our horizons to, and never venture beyond, our neighborhood,[6] hometown, or country. The great divides we visualize between women and men, children and adults, and blacks and whites[7] likewise promote our perception of such entities as discrete.

Mental gaps are often represented by token partitions. Like the ancient Assyrians, who used mere doorways to demarcate the borders of their empire,[8] we often use a partial wall or a column to create the illusion of a discrete work space or sitting area in a room.[9] And like the ancient Egyptians, who used cartouches to cut off visually the names of monarchs from the rest of the text in which they were embedded, thus substantiating the social gulf that separated royalty from ordinary folk, we often use lines to portray the mental gap between news and commercial ads in newspapers.

Often, however, we represent mental gaps quite literally by blank spaces. When we wish not only to rank entities but also to portray the relative magnitude of the mental distances among them,[10] a visual representation of the latter is of considerable help. I recall, for example, my eight-year-old daughter ranking her favorite restaurants and finding it necessary to "leave some space" between the first two and the third. The ability to visualize mental gaps is even more critical, of course, when we wish to depict the precise magnitude of such intervals.

A blank page at the end of a book similarly helps readers visualize the mental gap separating its framed contents from ordinary reality.[11] So do the blank spaces separating cartoons from other printed matter in magazines[12] and footnotes from ordinary text. The discreteness of categories such as "fruits," "vegetables," and "dairy products" is likewise implied by the blank spaces separating clusters of items on our shopping lists. Such spaces are clearly designed to substantiate the mental gaps they represent, thus making supposedly discrete mental fields more "visible."[13]

As evident from the way we usually leave the days immediately preceding or following the calendar month on wall calendars blank, as if they did not exist, blank spaces also help visualize discrete blocks of time. The experiential void separating such blocks from one another is usually designed to represent a mental gap, as when we break a book or a report into separate chapters or sections or indent new paragraphs to announce mental breaks among supposedly discrete clusters of ideas. The use of pauses as mental punctuation devices is even more evident in poetry. Not only do poets use blank spaces to represent actual pauses between stanzas. Some of them (for example, Stéphane Mallarmé) also allow considerable gaps between and even within lines as well as specify the exact amount of pausing they expect at various junctures of the poem.[14]

The somewhat similar "broken" phrasing so characteristic of the music of Anton Webern[15] or Miles Davis also demonstrates the role of silence (or "dead" space) in substantiating the mental void so critical to the experience of discontinuity. Silence also serves to feature discrete segments within theatrical and musical performances, and its visual counterpart, darkness, likewise helps delineate discrete scenes within films.[16] Moreover, the darkness that precedes the initial raising of the curtain in the traditional theater or the silence that precedes musical performances certainly highlights the discrete nature of the entire play or recital.

Often, however, we need more than a blank space or silence to substantiate mental gaps. Along with the rites of passage that help us articulate transitions from one mental entity to another, we also use various "rites of separation"[17] to highlight the gaps we visualize among them. Holidays, reunions, and parties, for example, inevitably dramatize the mental gap separating members who are invited to participate from nonmembers who are excluded. In so doing, they clearly promote our experience of ethnic groups, families,[18] and fraternities as insular entities.

Rites of separation are often designed to dramatize the mental gap between the old and new selves of people whose social identity is radically transformed as a result of crossing some critical mental partition.[19] Thus, for example, as they go through basic military training (in which they become soldiers), puberty rites (in which they officially become adults),[20] and initiations into monastic orders (in which they are symbolically transformed into brides of Christ), recruits, children, and ordinary girls practically undergo a symbolic death. To dramatize the considerable mental gaps (separating civilians from soldiers, childhood from adulthood, and so on) involved in such transformations, they must ritually destroy their old self

before they can assume their new identity. Men about to be married
thus attend bachelor parties given by their old friends,[21] newly en-
listed soldiers relinquish their civilian clothes and much of their
hair,[22] and new nuns renounce their entire former life. A ritual name
change helps monks, converts, slaves,[23] brides, and adoptees articulate similar symbolic metamorphoses and dramatize the gap between their old identity and the new one.

Similar rites of separation help substantiate radical transformations of collective identity. Thus, for example, as they cross the
mental gap separating political subordination from independence,
nations often change their name—from Basutoland to Lesotho, from
Dutch Guiana to Suriname. They likewise dramatize various critical
political transformations by changing their official calendar[24] or flag.
In order to dramatize the sharp symbolic break between their former
life in exile and current life in their homeland, Israelis similarly often
adopt Hebrew names instead of their birth names (and, in their
literature, often portray the native-born *sabra* as an orphan[25]).

Mental Quantum Leaps

Rites of separation help us dramatize the considerable magnitude
of the mental gaps we create. Though practically empty, the void we
visualize among mental entities is nonetheless experienced as substantial. Crossing it therefore requires a significant mental effort and
often involves giant mental quantum leaps.[26]

We generally become aware of boundedness and separateness
long before we learn to pay attention to distance. It is often assumed
that such a rudimentary "topological" mode of perceiving space is
later completely replaced by a "metric" awareness of distance.[27] In
fact, we never really lose it entirely and basically continue to experience space "metrically" as well as "topologically."

The topological layout of space inevitably distorts our ordinary
perception of distance. Most significantly, it leads us mentally to
inflate distances across boundaries; that is, between points that are
located in supposedly separate chunks of space—cities in different
states, buildings on separate blocks, and so on.[28] A very short trip is
thus perceived as monumental if it involves crossing some critical
mental divide: "For the well-traveled Pope John Paul II, this was the
shortest of trips—just across the river Tiber, about a mile from the
Vatican. Symbolically, however, the pontiff's visit to Rome's central

synagogue was a grand gesture, aimed at erasing nearly 2,000 years of enmity between Roman Catholics and Jews."[29] Crossing the critical symbolic (rather than just physical) divide separating our planet from the rest of the universe similarly transformed Neil Armstrong's first small step on the moon, the first ever made by a human on extraterrestrial land, into a "giant leap for mankind," while the mental gaps separating religious temples from their immediate surroundings likewise transform physically negligible steps across their thresholds into considerable mental leaps from the profane into the sacred.

Such a tendency to mentally "stretch" distances across boundaries often overrides even the ubiquitous "law of proximity"[30] that normally leads us to perceive things that are close to one another as parts of a single entity. Given the gaps we visualize among supposedly discrete chunks of space, we often experience even infinitesimal distances across them (such as between points B and C in the illustration on p.26) as considerably greater than much longer distances between points that are located within the same chunk (such as A and B). Thus, for example, given our common perception of rooms as insular, we can expect professors, who during class often cross quite casually the twenty-foot distance between the window and the door, not to make the mere two-foot step across the latter into the hallway. A somewhat similar result of perceiving any two points in the Americas as inevitably closer to one another than to any third point in another continent, namely a misperception of Santiago as closer to New York than Moscow, likewise led some Americans in the early 1970s to fear Chile's Salvador Allende, even more than Leonid Brezhnev, as a Marxist "on the U.S.A.'s doorstep."[31]

Given the way we experience minuscule physical distances across boundaries as wide mental divides, even the thinnest partition (for example, a tent) nonetheless serves as an insulation device and is, therefore, vital for our sense of privacy. By merely closing the door behind me when I enter the bathroom, I surround myself with an "envelope" of privacy that not even a thirty-foot distance from others could offer me. Indeed, those who cherish privacy often prefer a small office with a door over a larger, but exposed, work space. Thin but soundproof walls allow siblings to lead relatively insular lives in their rooms, and participants in conferences to attend entirely separate sessions while sitting only a few feet away from one another, separated by a wall. Furthermore, our ability to carry on a conversation in a crowded subway or a party suggests that even purely

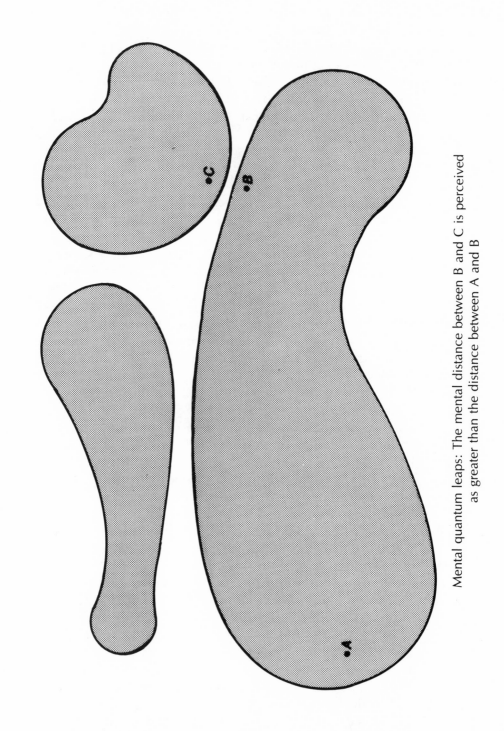

Mental quantum leaps: The mental distance between B and C is perceived as greater than the distance between A and B

social "walls" nonetheless provide the illusion of insulated pockets of privacy,[32] which is how we also come to experience the ten-foot distance from others sitting at our table in a restaurant as somehow shorter than the mere one-foot distance separating us from the waiter who is refilling our glass.

Our fundamentally topological perception of the world also distorts our experience of purely mental "distances." Partly a mental phenomenon,[33] distance is greatly affected by mental processes such as lumping and splitting. Whereas lumping involves playing down mental distances within entities, splitting entails widening the perceived gaps between entities so as to reinforce their mental separateness. Thus, while deliberately ignoring differences within mental clusters, we also pay special attention to differences between clusters. As a result, we often inflate "distances" across mental divides and perceive them as greater than even longer distances within the same entity.

Thus, despite the fact that the actual rest we take between appetizer and entrée is often shorter than those we take within each of them, stretching it mentally helps us experience appetizers as a discrete course. By the same token, on Monday we perceive the following Friday, which is four days away, as part of this week yet the preceding one, which is only three days away, as part of last week (and place it, accordingly, on a separate page of our appointment book).[34] Given the gaps we visualize between calendar months,[35] we likewise experience the interval from June 30 to July 1 as significantly longer than the one from July 1 to July 2[36] (just as we experience our thirty-ninth and fortieth birthdays as "light-years apart"[37]).

This also affects the way we mentally cluster people. The otherwise negligible difference between being born on November 21 or November 22, for example, involves a significant difference between being a Scorpio or a Sagittarius. By the same token, the mere one-year gap separating "undergraduate" seniors from entering "graduate" students often seems wider than the three-year distance between seniors and freshmen.

In order to accommodate our experience of some fundamental difference between "us" and "them," we likewise exaggerate in our mind "distances" across mental divides separating families, ethnic groups, religious denominations, races, species, and other chunks of identity from one another.[38] For example, in order to solidify our perceived distinctiveness as humans, we routinely "[lump] together beings as different as oysters and chimpanzees, while placing a gulf between chimpanzees and humans, although our relationship to those apes is much closer than the oyster's."[39] Experiencing such quantum leaps from outsiderhood to membership clearly enhances our ability to visualize the sharp divides separating supposedly discrete chunks of identity from one another.

By the same token, we also perceive four-star hotels as markedly different from their three-star relatives. The gap we perceive between these two supposedly discrete categories of quality is similar to the one athletes experience as separating various "levels" of achievement in sport.[40] For similar reasons, while clearly inferior to Herb Elliott's 3:54.5 run four years later in absolute terms as well as in the fact that it broke the existing world record by only 2.0 (as compared to 2.7) seconds, Roger Bannister's famous 3:59.4 mile run —which involved the first breaking of the legendary four-minute-mile "barrier"—nonetheless sank much deeper into our memory. Such a tendency to play up "distances" across mental divides also explains the willingness to pay $9.95 for products one might not purchase for $10.00.

Mental Images and Social Reality

There is a joke about a man whose house stood right on the Russian-Polish border. When it was finally decided that it was actually in Poland, he cried out: "Hooray. Now I don't have to go through those terrible Russian winters any more!"[41] His naive expectation that even nature would acknowledge the reality of the purely mental divide separating Poland from Russia reminds one of the little boy who expects nature to respect the mental gaps we visualize between purely conventional blocks of time and to make all June bugs, for example, totally disappear by the very first day of the month of July.[42] A similar attribution of naturalness to merely mental divides is made by those of us who expect to be almost magically transformed on purely conventional "critical" days such as our tenth or fortieth birthdays.[43] I still recall my daughter's disappointment the day she turned five, as she looked in the mirror and realized that she did not look any different from the day before.

Such reification[44] of the purely conventional is a result of our tendency to regard the merely social as natural. Despite the fact that they are virtually mental, most gaps—as well as the quantum leaps necessary for crossing them—are among the seemingly inevitable institutionalized "social facts"[45] that constitute our social reality. As such, they are in fact "real" in more than just an experiential sense, which explains how we come to perceive the insularity of purely mental entities as a natural, rather than a merely conventional, fact.

There is a good reason why we experience mental divides as part of nature, thereby reifying the purely mental quantum leaps we make across them and perceiving Nice as closer to other places in France than to Italy[46] and Houston as closer to Phoenix than to Mexico City. After all, it is in fact a lot easier for someone in Leningrad to arrange a seven-thousand-mile trip to Vladivostok than a mere two-hundred-mile excursion across the Soviet-Finnish border to Helsinki. Classic border-crossing scenes from Tony Richardson's *The Border*, Gregory Nava's *El Norte*, Alfred Hitchcock's *Torn Curtain*, and dozens of World War II films demonstrate time and again how the few feet right across Mexico's or Germany's borders have in fact been far more critical as well as resistant to refugees than the few miles before them. Scores of American detective novels likewise remind us how a mere step across a state line can instantaneously catapult fugitives from one legal reality into an entirely different one.

The gaps underlying such dramatic quantum leaps are clearly more than just mental figments. Those separating neighboring townships from one another, for example, are often responsible for considerable jumps in actual housing prices and property taxes from one block to the next. As a result of such gaps, children living just across the street from one another sometimes end up in separate schools, often of very different quality (which they attend together with other children who live miles away yet within the same school district). The gaps we perceive between contiguous time zones offer a similar illustration of the very real consequences of the way we "stretch" distances across mental divides. Despite the fact that they are only thirty miles away from each other, South Bend is actually a full hour "ahead of" Michigan City. The gap we perceive between a soccer field and its immediate surroundings likewise underlies the official exclusion of coaches sitting only a few feet outside the field from a game that at the same time includes two goalies standing three hundred feet away from one another.

Every long jumper expects an attempt that involves even a trifle half-inch transgression of the jumping board to be automatically disqualified, and every motorist is similarly aware of the very real consequences of stopping even one foot past a stop line at a street crossing. As he drew his famous "line of death" at the entrance to the

Gulf of Sidra, Libya's Muammar Qaddafi was basically asserting
what is known by any child who provocatively draws a line in the
dirt and dares his opponents to cross it, namely that crossing boundaries is a real, consequential act that usually takes place not only in
the mind.

Along similar lines, given the way we mentally inflate "distances" across the gaps we perceive among supposedly discrete
blocks of time, students often risk getting a lower grade when they
turn in a paper even a single day past a given deadline. By the same
token, hospitals usually bill patients a full extra day for staying even
a couple of hours beyond the end of the official billing day. They also
treat temporal distances between contiguous but separate workdays
as longer than mathematically identical intervals within the same
workday, thus officially regarding the eight-hour interval between
nurses' evening and following day shifts, for example, as somehow
longer than the eight-hour interval between their day and following
night shifts. As a result, though they may very well work on the
evening shift and eight hours later again on the day shift, nurses,
officially prohibited from working more than eight hours "a day,"
may not work on the day shift and eight hours later again on the
night shift (unless, of course, they work, and are paid, "over-
time").[47]

The social reality of the gaps that separate supposedly discrete
blocks of time from one another is also evident from the jerky—
almost convulsive—manner in which we officially move from one
phase of our existence on to the next, as illustrated, for example, by
the way society normally transforms mathematically negligible steps
across conventional cutoff points in time into critical quantum leaps
in "age." The minuscule interval separating the day immediately
preceding my twenty-sixth birthday from the birthday itself is in fact
far more critical than the 364-day interval that follows the latter as it
entails making a full-year quantum leap from being officially twenty-
five to being officially twenty-six. (By contrast, despite the fact that
we age continuously, we perceive time as actually stopping for a full
year between birthdays and regard a person as being twenty-five
until the day before his or her twenty-sixth birthday.) The practical
implications of such a manner of reckoning age can hardly be over-
stated, as evidenced by the way we actually cluster schoolchildren in
discrete classes separated from one another by full-year gaps. A child
born on January 1 must usually wait a full year longer than a child
born only a couple of hours earlier, on December 31, before he or she

can enter school. In much the same way, a 1991 car normally costs significantly more than a virtually identical 1990 model produced only a few days earlier.[48] Such actual quantum leaps are even more dramatic as one crosses the mental divides associated with particularly critical birthdays. A single day is officially regarded as significantly longer than even several years when it entails crossing any of the birthdays on which one *suddenly* becomes legally eligible to drink in a bar, obtain a driver's license, vote, join the army, run for office, or retire and receive a pension.[49] As a result, eighteen-year-old "adults" are often regarded by the law as somehow "closer" to sixty-one-year-olds than to seventeen-year-old "minors." By the same token, from a strictly legal standpoint, the single moment at which a person is pronounced medically dead is far more critical than the six previous years when that person was in a coma, attached to some life-support system.

The way we reckon age is but one manifestation of the general spasmodic manner in which we officially structure any social mobility in time. Though they are usually quite short, wedding ceremonies, for example, nonetheless involve a momentous quantum leap across the mental divide separating marriage from singlehood. As a result, even couples who have lived together for several years officially undergo a substantial transformation of their relationship during the brief moment in which they exchange their vows. Along similar lines, given the gaps we perceive between them, we expect any move from one supposedly discrete phase of one's professional career on to the next one to entail a dramatic quantum leap in one's professional capabilities, thereby essentially treating the infinitesimal interval between doctors' last day of internship and first day of residency, for example, as even more critical than their entire internship year. As a result, on the day they are officially transformed into residents, we expect young physicians *immediately* to assume significantly higher degrees of professional responsibility—which they were systematically denied throughout their internship, not to mention only a few hours earlier. By contrast, despite the considerable professional experience they have obviously gained during their internship, on the last day of that year interns are nonetheless officially assigned the same degree of responsibility they were given on its first day.[50]

To further appreciate the social reality of quantum leaps across mental divides, note that the difference between placing third and fourth in the Olympic trials is also the difference between competing and not competing in the actual games. By the same token, when a law school admits only 270 applicants every year, the difference between being ranked 270th and 271st is clearly far more critical than the difference between being ranked 270th and 1st. Along similar lines, when the official rules of track and field specify that any favoring wind over 4.473 miles per hour (2 meters per second) would automatically invalidate a record, the infinitesimal difference between 4.472 mph and 4.474 mph winds is far more consequential for runners than the difference between any of them and having no favoring wind at all.

Mental reality, in short, is deeply embedded in social reality. The gaps we perceive among the supposedly discrete entities that constitute social reality as well as the quantum leaps necessary for crossing them are admittedly mental. Nonetheless, once they are institutionalized, they become seemingly inevitable facts that we can no longer ignore or wish away. Along with the islands of meaning they help delineate, they are the very stuff that our social life is made of. Given their centrality to the way we organize our everyday life, such gaps are therefore quite real in their felt presence. Thus, if we perceive the world as made up of discrete entities, it is because, in a way, they indeed *are* discrete.

3

The Rigid Mind

Thou shalt not sow thy vineyard with two kinds of seed. . . . Thou shalt not plow with an ox and an ass together. Thou shalt not wear a mingled stuff, wool and linen together.[1]

In order to maintain our experience of the world as made up of discrete islands of meaning, we must preserve the insular character of mental entities—that is, carefully insulate them from one another. The stretches of void we visualize among them clearly enhance our perception of their separateness. The existence of such gaps must therefore be constantly reaffirmed.

The ability to perceive gaps among mental entities is part of a particular mind-set, whose distinctive characteristic is its rigidity. The presence of such a mind-set is most evident with regard to the mental divides that help us delineate both individual and collective chunks of identity. A clear, sharp experience of our self and of the groups to which we belong presupposes a rigid perception of the contours separating them from other selves and groups. In order to better understand the way we perceive the world, it is essential that we examine the way the "rigid mind" operates as well as its psychological, cultural, and social origins.

Purity and Order

The most distinctive characteristic of the rigid mind is its un-yielding, obsessive commitment to the mutual exclusivity of mental entities. The foremost logical prerequisite of a rigid classification is that a mental item belong to no more than one category. Such either/or logic presupposes a digital mode of thinking, which, unlike its analog counterpart,[2] does not tolerate any "gray" shadings among mental fields. "Digital thinking" has a staccato character somewhat evocative of the on/off nature of the conventional light switch or the convulsive progression of time on digital clocks, in marked contra-distinction to the smooth, legato style of the dimmer or the tradi-tional analog clock.

Firmly committed to the indispensability of the perceived gaps among mental entities, the rigid mind allows no "contact" among them. Its obsessive need to literally segregate islands of meaning from one another so as to preserve their insular character is most clearly manifested in pigeonholing, a mental process that leads to the practical partitioning of reality into discrete "mental ghettos" that never "touch" one another. A classic manifestation of this kind of compartmentalization of our experience is the way we use the bed-room, the "adult" bookstore, and nighttime as "ghettos" that pro-mote, in space as well as in time, the actual segregation of the erotic from the ordinary.[3] Such an effort to segregate supposedly insular mental "domains" from one another is also evident from the way we relegate the "worlds" of children and adults to separate rooms or floors of department stores, video stores, and libraries. The rigid clustering of "classical," "jazz," "heavy metal," "New Age," "rhythm and blues," "salsa," "country," "rap," and "easy listen-ing" music in separate radio stations or specialized programs on the same station likewise enhances our perception of such conventional "kinds" of music as discrete and separate from one another.

As we might expect, the rigid mind cherishes sharp, clear-cut distinctions among mental entities. Thus, apart from partitioning reality into insular mental ghettos, it also leads a vigorous campaign against "the in-between, the ambiguous, the composite,"[4] in an at-tempt to create a "world without twilight."[5] Being mixtures of supposedly mutually exclusive mental entities, such anomalies nec-essarily threaten the cognitive tranquility of anyone committed to a rigidly compartmentalized world. Occupying the proverbial "gray areas" of classificatory schemata, they blur the distinctions among supposedly discrete compartments of reality, thereby disputing the notion that they are indeed separated from one another by inevitable divides.

The objection of the rigid mind to the intermediate has a critical extracognitive dimension, often manifested in the form of a deep anxiety, even panic, at the very idea that supposedly insular mental entities might actually "touch" one another. Being situated within several mental fields at the same time, intermediate entities necessarily defy the either/or logic underlying the perceived mutual exclusivity of categories, thereby questioning the very viability of the boundaries separating them from one another. Essentially ambiguous, they present a serious threat to rigid classificatory structures, since, by their very existence, they call attention to the inadequacies of such structures.[6] As such, they are often perceived by the rigid mind as quite dangerous.[7]

Hence the deep fear—usually manifested in the form of superstitions—that often surrounds twilight, a stretch of time that has elements of both day and night yet is neither, or the equally ambiguous transitions between the seasons. Similar fears are elicited by spatial "twilight zones." Thus, around the world, people often place in doorways all sorts of charms and amulets to drive away evil forces that haunt thresholds.[8] For similar reasons, they also fear "twilight persons" such as witches (once known as "fence riders")[9] who straddle the perceived boundary between civilization and wilderness or the essentially transitional (and, therefore, ambiguous) yet unborn and just deceased, both of whom clearly defy the mental divide separating the living from the nonliving.[10]

The anxiety and fear provoked by the intermediate often lead to taboos and other forms of avoidance.[11] They are manifested, for example, in the various avoidance practices surrounding thresholds around the world[12] as well as in the attempts made by various societies to ritually seclude preinitiates who straddle the boundary between the categories "child" and "adult" so as to prevent them from even entering other members' consciousness.[13] In a last-ditch effort to avoid ambiguity, the rigid mind also tries to force mental "monsters" into one of the conventional categories available.[14] A classic example was the desperate attempt made by the North American colonists who objected to miscegenation to suppress the inevitable presence of mulattoes by lumping them together with "full-blooded" blacks.[15]

In an attempt to avoid it, we often develop a strong aversion to the ambiguous. Thus, for example, we are usually revolted by the sticky, an intermediate state betwixt and between the solid and the liquid.[16] The forms of life we detest most are, likewise, those that "make our skin crawl because they slip in between categories."[17] Thus, we are appalled by ambiguous creatures that straddle the boundaries of our conventional categories, a classic example of which is the bat, a sort of combination of a bird and a rat. Along similar lines, we abhor dwellers of twilight zones that "offend the necessity of clear distinction" and, thus, defy our desperate attempts to create order—reptiles that inhabit both land and water, "nasty rodents that live in houses yet remain outside the bounds of domestication," insects that dwell in "cracks that are zones of separation" and that, as parasites, are both part of and separate from us.[18] Our intense abomination of such ambiguous creatures highlights the inverse relation between order and anxiety:

> We become agitated when [they] seem not to fit the taxonomic system. Such incompatible animals shock us. The degree of our upset indicates that something more is disturbed than the plan of animal classification. Exceptions to the system threaten not only animal order but our basic model for order. . . . [T]hose anomalies signify . . . alarming forces of disorder and evil, much worse than flawed classification.[19]

Moreover, even the most attractive objects can be quite disgusting when encountered in places other than where they normally "belong." After all, even lovers shudder at the sight of each other's hair floating in their soup bowl or bathtub. The same fawn or raccoon that looks so cute in the zoo would likewise appall us in our bedroom, and nothing on our plate would disgust us more than our favorite pet.

The aversion to ambiguity is often manifested in a pseudohygienic avoidance of "filth." As Mary Douglas has shown, dirt is basically "matter out of place," "the by-product of a systematic ordering and classification of matter, in so far as ordering involves rejecting inappropriate elements. . . . [It is] a kind of omnibus compendium which includes all the rejected elements of ordered systems. . . . [O]ur pollution behavior is the reaction which condemns any object or idea likely to confuse or contradict cherished classifications."[20] Cleaning, thus, is, before anything else, a process of putting things back in their mental "place," where they "belong." It is the fear of mental contagion that likewise leads groups to prohibit intermarriage or launch symbolic crusades against contact with "impure" elements. In allowing overlaps among mental fields, ambiguous entities essentially "contaminate" well-ordered systems of meaning, thereby evoking a sense of pollution.[21]

Purity, in short, is the antithesis of ambiguity. Purists are those who refuse to mix different styles of furniture in their living room, never serve white wine with steak, and protect their national language or cuisine from any foreign influence. Avoiding the unclean is essentially avoiding the unclear. It is an attempt to preserve the mental "purity" of a rigidly classified universe.

Self and Environment

The notion of "filth" applies to most of our bodily discharges. Thus, we are usually appalled by the very thought of touching, or even stepping on, spittle that only seconds ago was in our own mouth. Along similar lines, an instant after our urine, sweat, feces, and snot stop being a part of us, we already experience them as detestable waste.

It is their ambiguous nature that explains our aversion to our bodily discharges.[22] They are repulsive because, though already separate from our body, they are still experienced as part of it.[23] As parts of both our body and its environment, they certainly challenge our image of the self as an insular, free-standing entity.

Separating the body from its immediate surroundings is necessary for preventing the self from "melting" into them and practically disintegrating as a distinct entity. Keeping the body hermetically sealed off is thus one of the foremost obsessions of the rigid mind, as manifested, for example, in its traditional artistic portrayal as

> isolated, alone, fenced off from all other bodies. All signs of its unfinished character . . . were eliminated; its protuberances and offshoots were removed, its convexities (signs of new sprouts and buds) smoothed out, *its apertures closed.* . . . Corporal acts were shown only when the borderlines dividing the body from the outside world were sharply defined. The inner processes of absorbing and ejecting were not revealed.[24]

> That which protrudes, bulges, sprouts, or branches off (when a body transgresses its limits . . .) is eliminated, hidden, or moder-

ated. . . . The basis of the image is . . . a *closed individuality that does not merge with other bodies and with the world.*[25]

The rigid mind has likewise generated numerous etiquette rules designed to protect the self from blending with its immediate surroundings.[26] Such rules keep us, for example, from leaning on tables and walls and severely restrict acts that involve ejecting parts of the body into the environment—spitting, nose-blowing,[27] farting, defecating, ejaculating. To promote the image of the sealed self, they also make us keep our mouth shut when we eat or laugh and cover it when we cough, sneeze, or yawn. In fact, most body-related taboos concern the openings through which matter exits our body—our genitals, anus, mouth.

The image of an insular self is also threatened by any matter that enters the body. Just as we transgress our corporeal limits and flow into our surroundings when we spit, defecate, or blow our nose, we also literally let the environment into our body whenever we eat. Like feces and urine, the food we eat is ambiguously experienced as both me and not me. To maximize their separateness, the rigid mind minimizes the number of occasions on which we incorporate the environment into the self, as evident from various taboos on snacking between meals. Numerous taboos also surround the act of eating as well as the definition of what is edible.

In allowing us to literally merge with others through ejection or absorption, sexual intercourse, too, threatens the image of an insular self,

> sharply bounded [and] separated from the selves of others . . .
> [Such self is] easily punctured during copulation. The alien elements that intercourse can inject into an individual's essence may
> disrupt its existing structure and produce a new one. . . . [T]he
> human body—like the human self—is a clearly demarcated vessel,
> strictly segregated from the world by an impermeable membrane.
> The physical aspects of sex seem so fearsome precisely because they
> breach this boundary of the body. . . . [I]ntercourse reveals the
> individual to be not the closed container [that the rigid mind envisions] but rather an open sieve, liable to contamination. . . .[28]

The deep fear that aspects of our essence might actually "leak out" or "trickle in" through our genitals[29] is manifested in the numerous taboos that surround the sexual act. It also underlies the perception of sex as polluting and the association of abstinence (which clearly precludes any possible "contamination" of the self by other selves) with purity.

In order to remain discrete, selves must be unequivocally separated from their surroundings.[30] It is our most immediate environment, of course, that also presents the most serious threat to our selfhood and that we must be particularly careful never to incorporate into our bodies. It is precisely those animals perceived as "closest" to us that we must therefore avoid most as food,[31] which is why we indeed normally regard pets as inedible, thus eating pigeons but not canaries, sardines but not goldfish (and why films that show people eating their own dog [Bryan Forbes's *King Rat*] or a fish straight out of an aquarium [Charles Crichton's *A Fish Called Wanda*] are so revolting). Along similar lines, it is our "closest" relatives (parents, siblings) that we must particularly avoid as sexual partners. As any victim of parental child abuse must know, such sexual contacts are absolutely detrimental to one's selfhood. The incest taboo, of course, is the quintessential expression of our "endophobic" need to maintain some psychological distance from those who are "closest" to us, a need that accounts for various milder forms of exogamy as well. A somewhat similar need to avoid blending with one's "own kind" underlies the homophobic taboo on sexual contacts with members of one's own sex.

Both the origin and function of the incest taboo are fundamentally cognitive. By avoiding the immediate, we basically surround the self by a mental gap that enhances its image as discrete and separate from other selves. Our avoidance of incest, we may recall, certainly antedates our awareness of its genetic hazards. In much the same way, we also developed the idea of contagion before we discovered bacterial pathogenicity[32] and feared sexual contamination long before we knew about sexually transmitted diseases. Such ideas, fears, and pollution-related taboos were all generated—long before their current supporting medical evidence—by our fundamentally cognitive anxiety about ambiguity.

Social Segregation

The incest taboo and other forms of exogamy are all expressions of our fundamental "endophobic" need to maintain some "distance" from our "closest" relatives. Yet our sexual choices are also restricted by "exophobic" taboos on contacts with anything perceived as too "distant" from us.[33] We are by and large situated at the center of a doughnutlike constellation of taboos designed to keep both personal and collective chunks of identity tightly bounded. By preventing us from blending with those immediately around us, endophobic taboos help protect the integrity of our selfhood. By keeping us from venturing "too far," exophobic taboos likewise help delineate supposedly discrete collectivities, from ethnic and religious groups to social classes, nations, and species. (See illustration.)

Our bent for venturing "too far" is for the most part checked by various exclusionary practices that basically designate some objects as strictly off limits. A classic example is the way we normally regard as perverse sexual contacts that transgress boundaries of social categories to which we belong.[34] After all, even parents who pride themselves on allowing their children to marry Jews, blacks, or blue-collar workers would nonetheless find the idea of their being sexually involved with an infant or a goat absolutely offensive. "Liberals" who are generally appalled by the apartheid or Nuremberg antimis-

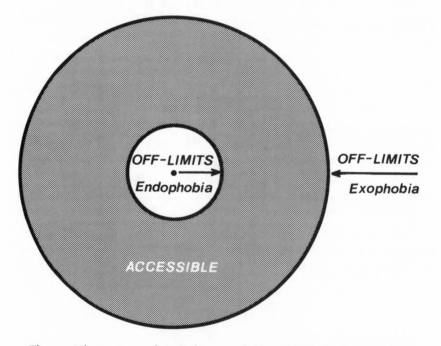

The social structure of sexual accessibility: While the incest taboo helps protect the integrity of the self, xenophobia helps delineate the boundaries of social groups

cegenation laws would probably be just as appalled by transgressive sexual contacts with carrots or baboons. They basically differ from advocates of such pronouncedly exclusionary policies only in where they draw their lines.

Along somewhat similar lines, even our supposedly unbounded ethical notion of "universalism" is actually bounded by the tacit limits of some conventional "universe." "Altruists," for example, usually restrict their definition of "other" to humans, rarely extending it so as to also include, for instance, the weeds we so passionately remove, the cockroaches we so zealously spray, or the dartboards and bowling pins we so violently attack. All in all, we are not that different from the ancient Romans, whose bloody gladiatorial games clearly showed that there is "a sharp limit to . . . moral feelings. If a being came within this limit, activities [that] occurred at the games would have been an intolerable outrage; when a being was *outside the sphere of moral concern,* however, the infliction of suffering was merely entertaining. Some human beings—criminals and military captives especially—and all animals fell outside this sphere."[35] The Romans certainly did not lack moral sentiments. At least, not more so than we, who so casually pick flowers, poison moths and rats, and eat chicken and sardines. Such sentiments, however, are hardly ever boundless.

Social identity is always exclusionary, since any inclusion necessarily entails some element of exclusion as well: "*The very same activities that are, to those privileged to partake in them, unambiguous acts of social inclusion are . . . to those who are not so privileged equally unambiguous acts of social exclusion. . . .* When we single out a friend and take him into our confidence, we are thereby deliberately choosing not to confide in our other friends."[36] In order for any group to be perceived as a separate entity, it must have some nonmembers who are excluded from it.[37] That is why one of the very first things boys often do when they form a club is put up a No Girls Allowed sign on their clubhouse. If membership in the French nation, the American Bar Association, the Presbyterian church, or the Vanderbilt family is to be meaningful, there must be at least some individuals who are explicitly excluded from such collectivities.

Some "shell of exclusion"[38] is therefore necessary for any group to experience itself as a separate entity. Like selfhood, group identity presupposes a clear differentiation of the group from its surroundings.[39] Hence, it involves playing up the ways in which group members are different from nonmembers.[40] Such obsession with distinction is particularly present among groups that try to protect their perceived superiority over other groups, a classic example of which is the need of elites to differentiate themselves from "the masses."[41] Likewise, as blacks enter their neighborhoods, white residents often redefine their community boundaries in a way that excludes them. As one such resident explained when asked to draw the boundary of his neighborhood, "it used to be the tracks, but blacks have moved this side of them, so I guess now you would have to say it's Cicero Avenue."[42]

The inevitable embeddedness of group identity in negative sentiments toward outsiders[43] also leads groups particularly anxious about their distinctiveness to generate and perpetuate conflicts with other groups.[44] Before they can develop any class consciousness, claim Marxists, workers must perceive their own interests as antithetical to those of their employers. Persecuted Protestant sects in fact went as far as to reject gestures of tolerance from their persecutors in order to avoid being assimilated by them.[45] To groups *that* concerned about their separateness, even a complete victory over their enemies is perceived as dangerous.[46] Such groups might even cultivate some chronic enemy just in order to maintain their distinctive identity. George Orwell's classic portrayal of the relations among Eurasia, Eastasia, and Oceania in *1984*[47] is quite evocative of this kind of indispensability of "communists" for fascists, "antirevolutionaries" for communists, and "heretics" for the church.

Just as it tries to curtail the amount of "traffic" between self and environment, the rigid mind also devises various barriers to keep group members from being "contaminated" through contact with nonmembers. The most conspicuous expression of this effort, of course, is physical segregation. Sealed borders kept both imperial Japan and modern Albania for long periods practically segregated from the rest of the world. High walls have likewise protected many monastic orders from any external "pollution." Discrete enclaves such as pales, ghettos, prisons, asylums, quarantines, and leper colonies have similarly allowed many societies effectively to "contain" their excluded social refuse.

Avoidance rules keeping "untouchable" Pulayans at least ninety-six paces away from Brahmans, and Ernadans at least four hundred yards away from villages of higher castes,[48] likewise help substantiate the mental gaps among social groups in India and keep higher castes from being "polluted" through contact with lower ones. In a similar way, until quite recently, blacks and whites in America were forced by various segregation laws to commune separately, use separate schools, courts, hospitals, parks, inns, and restaurants, and enter the same buildings only through separate entrances. In accordance with the infamous Jim Crow laws, they were also physically segregated on boats, streetcars, buses, and trains by being assigned separate seats, separate compartments of cars, and even separate cars.[49] (Separate dining rooms and bathrooms likewise help segregate executives from everyone else in corporations.) Such exclusionary practices, of course, are part of the apartheid between the races in South Africa to this day.

Yet physical segregation is certainly not the only way to keep group members from being "contaminated" by contact with nonmembers. Exclusionary measures far more subtle than either incarceration or ghettoization effectively prevent social "pollution." Excommunication, after all, need not always entail actual deportation, and "exclusive" social clubs rarely need to rely on barbed wire to protect their "purity."

Many groups, for example, manage to maintain their ethnic identity by preserving a separate language as well as distinctive clothes, dances, and food. Titles and diplomas likewise enhance the perception of mental gaps among professions as well as among different ranks within professions. They help to distinguish physiotherapists, for example, from mere masseurs,[50] psychiatrists from psychologists, first lieutenants from second lieutenants, and full professors from associate professors. In fact, many conceptual distinctions would probably not have existed were it not for the need of elites to differentiate themselves sharply from "the masses."[51] It is the essentially purist wish to establish such a mental chasm that leads them to cultivate and passionately defend aesthetic distinctions between "refined" and "vulgar" books (*Madame Bovary* versus *Valley of the Dolls*), films (a Bergman movie versus *Rambo III*), stores (Saks Fifth Avenue versus K Mart), vacation sites (Martha's Vineyard versus Atlantic City), topics of conversation (postmodernism versus garage sales), food (sushi versus hot dogs), drinks (cognac versus beer), cars (Saab versus Ford), newspapers (*Wall Street Journal* versus *National Enquirer*), music (Debussy versus Ray Conniff), television personalities (Bill Moyers versus Johnny Carson), and sports (squash versus bowling).[52]

Social closure[53] is even more explicitly maintained by various formal restrictions on access to membership. Tough entrance requirements[54] and rigid definitions of professional tasks and jurisdictions[55] are classic examples of such institutionalized exclusion. Strict immigration quotas thus help nations maintain their "purity," while stringent licensing procedures and a pronouncedly exclusionary distinction between the tasks of prescribing and dispensing drugs likewise help separate physicians from chiropractors and pharmacists.[56] Barring mobility across social strata serves a similar function, and many social systems indeed include impenetrable "membranes or hymens which separate one stratum from another [that] do not have any 'holes' through which, nor any stairs and elevators with which, the dwellers of different strata may pass from one floor to another."[57] The traditional relegation of women and minorities to nonprestigious, low-income occupations, for example, suggests that even seemingly "open" labor markets are in fact segmented into relatively segregated sectors among which there is little, if any, mobility.

An even more extreme form of social segregation is endogamy. Keeping members sexually confined to its boundaries allows a group to maintain an "uncontaminated" gene pool. Prohibiting all sexual contacts between Aryans and Jews, the infamous Nuremberg laws[58] were designed to protect the "purity of German blood." Such purism also generated the laws against miscegenation among whites, blacks, Native Americans, and Orientals in America.[59] (Only in 1967 did the Supreme Court define such racist laws as unconstitutional, but statutes prohibiting sexual unions between whites and blacks in fact remained on the books for some time after that.)[60] In these and similar cases, the vehement objection to mixing "blood" has been fundamentally cognitive. Essentially transgressive, intermarriage blurs the distinction between member and nonmember, thus making it difficult to perceive the group as an insular entity. Groups that prohibit sexual contacts across their boundaries basically apply the biological reasoning by which lack of interbreeding proves that a group of organisms constitutes a discrete species. By keeping members from transgressing their limits, they try to highlight the mental gap separating them from other groups. Endogamy, in short, enhances our ability to perceive any group as differentiated from other groups[61] (whereas intermarriage, by contrast, brings separate groups "closer" together and promotes their assimilation in our mind).

Cultures vary in the way they define endogamy, yet they nearly always condemn bestiality. In order to perceive humankind as a discrete entity, the rigid mind highlights the mental gulf separating us from animals. (That is also why, in supermarkets, tuna for humans and for cats is kept in separate aisles.) Such a divide is central to the biblical theory that we were created quite separately from other life forms.[62] It also underlies the idea that, in sharp contrast to humans, animals have no consciousness or soul, a claim often used to justify experimenting with them.[63] Even the word "it" presupposes a wider mental gap separating apes from humans than from peaches or paper clips.

As with both incest and endogamy, the cognitive need to separate generates specific normative proscriptions. In order to preserve our mental separation from animals, we deliberately avoid, for example, eating "like a pig." In fact, "good manners" also entail refraining from opening our mouth wide like a dog, licking our plate like a cat, and gurgling down our drinks like a horse.[64]

The rigid mind also detests any ambiguous creature that might threaten the mutual exclusivity of the categories "human" and "animal."[65] That explains the horror of freaks like "wolf children" and the "elephant man,"[66] the killing of twins and "monstrous" babies,[67] the fear of being inoculated with cows' fluids,[68] as well as the seclusion of the insane.[69] For the same reason, the rigid mind also abhors the ape, which, having "either man's face and an animal body or the other way around," is "uncomfortably close as an animal and disgustingly far away as a human."[70] "One of the most oddly disquieting events of my life," admits a well-known biologist, was an encounter with a young chimpanzee: "The episode was unnerving. It wasn't the same as making friends with the neighbor's dog. I had to ask myself: was this really an animal? . . . I had responded to him almost exactly as I would to a two-year-old child."[71] The ape is, at the same time, "the most insulting, degrading, obscene of creatures and yet the most intelligent . . . member of the animal kingdom. The tension between these two aspects is indicated by our laughter—that uniquely human convulsion of air arising from the contradictions of our own thought."[72] Hence our nervous giggling around the ape cages in the zoo, as we watch with both fascination and deep anxiety those ambiguous creatures that, despite being animals, have such "human" gestures and expressions. A joke depicting her picking lice off other babies in the nursery[73] likewise betrays the anxiety many must have felt a few years ago when Baby Fae lived for three weeks with a baboon's heart. Our deep awareness of our embarrassing proximity to apes also explains better than any religious sentiment the furor created by *The Descent of Man*. Had Darwin claimed that men were most closely related to and descended from raccoons or elephants, things might have gone more smoothly for his theory. . . . [T]he storm which broke over the theory released great pressures that had been building for centuries, having less to do with intellectual disagreement or even with the Bible . . . and more to do with our native unease about borderline creatures. . . . [H]umanism has never forgiven Darwin for shattering the classical/ Christian illusion of human separatism.[74]

The rigid mind is just as anxious about separating the masculine from the feminine and often insists on keeping males and females literally segregated from each other—in separate schools, restrooms, sports. (A classic example of their almost total physical segregation is the South Asian purdah system, whose essence is aptly encapsulated in the title of Rabindranath Tagore's novel *The Home and the World*.)[75] It further dichotomizes the world into separate male and female domains by "genderizing" it, whether in the form of segregating the world of "work" from that of homemaking or by inspiring the production of gender-specific watches, razors, and handkerchiefs. (Some languages assign gender to inanimate objects through a formalized use of a special gender suffix.) In order to further promote the mutual exclusivity of masculinity and femininity, boys are often taught to avoid dolls and "girls' talk" while girls are urged to cultivate "feminine" hobbies (sewing) and interests (fashion) and shun "masculine" ones (wrestling, politics). Being socialized to develop gender-specific ambitions, they also tend to enter some professions and avoid others. As a result, men and women often end up occupying "separate spheres"[76] of the social world.

In order to maintain the mutual exclusivity of masculinity and femininity, the rigid mind also tries to polarize both behavior and appearance along gender lines so as to make males and females more obviously distinct from each other. Applying "the law of the excluded middle," it promotes the exaggeration of the natural differences between the sexes,[77] prompting women to shave their legs and cultivate a somewhat squeaky voice and men to pump up their muscles and grow beards. For the same reason, we also socialize girls to cultivate a distinctively "feminine" way of sitting and walking, and we avoid dressing boys in pink. We likewise "genderize" various other aspects of our clothing (line, position of buttons)[78] as well as body ornaments (pipe, ankle bracelet) and modes of displaying our hair.[79] Eliminating any overlaps between masculinity and femininity certainly facilitates their perception as discrete entities separated from each other by a real divide.

Obviously threatened by any possible confusion between the masculine and the feminine, the rigid mind clearly abhors hermaphrodites,[80] often leading such ambiguous "monsters" to undergo surgery in order to become fully male or female.[81] Similarly threatened by any gender switching other than as part of masquerading or play-acting,[82] it is also averse to *trans*vestites, who far too often and much too casually cross the line separating the masculine from the feminine. It likewise loathes anyone who threatens the mutual exclusivity of conventional gender roles (male nurses and female executives, wimpy husbands and domineering wives) as well as homosexuals, who defy its view of male and female as complementary opposites[83] (and also portrays the gay male as the diametrical opposite of the straight male.[84]) To further separate masculinity from femininity, it also promotes pejorative concepts such as "effeminate" and "sissy." Introducing children to such concepts is one of the subtlest ways of socializing them to reify the mental divide separating the masculine from the feminine.

The Psychological Roots of Rigidity

Many people's gender identity is at least somewhat out of line with their biological sexual membership. Only the most rigid among them, however, actually change their sex. Transsexualism is a product of an exceptionally rigid definition of masculinity and femininity.[85] In marked contrast to both homosexuals and transvestites, transsexuals obviously cannot tolerate ambiguity. It is their rigidity, more than any clinical necessity, that leads most of them to "migrate" surgically from one sex to the other.

Rigidity is a mind-set that is more characteristic of some individuals than of others. We all think in categories, yet only the particularly rigid among us would actually refuse even to taste a sweet potato dessert just because sweet potatoes are ordinarily served only as part of entrées. They are the ones who are always so careful to leave wide gaps among figures they arrange in simulated social scenes and who so religiously keep their drawings from visually flowing into their surroundings by always framing them.[86] They are the ones who also avoid stepping on sidewalk cracks or carpet seams and who so obsessively keep the different food items on their plate from touching, lest they might "contaminate" one another.

There are a number of psychological environments that normally generate a particularly sharp distinction between self and environment. For example, during periods of illness, we tend to be experientially confined to our body, and even the most empathetic among us are usually unable to concern themselves with anything that occurs beyond its edges. Likewise, when we are in pain, we tend to withdraw into a barricaded shell or cocoon[87] and have difficulty maintaining contact with anybody outside it. In fact, we sometimes deliberately inflict pain on ourselves in order to sharpen the experiential split between self and environment. The pain that results even from mild self-mutilation (lip biting, scab picking, skin peeling,[88] nail biting) certainly reminds one constantly precisely where one begins and ends, thereby dramatizing the separateness of one's self as an insular entity.

Major identity crises likewise tend to rigidify our perception of the boundaries of our selfhood. It is their attempt to establish a distinct identity that is clearly separate from those of their parents and siblings that makes children so obsessed with ownership, which presupposes a rigid distinction between "mine" and "not mine." It is their effort to literally seal their self so that it will not "leak" that likewise makes them so addicted to Band-Aids.[89] A similar concern with separateness from their parents makes adolescents so obsessed with privacy, to the point of treating their room as practically detached from the rest of their home. Such a rigid definition of one's selfhood produces a general rigid mind-set. As clear from their rigid notions of masculinity and femininity, as well as inflexible definitions of "jocks," "brains," and "nerds," adolescents are extremely intolerant of ambiguity. They have just as little taste for political nuance and compromise.[90]

Various early formative experiences also generate rigidity. A perfect case in point are early attempts to suppress ambivalence.[91] Children who feel both affection and hostility toward their parents, yet are not allowed to express the latter, may try to keep it from "breaking out" by tightening their muscles[92] and thus maintaining a rigid posture. Those who are unable to "contain" their hostility, however, often try to deny its very existence. Eschewing their ambivalence, they learn to "split" their feelings so as to never experience both love and anger toward the same person, thereby dividing people into wonderful ones whom they love and terrible ones whom they hate, allowing for no nuance whatsoever.[93] In their effort to deny their ambivalence, they also come to rely on rigid mental structures that exclude any gray shadings.[94] They thus abhor ambiguity and try to force intermediate essences into "pure" categories.[95] They likewise tend to compartmentalize the world, strictly separating work from pleasure, the proper from the distasteful, and objects of sensual desire from those of mere romantic attachment.

A craving for rigid structures also stems from not having had limits set on one's actions early on. Children need to learn that transgressing certain physical (playing too close to the stairs, touching the hot stove) or moral (stealing, being rude) lines is bound to hurt them, and only when their repeated attempts to test such limits are consistently curbed do they come to appreciate the comforting presence of boundaries that constrain and protect at the same time. The absence of such limits leaves children feeling totally unprotected, and when parents never say No, a child may experience the world as limitless and develop an agoraphobic fear of boundlessness. Agoraphobia is an expression of a desperate need for some closure. Its victims experience great anxiety in unbounded environments and dread all forms of open-endedness—wide highways and boundless expanses of water, long silences, darkness (when even familiar outlines cannot be seen[96]), situations that lack clear rules or agendas. They feel comfortable only when they can cling, tangibly as well as visually or mentally, to entities with clear edges.[97] They thus tend to swim only near the wall of the pool, drive only in the right lane, and surround themselves with rigid schedules and deadlines,[98] all in order to avoid the dreaded sensation of "free-floating" in some boundless void.

Yet an agoraphobic yearning for closure is also generated by fear of being assimilated into one's environment and "melting" away as a distinct entity. Such fear usually stems from children's inability to separate fully from parents who are extremely possessive[99] or simply unable to draw a clear line between the child and themselves. Being too young to draw that line, such children come to experience themselves as mere extensions of their parents and tend not to trust their own ability to circumscribe a distinct self. The fear of "dissolving" into one's surroundings tends to generate stiffness.[100] One feels an urge to tighten one's muscles if one does not trust one's own body to "contain" one's self. By preventing it from "leaking" out, stiffening one's muscles sharpens the experience of one's self as a bounded entity. Yet the fear of "melting" away leads one to avoid relaxing not only physically but also mentally (by staying away from alcohol)[101] as well as socially (by tightening one's lips and refraining

from "opening up" to others). A wall of privacy that precludes
intimacy certainly helps anyone who fears "blending" with others
establish a sense of separate selfhood. So does a propensity to think
analytically and decontextualize,[102] which makes one mentally pre-
disposed to keeping things separate. It may well be the fear of "dissolving" into their surroundings that makes some people
exceptionally good at playing Boggle or solving "Word Seek" and
"Find the Faces in the Tree" puzzles, both of which call for an ability
to identify the boundaries or outlines of camouflaged words or figures that are not clearly separated from their surroundings by actual
gaps.

Fear of intimacy, however, is also generated by precisely the
reverse condition of overindividuation. We all begin life by being
pulled out of an ever-present amniotic sea, the first of many repeated
experiences of feeling totally detached from our surroundings,[103] yet
being separated too early from our parents makes such experience of
detachment particularly acute. Overindividuation generates an obsession with privacy (a need to be alone most of the time, an aversion
to sleeping in the same bed even with one's lover) and, in extreme
cases, a total autistic withdrawal into an insulated "shell" that allows
little if any contact with one's environment. Highly protective of
their separateness, autistic persons keep the orifices of their body
(mouth, ears, nostrils) tightly closed and are extremely anxious about
the food that enters as well as the waste that exits it: "How could
something that was part of his body be outside of his body? Where
were the boundaries of his physical existence? Did this mean that his
body had no limits?"[104] For the same reason, they also tend to avoid
interacting with others around them.

No wonder there are more autistic boys than girls.[105] After all,
separateness from one's parents is far more intensely experienced by
boys, who are more fundamentally different sexually from the parent
who usually raises them: "Women and men grow up with personalities affected by different boundary experiences. . . . Boys come to
define themselves as more separate and distinct, with a greater sense
of rigid ego boundaries and differentiation. The basic feminine sense
of self is connected to the world, the basic masculine sense of self is
separate."[106] This often leads to a general preoccupation with boundedness and separateness. In their effort to maintain an identity separate from their mothers', it is men who create the rigid mental
divide between masculinity and femininity. They also tend to develop a higher propensity to decontextualize than women[107] and

seem to have a greater need for closure, as evidenced by their greater tendency to draw closed forms as well as their greater compulsion to close off incomplete ones.[108] Men also tend generally to "open up" to others less than women.[109]

Yet rigidity is by no means an exclusively male trait. An aversion to eating, anorexia is the feminine version of autism, since not letting food into one's body is analogous to not letting others into one's self. Along similar lines, bulimia is the feminine equivalent of Don Juan–style bed-hopping, as both entail a promiscuous fusion with one's environment followed by an almost immediate expulsion of all foreign matter from one's self. Like autism and bed-hopping, both anorexia and bulimia are expressions of an obsession with maintaining a rigidly bounded self.

Rigid Social Environments

Yet rigidity is not only part of individuals' psychological makeup. Xenophobia, for example, is much more widespread in England and Japan than in Hawaii, and overindividuation is far more prevalent in societies in which people are born in hospitals rather than at home and in which the first experience of the self as detached from its surroundings, is, therefore, much more acute.[110] In calling attention to a rigid "mind," I do not mean to imply an exclusively psychological account of rigidity. Collectivities, too, have distinctive mentalities,[111] and rigidity clearly characterizes some of them more than others.[112] Having examined the psychological roots of rigidity, we can proceed to identify some social environments that feature a particularly strong bent toward a rigid manner of classifying reality.

A particular obsession with boundaries usually characterizes groups that perceive themselves as minorities in constant danger of extinction. They regard their boundaries as critical to their survival and feel that, unless they seal them off so as to preserve their distinctiveness, they will inevitably be assimilated into their surroundings and cease to exist as a distinct entity. Firm boundaries that set them clearly apart from their social surroundings are thus central to the very definition of communes,[113] nations,[114] ethnic groups, and social elites. It is precisely their distinctive and essentially exclusionary language, script, religion, cuisine, holidays, music, dances, and folk costumes that help Ukrainians and Chinese, for example, preserve their "ethnic" identity in America, the cultural "vaccine"[115]

they use to immunize themselves against melting away into their
social surroundings. "Purifying" the collection and repertoire of the
Boston Museum of Fine Art and the Boston Symphony Orchestra
from all forms of "popular" culture likewise helped that city's Brah-
mins preserve their distinctiveness despite the massive influx of "rab-
ble" into their city during the nineteenth century.[116]

The manner in which groups distinguish insiders from outsiders
often reflects the way they classify people in general. Both the clergy
and the military, whose extremely rigid definition of membership
has led them to lump all nonmembers as an undifferentiated lot
("laymen," "civilians"), also maintain strict boundaries among different ranks within them as well as between men and women.[117]
They have traditionally also been particularly hostile to homosexuals, who blur the distinction between masculinity and femininity and
therefore undermine the identity of men as masculine.[118] Aversion to
homosexuality, as well as to both transvestism and bestiality (which
involves transgressing the mental divide separating humans from
animals), likewise coincides with a particularly rigid definition of
ethnic or religious boundaries.[119]

The way groups classify people also resonates in the way they
classify other things in the universe,[120] and the rigid manner in which
some of them draw their own boundaries is usually part of a general
mind-set[121] characterized by a strict adherence to an either/or logic
and an aversion to ambiguity.[122] Any transgression of boundaries
can serve as a metaphoric allusion for a group whose own boundaries
are threatened,[123] and groups that are particularly obsessed with their
social "purity" indeed often take the integrity of the body to represent their own and are therefore particularly careful to maintain its
separateness from its surroundings.[124] Zoroastrians, for example,
actually bury the hair and fingernails they trim off their body. They
likewise regard even breathing as polluting and perform purificatory
rites both before and after urinating and having sexual intercourse.[125]
Their need to keep categories separate likewise generates an aversion
to meteorites, which defy the separation of earth from heavens.[126]

Rigidity as a general mind-set, featuring a pronounced purist
obsession with boundaries and distinctions that manifests itself in
many different substantive contexts, is even better exemplified by
Gypsies. In a collectively "autistic" manner, Gypsies do everything
possible to maintain a wide gap between the hermetically sealed
bands in which they live and their social surroundings. In order to
preserve their "purity," they try to limit all their contacts with non-

Gypsies (whom they mentally lump together as *gaje* or *gorgios*) to sheer political or economic necessity. Not only do they practice strict endogamy; to avoid any possible "contamination," they also refrain from eating food prepared by non-Gypsies and keep a special set of eating utensils that they use only to serve non-Gypsy guests and wash as well as store separately from their own. Along similar lines, they also avoid using furniture that has been used by non-Gypsies and keep special chairs exclusively for non-Gypsy guests.[127] Such precautionary measures are all part of a general obsession with pollution, which they themselves consider their foremost distinctive feature[128] and the perceived lack of concern with which makes non-Gypsies so repulsive to them. Such purism is manifested, for example, in the fact that Gypsy men and women sit, eat, talk, and dance separately and that even their clothes are washed separately.[129] It is also evident from the fact that they abhor any contact between the upper and lower parts of their body, thereby washing them—as well as clothes associated with them—separately (using separate soaps, towels, and washbasins) and regarding oral sex as one of the most dreadful forms of impurity.[130] Anxiety about social "purity" also goes along with a tendency to view food as polluting,[131] and Gypsies are indeed extremely cautious about the food they allow into their bodies as well as about the utensils they use for eating it, surrounding both with numerous taboos.[132] They likewise guard quite zealously the orifices of their bodies and make every effort to segregate their interiors and exteriors from one another.[133] In fact, they even detest animals that blur the distinction between their interior and exterior by licking their fur (cats, dogs) or shedding their skin (snakes, lizards).[134] At the same time, they are particularly fond of animals with bristles, especially of the hedgehog,[135] a creature that, in literally maintaining an actual gap between self and others, is probably the most glaring representation possible of "autistic" insularity.

Like Gypsies, Jews, too, perceive themselves as an island engulfed by an ocean of non-Jews[136] and, in an attempt to maintain the mental gap between the categories "Jew" and "non-Jew," have traditionally avoided any "contaminative" contact with non-Jews (typically lumped together, like non-Gypsies, in a single category—first as idolaters and now as Gentiles [*goyim*]). According to the Mishnah, the compiled rabbinical interpretations of scriptural ordinances, Jews may not even have their hair cut by Gentiles,[137] and numerous dietary restrictions prevent them from eating in Gentiles' homes, thus practically limiting their opportunity to establish intimate contacts with them. Following purist decrees introduced twenty-five centuries ago,[138] they have largely practiced strict endogamy, marrying even first cousins to avoid intermarriage. Their pronounced separatism has generally also led them to avoid proselytizing. In fact, in its Orthodox version, Judaism admits converts only reluctantly and after a long process that requires them to sever their original family ties.[139] That, as well as the practice of mourning and even mock-burying Jews who marry Gentiles,[140] further bolsters the mental gap between the categories "Jew" and "non-Jew."

Such a purist obsession with group boundaries is, again, part of a general rigid mind-set that manifests itself in many different contexts. The culture that maintains such a sharp distinction between member and nonmember is also rigid, for example, in the way it classifies animals, as clearly evident from its aversion to zoological anomalies. Orthodox Jews, for instance, may not eat the pig, which has parted hooves and cloven feet yet does not chew its cud, or the shrimp, which lives in water yet has no fins or scales. It is their ambiguous status as composites of categories regarded as mutually exclusive that makes them abominable,[141] and the Scriptures are quite explicit about the symbolic relationship between such culinary and social purism: "I am the Lord your God, who have set you apart from the peoples. Ye shall therefore separate between the clean beast and the unclean."[142] For similar reasons, Jews also may not tie a horse to a wagon drawn by oxen or harness asses with camels.[143] In general: "one kind of cattle with another, one kind of wild animal with another, cattle with wild animals, wild animals with cattle, one kind of an unclean beast with another, one kind of a clean beast with another, an unclean beast with a clean, a clean beast with an unclean—it is forbidden to plough with them, draw with them, or drive them."[144]

Jewish *kashruth* laws disqualify many other food items that involve mixing categories.[145] To this day, observant Jews keep two separate sets of dishes and cooking and eating utensils—one for meat products and the other for milk—and are careful never to mix them within any single meal. After all, "no flesh may be cooked in milk . . . and no flesh may be served up on the table together with cheese. . . . If a drop of milk fell upon a piece of flesh that was cooking in a pot . . . that piece is forbidden."[146] Such purism is manifested in numerous other domains as well. In fact, there are two tractates in the Mishnah, literally named *Kilaim* ("hybrids") and *Erubin* ("mixings"), which basically consist of injunctions such as the following:

Grain may be sown alongside another kind of grain only if a quarter-*kab*'s space intervenes; vegetables may be planted alongside other vegetables only if six handbreadths intervene.[147]

A cord of wool may not be tied onto one made of linen.[148]

A man may not stand within a private domain and drink in the public domain, nor may he stand within the public domain and drink within a private domain unless he has inserted his head and the greater part of his body into the place where he drinks.[149]

No wonder Jews thought up a purist God who spends the first three of only six days he has in which to create the entire world just making distinctions. Judaism's aversion to mixtures and ambiguity is manifested in its explicit condemnation of transvestism[150] as well as in its highly ritualized articulation of passages from one life stage to the next. Not only does it explicitly prohibit bestiality; in marked contrast to so many other cultures, it has also conspicuously avoided ambiguous mythic hybrids (such as centaurs and mermaids) that blur the distinction between humans and animals.[151] A particularly rigid Jewish conception of selfhood likewise underlies the attribution of impurity to bodily discharges[152] as well as the association of sex with dirt.[153]

None of the above by itself, of course, would warrant calling a group rigid. The cultural juxtaposition of such diverse manifestations of a purist obsession with boundaries and distinctions, however, is quite overwhelming. It is hard not to see the mental affinity between the attribution of impurity to bodily discharges, the abomination of ruminants that have no parted hooves, the taboo against wearing clothes made of both wool and linen, and the practice of mourning and mock burying members who marry nonmembers. These are all different manifestations of a single rigid mind-set.

Inherently conservative and antithetical to change, rigidity clearly helps maintain the status quo. It is especially during periods of great instability, therefore, that groups tend to hang on to rigid structures. As they go through a major identity crisis, for example, groups, just like individuals, become much more protective of their boundaries.[154] Particularly anxious about their identity, they tend to become obsessed with treason, heresy, and other transgressions and often resort to various "rites of exclusion," including persecution, as a way of reaffirming them.[155] (Such rites also help separate new identities from old, discarded ones. The political witch hunts perpe-

trated by Robespierre, Khomeini, and the communists in Eastern
Europe as well as the postwar trials of the Nazis in Germany and the
military in Argentina were at least partly designed to signal breaking
with an old identity and clarify who and what the group would no
longer include or allow.) Thus, it was during periods when it felt
threatened (such as during the thirteenth century) that the church
was particularly hostile to homosexuals.[156] Similarly, though purism
was clearly a general Puritan trait (as evident from the very name
they chose for themselves as well as from their reluctance to admit
new members[157] and their objection to even mere fantasies about
human-animal transformations[158]), it was special threats to their collective survival—and, therefore, the need to reaffirm their identity—
that led the Puritans to banish Anne Hutchinson, persecute the
Quakers, and hang the "witches" of Salem.[159] Along similar lines,
though Germans may have a general predilection for rigid partitions,[160] it was its defeat in World War I and humiliation at Versailles
that made Germany particularly anxious about its physical borders as
well as social purity. (Restricting citizenship to people "of German
blood" and preserving the cultural purity of German art were part of
the Nazis' platform as early as 1920, early manifestations of the
rigidity that would later inspire the persecution of homosexuals, the
Nuremberg laws, and the use of color coding to distinguish Jews,
homosexuals, criminals, and political prisoners from one another
even in concentration camps.)

It was a conservative effort to protect the boundaries of the me-
dieval world from the onslaught of the Renaissance, Reformation,
and scientific revolution that likewise ignited the fifteenth- through
seventeenth-century witch hunts in Europe, which indeed occurred
mostly in societies that underwent serious upheavals (Germany).
They were almost absent from those where the church remained
strong (Spain) and were pretty much over as soon as the contours of
the religious domain were redefined.[161] Along similar lines, it was
the realignment of allies and enemies after World War II that generated the McCarthyite need to reaffirm America's political essence,[162]
and it was identity-shaking events such as the American Revolution[163] and the Civil War that widened the racial cleavage in the
South. The Jim Crow laws, for instance, quite unnecessary when
"everyone knew his place," evolved only after the abolition of slavery, as the white South tried to reaffirm its identity. The antebellum
and postbellum pressure to narrow the social gap between whites
and blacks likewise inspired the "one drop rule,"[164] whereby a single

"drop of black blood" would suffice to define one as black. It was their increasing insecurity that led white Southerners to bolster the mental gap between "white" and "black" by defining everyone who was not fully white as black.

Groups undergoing identity crises persecute not only people. As evident from the nativist crusades carried out in our own times by China, Libya, and Iran, xenophobic sentiments are also unleashed against languages[165] as well as other cultural (religious, literary, aesthetic) traditions. In an effort to redraw the boundaries of the *polis* after the Peloponnesian War, Athens even launched a symbolic crusade against ambiguous mythical creatures that confounded its gender and species categories (Amazons, centaurs),[166] and the period when conservative Europe was trying to resist the Renaissance, Reformation, and scientific revolution also saw a considerable rise in the number of animals prosecuted by criminal courts.[167]

Our search for rigid social environments need not confine us, however, to rigid societies. In every society, some domains clearly exhibit more than their share of rigidity. A classic example of such a domain (and, in fact, where the very idea of "contamination" originally evolved, thousands of years prior to the medical discovery of bacterial pathogenicity) is religion. One of the foremost characteristics of the religious mind is the rigid manner in which it compartmentalizes the world into sacred and profane spheres.[168] Since the sacred is essentially defined as that which is not profane, the two are regarded as mutually exclusive and are separated from each other by the widest mental gulf imaginable.[169] "Profaning" the sacred is thus an abominable sin,[170] and even the slightest possibility of such "mental promiscuity" horrifies the rigid mind:

> Since the idea of the sacred is always and everywhere separated from the idea of the profane . . . and since we picture a sort of logical chasm between the two, the mind irresistibly refuses to allow the two . . . to be confounded, or even to be merely put in contact with each other; for such a promiscuity . . . would contradict . . . the dissociation of these ideas in the mind. The sacred thing is *par excellence* that which the profane should not touch, and cannot touch with impunity.[171]

To preserve the mental gulf between them, religion segregates the sacred and the profane spatially as well as temporally from each other. By placing one on the right (or at the top) and the other on the left (or at the bottom) and creating rigidly bounded sanctuaries (temples, holy cities) as well as "holy days,"[172] it keeps them literally apart from, and ensures that they will not touch, each other. Specifically designed to keep the sacred from being "contaminated" through contact with the profane, such segregative measures are part of a "negative cult"[173] that is also responsible for various contact taboos (on talking in sanctuaries, eating ordinary food on holy days, or touching or even looking at sacred objects) as well as for the preservation of languages such as Hebrew (for nearly two millennia) and Geez (Ethiopic) almost exclusively for sacred use.

To further promote such mental separation, religion also devises special rites to help "decontaminate" those entering the sacred domain from any previous contact with the profane. "Put off thy shoes from off thy feet, for the place whereon thou standest is holy ground,"[174] God tells Moses as he approaches the burning bush. That is why Muslims indeed remove their shoes before they enter a mosque while Christians sprinkle water on themselves on entering church. Along similar lines, Jews burn all their leaven before Passover and clean their homes, wash themselves, and put on fresh clothes (which they do not wear during the week) before the Sabbath begins.[175] Similar purificatory rites help "polluted" Zoroastrians,[176] repenting Jews,[177] and born-again Christians shed their former, profane selves. The mental gulf between the sacred and the profane is likewise dramatized during the passage from the former back into the latter. Thus, for example, at the conclusion of the Sabbath, Jews perform a special "separation" (*havdalah*) rite in which they bless God essentially for making distinctions.[178] Any passage from the Sabbath back into the profane weekdays before they are ritually separated from each other is strictly prohibited; and, even on the rare occasions when Jews may break the Sabbath laws, they must first "exit" the holy day by performing a *havdalah*.[179]

Sanctuaries, holidays, and contact taboos are among the hallmarks of religion, yet one can easily recognize their secularized counterparts in bureaucracy, which harbors a "negative cult" that clearly emulates the religious original. The mental underpinnings of religion and bureaucracy are strikingly similar. Whereas one tries to preserve the mutual separateness of the sacred and the profane, the other promotes an equally rigid segregation of the formal, official, public, and impersonal from the informal, unofficial, private, and personal. To maintain such segregation, bureaucracy insists that public moneys and equipment be clearly separate from officials' private assets and that personal matters be strictly excluded from official discourse[180] (which explains the meaning of using official rather than ordinary stationery or, conversely, adding an informal handwritten "P.S." at the end of a formal typed letter). It likewise promotes a sharp distinction between public and private space and time, separating office from home[181] and confining official commitments to rigidly bounded "duty periods"[182] (which accounts for the special meaning of meeting or even calling officials at home, especially in the evening, on the weekend, or when they are on vacation[183]). Such a sharp break between one's "on-duty" and "off-duty" time often coincides with a rigid distinction between the people with whom one works and the ones with whom one socializes.[184] Like the separation of business from personal letters and public from private moneys, both, after all, are products of the same purist mind. Such purism also gives rise to a highly pragmatic style of mental focusing distinctively characterized by a sharp break between what one attends and what is excluded from one's attention as "irrelevant."

Another institutionalized hotbed of rigidity is law, which rewards its practitioners for thinking analytically and decontextualizing and admonishes them for being "wishy-washy" or "fuzzy." So is science, which dreads anomalies and makes every effort to deny their existence (or at least their anomalous nature).[185] (The very same rigorous mind-set that generated the scientific revolution also inspired in 1474 in Basel the criminal prosecution and burning of a cock that transgressed the "laws" of nature by laying an egg.)[186] Traditionally expected to caulk any crack in the mental wall separating the natural from the "supernatural,"[187] it likewise excludes whatever transgresses the conventional limits of its discourse or methodology (acupuncture, astrology) as "nonscientific." Academic science also breeds intellectual provincialism in the form of insular "disciplines" that are largely oblivious of scholarly activity that takes place beyond their boundaries.[188] With very few exceptions, maverick scholars who transgress the boundaries of their "field" by doing *cross*-disciplinary work usually pay a heavy price for their lack of disciplinary discipline.

Traditionally obsessed with classifying, science has also inspired the evolution of many cultural "texts"—both scientific (the zoo, the botanical garden, the museum, the encyclopedia, the Dewey decimal system)[189] and nonscientific (the supermarket, the department store, the restaurant menu, the *Yellow Pages,* the catalog, the stamp collection)—that embody the purist effort to force reality into mutually exclusive mental compartments (as well as promote decontextualization[190]). The catalog, the menu, and the Dewey decimal system serve to remind us that rigidity is likewise enhanced by the very act of listing: "The question, is a tomato a fruit *or* a vegetable? is the kind that would seem pointless in an oral context [yet] is the kind of question generated by written lists."[191] The current ubiquity of the digital computer, of course, seems to suggest that, at least for the foreseeable future, such a rigid either/or logic is here to stay.

4

The Social Lens

*But how could there not be arbitrariness? Nature presents [things] . . .
without firmly established divisions. Everything shades off into everything else by imperceptible nuances. And if, on this ocean of objects
surrounding us, there should appear a few that seem to break through the
surface and to dominate the rest like the crest of a reef, they merely owe
this advantage to . . . conventions . . . that have nothing to do with the
physical arrangement of beings.*[1]

I have thus far drawn a deliberately one-sided picture of reality
as an array of insular entities neatly separated from one another by
great divides. Such discontinuity, however, is not as inevitable as we
normally take it to be. It is a pronouncedly mental scalpel[2] that helps
us carve discrete mental slices out of reality: "You get the illusion
that [entities] are just there and are being named as they exist. But
they can be . . . organized quite differently depending on how the
knife moves. . . . It is important to see this knife for what it is and
not to be fooled into thinking that [entities] are the way they are just
because the knife happened to cut it up that way. It is important to
concentrate on the knife itself."[3] The scalpel, of course, is a *social*
scalpel. It is society that underlies the way we generate meaningful
mental entities.

Reality is not made up of insular chunks unambiguously separated from one another by sharp divides, but, rather, of vague, blurred-edge essences that often "spill over" into one another. It normally presents itself not in black and white, but, rather, in subtle shades of gray, with mental twilight zones as well as intermediate essences connecting entities. Segmenting it into discrete islands of meaning usually rests on some social convention, and most boundaries are, therefore, mere social artifacts. As such, they often vary from one society to another as well as across historical periods within each society. Moreover, the precise location—not to mention the very existence—of such mental partitions is often disputed even within any given society.

Culture and Classification

There is more than one way to carve discrete chunks out of a given continuum, and different cultures indeed mold out of the same reality quite different archipelagos of meaning. While all cultures, for example, distinguish the edible from the inedible or the young from the old, they usually differ from one another in where they draw the lines between them. The distinction between the sexually accessible and inaccessible is likewise universal (all cultures, for example, have an incest taboo), yet the specific delineation of those who are considered off limits often varies from one culture to another. Surrounding oneself with a bubble of "personal space," too, is a universal practice, yet, in marked contrast to other species, humans exhibit substantial subspecific cultural variations in where they draw its boundaries.[4] (Along similar lines, the precise delineation of one's "personal" circle of intimates also varies from one culture to another.)[5] By the same token, not everyone who is considered "black" in America would necessarily be classified as such in the West Indies or Brazil.

Moreover, cultures often make certain distinctions that other cultures simply do not. Whereas West Germans, for example, perceive Holland and Belgium as two distinct residential regions, Swedes and Italians both tend to regard them as a single undifferentiated whole.[6] Even purely phonic differences that are quite critical in one language are sometimes totally ignored in others, as the same sound range covered by several distinct phonemes in one language may very well be covered by a single phoneme in another. Thus, for example, though they clearly constitute two separate phonemes in both Polish and Romanian, "c" and "q" are fully interchangeable allophones in French.[7] For quite similar reasons, Hebrew speakers usually treat *list* and *least* (or *pull* and *pool*) as homonyms, Spanish speakers often fail to hear the difference between *race* and *raise*, and Koreans may use *rule* and *lure* interchangeably (just as Americans may have trouble distinguishing the French *peur* from *père* or the Spanish *pero* from *perro*).

Languages likewise differ from one another in the way they generate distinct lexical particles,[8] and it is not unusual that a single word in one language would cover the semantic range of several separate words in another. Thus, for example, while there is a single word for both rats and mice in Latin, insects and airplanes in Hopi, and brothers-in-law and grandnephews in the Algonquian language of the Fox, there are separate words for blankets that are folded and spread out, for water in buckets and in lakes, and for dogs that stand and sit in Navajo.[9] Such differences have considerable cognitive implications. After all, it is much easier to isolate a distinct mental entity from its surroundings when one has a word to denote it.[10] That explains why the Navajo, who use different verbs to denote the handling of objects with different shapes, indeed tend to classify objects according to shape much more than English speakers.[11] By the same token, lacking the necessary lexical tools for differentiating, it took me, a native speaker of Hebrew, a long time before I could actually notice the mental gaps—so obvious to English-speakers—that separate jelly from jam or preserves.

While such cross-cultural variability often leads us to look down on other cultures' classificatory schemas as primitive or "confused," it ought to help us recognize and accept the relative validity of our own. Only their ethnocentric blinders prevent those who claim that "savages" fail to notice obvious mental discontinuities[12] from appreciating the highly sophisticated classificatory skills of these people, who clearly do make distinctions, though rarely among the things that we do.[13]

Classifying presupposes an ability to ignore "trivial" differences among variants of the same mental entity,[14] and what often looks like an inability to differentiate may very well be a deliberate disregard for negligible differences that "make no difference." The Hopi are certainly not blind to the physical dissimilarity of insects and airplanes. Nonetheless, their culture has no significant conceptual distinction that corresponds to such a difference. Along similar lines, when mental distance is a function of the way items are totemically associated with social groups, there is a good reason to ignore differences among items that are regarded as interchangeable manifestations of the same totem.[15] Thus, for the Australian aborigines, who classify the universe by "dividing" it among their various clans, it is far more logical to note the mental affinity between the rosella parrot and the cat, which is associated with the same clan, than its physical resemblance to the cockatoo, which is associated with a different one.[16] Since the "obvious" physical difference between the parrot and the cat is socially irrelevant, it is deliberately ignored. By the same token, while they probably never confuse the parrot with the cockatoo, aborigines may "fail" to differentiate the kangaroo rat from the gum-tree grub or the planet Venus, which are associated with the same clan.

Like these "savages," though we are obviously aware of the differences in taste between milk and sardines or meat and eggs, it makes a lot of sense to ignore them when what concerns us is our calcium intake or cholesterol level. It is likewise more logical to lump shrimps with pigs than with fish if we observe the Jewish dietary laws. To most "savages," however, our ways of classifying must seem as confused as theirs seem to us:

> We order the world according to categories that we take for granted simply because they are given. They occupy an epistemological space that is prior to thought, and so they have an extraordinary staying power. When confronted with an alien way of organizing experience, however, we sense the frailty of our own categories. . . . Things hold together only because they can be slotted into a classificatory scheme that remains unquestioned. We classify a Pekinese and a Great Dane together as dogs without hesitating, even though the Pekinese might seem to have more in common with a cat and the Great Dane with a pony.[17]

Thus, though they themselves have only one word for both insects and airplanes, the Hopi must find it odd that English uses a single word to denote water in nature and in containers.[18] They must likewise find it peculiar that it "fails" to differentiate mothers' brothers from fathers' sisters' husbands, maternal from paternal grandfathers, and first from third cousins. Along similar lines, West Indians indeed find it odd that the English perceive all the various shades of dark skin as "black."[19] Most "savages" must also find it bizarre that we keep hamsters and gerbils as pets while ridding our homes of mice.

Any notion of logic is valid only within a particular cultural milieu,[20] and our own classifications are no more logical than those of "savages." We must therefore resist the ethnocentric tendency to regard our own way of classifying reality as the only reasonable way to do it. That entails giving up the idea that some ways of classifying are more correct and "logical" than others[21] and, therefore, also reconsidering the standard tests through which we usually measure intelligence. Thus, for example, "a person, asked in what way wood and alcohol are alike [should not be] given a zero score if he answers: 'Both knock you out' [just] because the examiner prefers logical categories of scientific classification."[22] By the same token, nor should we penalize someone who maintains (as did my daughter, when she was five) that the difference between a bus and an airplane lies in the fact that we need not pay the pilot on boarding a plane.

Ways of classifying reality vary not only across cultures but also across historical periods within the same culture. The last couple of centuries, for example, saw substantial shifts in the location of the lines we draw between the sexes,[23] the "races,"[24] public and private, family and community. Along similar lines, our calendar year did not always begin on January 1,[25] opiates were still legal in America only eighty years ago,[26] and lungs and gills did not become "similar" until comparative anatomists began classifying organisms according to functional rather than morphological features.[27] Even the location of the line separating art from life changes over time—the Romans, for example, would often execute real-life convicts on stage as part of theatrical shows.[28] A few decades ago, Americans were taught to regard the color of one's skin (and Germans the color of one's hair) as most salient for social exclusion. Today they learn to ignore it as socially irrelevant.

In 1792, when Mary Wollstonecraft published her *Vindication of the Rights of Women,* a distinguished Cambridge professor rebutted with a satirical *Vindication of the Rights of Brutes.*[29] Only two centuries ago, the mental gap between the sexes was so wide that women were perceived as "closer" to animals than to men and granting them political rights seemed as ludicrous as extending such rights to beasts. That this sounds so utterly absurd today only comes to show that absurdity is a function of where we draw lines, and that mental distances may change over time. Before the Civil War, when blacks were regarded in the United States as objects rather than persons, granting them civil rights would have legally been just as ludicrous. (In fact, public signs such as Negroes and Dogs Not Allowed suggest that, until quite recently, they were still perceived in the South as "closer" to animals than to whites.)[30] Only a few decades ago, the idea that homosexuals should be regarded as a distinct political minority would have been as absurd as granting such status to music teachers, baseball fans, or vegetarians. Rights have historically been extended to new social categories (prisoners, noncitizens, children, the insane, the preborn) whose legal standing prior to that would have been inconceivable.[31] (By the same token, for many centuries, European criminal courts also prosecuted pigs, rats, bees, and other animals.[32] In 896 Pope Stephen VI put on trial the dead body of his predecessor, and in 1591 a Russian town bell was sentenced to banishment in Siberia, where it was kept in solitary confinement until fully pardoned three hundred years later, for ringing the signal of an insurrection.[33]) The Nazi experiments with Jews and the mentally retarded likewise presupposed (and, in turn, promoted) the idea that the mental partition between true Aryans and such "subhuman" groups was as thick as the one separating person from object. To anyone brought up in such ideological climate, objecting to experimentation with Jews would have been as absurd as the objection to experimentation with animals seems to many of us today.

The lines we draw vary not only across cultures and historical periods but also within cultures at a given point in history, as one can tell from the joke about the Orthodox Jew from New York who asks a Southerner who is obviously intrigued by his traditional garb and heavy accent, "What's the matter, you've never seen a Yankee before?" At the same time that one needed seven-eighths "white blood" to avoid being considered a "person of color" in Florida, a mere three-quarters would suffice in Nebraska,[34] and in universities that rarely tenure their young faculty, the line normally separating faculty from students may not be as pronounced as the one separating tenured faculty from both students and nontenured faculty. The lines believed by residents of fancy neighborhoods to separate them from those who live in less prestigious neighborhoods nearby are likewise often blurred by the latter.[35] (When I asked the man from whom I bought my house about the nearest train station, he mentioned a station located six minutes away in a fancier neighborhood, yet "forgot" to mention a station located only two minutes away in a much less prestigious one.) Likewise, within the same culture, meat eaters draw the line between what is edible and inedible quite differently than do vegetarians. (Whereas Bertrand Russell would claim that this line ought to be drawn "at the level of the species," vegetarians may not find ordinary meat eaters that different from cannibals.) Similarly, though "*inter*marriage" normally denotes unions between blacks and whites or Jews and Christians, Ashkenazic Jews also use it to refer to marrying Sephardic Jews.

Of course, from the proverbial Martian's standpoint, since we only marry other humans, we are all "boringly endogamous"[36] and any cross-racial or interfaith "intermarriage" is embarrassingly trivial, yet even within the same culture, lines that seem obvious to some groups may be totally ignored by others. Thus, for example, despite their obvious ubiquity to their own members, the boundaries of communes are usually ignored by the state.[37] And the wide mental gaps that nine-year-olds believe separate them from eight-year-olds, or that rat breeders perceive as separating their own "refined" show animals from ordinary rats, are not appreciated by anyone but them. Along similar lines, whereas no radical bookstore would place a book on the women's movement alongside books on beauty or homemaking, bookstores less sensitive to the distinction between feminist and traditional notions of womanhood might well do so.[38] The distinction some current college students make between "stylish radical-chic" and "granola" lesbians is likewise lost on many alumni, "to whom the shadings of lesbian politics are as irrelevant as the difference between Sodom and Gomorrah."[39]

Such diversity also generates discord. As we carve mental entities out of reality, the location as well as the very existence of the lines separating them from one another is quite often disputed.

The prototypical border dispute is a battle over the location of some critical line in actual space, as manifested in disputes ranging from local turf feuds between neighbors or street gangs to full-scale international wars. It is the original on which numerous battles over the location of various partitions in mental space are modeled. Controversies regarding the location of group divisions (the eighteenth-century debate over whether blacks are "closer" to whites or to apes,[40] family fights over who should be invited to a wedding) or moral boundaries (the line separating legal from illegal drugs,[41] the ethical limits of euthanasia) are perfect examples of such border disputes. So are the battles over the fine line between politicians' private and public lives, the definition of work (the distinction between mere "chores" and actual "labor,"[42] the status of housework), and whether phrenology or chiropractic are part of science.[43] Just as disputable is the delineation of frames, as evident from heated arguments between comedians and their audience over whether personal insults are within the limits of the comedy show frame.

Similar in essence are battles over the temporal delineation of historical narratives, such as the debate over the actual beginning of America's involvement in Vietnam (the various versions of which obviously implicate different administrations) or the dispute between Jews and Arabs over the acceptable limits of each side's historical claim to Palestine. The political significance of where we begin and end such narratives is tremendous. Whereas the story of a battle that ends with the evacuation of a settlement will most likely be remembered as a defeat, concluding it with the rebuilding of that settlement several months later allows a nation to define the evacuation as only temporary and preserve the entire event in its collective memory as a heroic symbol.[44] Equally controversial is the temporal delineation of "life." The different medical and legal definitions of the fine line separating life from death,[45] for example, often generate heated battles over the precise point when doctors may turn off life-sustaining respirators. The definition of the precise point when life begins is, likewise, at the heart of the battle over abortion. That point "is not something that is verifiable as a fact. . . . It is a question of labels. Neither side in this . . . debate would ever disagree on the physiological facts. Both sides would agree as to when a heartbeat can first be detected. Both sides would agree as to when brain waves can be first detected. But when you come to try to place the emotional labels . . . that is where people part company."[46] The battle, of course, is over the precise location of the point at which a mere "conceptus" becomes a "fetus" and a pregnant woman's body is transformed from a single into a dual entity. While pro-choicers insist that an abortion involves only the woman's own body, pro-lifers argue that it involves another living being as well. The definition of that critical point has been disputed even within the church, and while some church fathers claimed that ensoulment occurs at conception,[47] leading theologians such as Thomas Aquinas contended that it occurs only forty days (or even eighty, in females) later. If one accepts this view, of course, aborting a still-"inanimate" eleven-week-old female preborn can hardly be called homicide. As Justice John Paul Stevens recently cautioned the United States Supreme Court, there is no reason why we should protect "the potential life of an embryo that is still seed" any more than that of a sperm or an unfertilized egg.[48] (The rhetorical use of terms like *seed* and *potential,* as well as of others such as *baby,* is obviously of critical moral significance in legal battles over abortion.)[49]

Even when we do not dispute its location, we often still disagree with one another on how impenetrable we expect a given boundary to be. Such disagreement is at the bottom of disputes over the walls of prisons (whether prisoners may take weekend leaves, how often they may be visited, the conditions for paroling them) and nation-states (immigrant quotas, the status of guest workers,[50] the right to travel abroad), battles over the extent to which groups ought to allow their languages to be "contaminated" by foreign words, and family fights over whether children may close the doors to their rooms.[51] Moreover, we often wage battles over the very existence of a given boundary. States, for example, usually ignore boundaries drawn by separatists, while conservatives and liberals fight over the necessity of drawing a line between "X" and "R" rated films and evolutionists and creationists debate the distinction between science and ideology. Along similar lines, animal rights activists defy the "experiment" frame that allows the killing of animals,[52] whereas feminists question the distinction between erotic art and pornography and object to sexism even in fiction or jokes. Governments and dissidents likewise often debate the legitimacy of the frames that distinguish "religious" sermons, "satirical" plays, and "academic" discourse from explicit political protest.

Such battles are basically about whether what may look like several separate entities are indeed just different variants of a single entity. The entire debate over the reunification of East and West Germany or North and South Korea, for example, was basically over whether there should be one or two of each. Such disagreements also led some people to reproach those who found John Poindexter's and Oliver North's reasoning at the Iran-Contra hearings, for example, evocative of the Nuremberg trials, as well as those who compared the secession of Lithuania from the Soviet Union in 1990 to that of South Carolina from the Union in 1860,[53] with "How can you even compare?" The current battle between Israeli liberals and ultranationalists over whether or not to prosecute Jewish vigilantes in the West Bank is, likewise, basically about whether they and others who break the law constitute one moral entity or two separate ones ("lawbreakers" and "overzealous patriots").

Language certainly plays a major role in such disputes. That is why Israel has traditionally refused to recognize Palestinians as a distinct entity and why a seceding East Pakistan immediately renamed itself Bangladesh. When sociology conference organizers debate whether to include a single "Race and Ethnicity" session or two separate ("Race" and "Ethnicity") ones, they are actually fighting over whether or not being black or Oriental is different from being Irish or Italian, and when Czechs and Slovaks debate whether to name their union "Czechoslovakia" or "Czecho-Slovakia,"[54] the separatist overtones of the latter name are quite obvious. The label "*para*psychological" clearly excludes phenomena from the realm of science, whereas the label "nonhuman animals"[55] clearly defies the conventional distinction between human and animal. Moving away from the discrete labels "homosexual" and "heterosexual" to a continuous homosexuality-heterosexuality scale[56] likewise helps rid the gay of their "specialness" stigma, whereas using "Ms." as the counterpart of "Mr." clearly helps feminists downplay the distinction between married ("Mrs.") and unmarried ("Miss") women (which, since it does not apply to men, implies that marriage transforms women more than it does men).

Such labeling politics reveal how attitudes toward (protecting or defying) boundaries and distinctions betray deep sentiments (conservative or progressive) toward the social order in general. Like the heated battles over drugs, censorship, and abortion, they show that not only does the way we cut up the world underlie the way we think, it clearly also touches the deepest emotional as well as moral nerves of the human condition.

The Color Gray

That the location as well as the very existence of boundaries is often disputed is even more understandable given the pervasive presence of ambiguity in our life. To the rigid mind, the world is a set of discrete entities separated from one another by gaps. Crossing these gaps entails sharp, dramatic breaks. Movement between islands of meaning therefore has a jerky, staccato nature characterized by abrupt transitions. That is why we gain or lose a full hour as we cross time-zone boundaries[57] or experience some shock upon waking up from a daydream.[58] Such experience of reality obviously allows no room for ambiguity. Yet "things," noted Anaxagoras, are rarely "cut off with an axe."[59] In reality, there are no discrete entities literally detached from their surroundings by actual gaps. Nature "refuses to conform to our craving for clear lines of demarcation; she loves twilight zones."[60] Our neat and orderly classifications not-withstanding, the world presents itself not in pure black and white but, rather, in ambiguous shades of gray, with mental twilight zones and intermediate essences. Despite the stubborn efforts of the rigid mind to deny it, at least some element of ambiguity in our life is inevitable.

Differentiating discrete, insular entities from their surrounding environment is certainly not our only mode of perceiving the world. Hearing, taste, and smell, for example, do not allow a sharp delineation of "things" as do touch or vision.[61] Listening to music, for instance, is an entirely different perceptual experience than looking at a map, as sounds, in marked contrast to countries or school districts, cannot be confined within limits. By the same token, it is much easier mentally to detach a camouflaged figure from its surrounding ground than to isolate the distinctive taste of turmeric in a curry. Nor will an olfactory "map" "have the sharp edges of a visual map—it will be fluid . . . literally drifting on the wind, with eddies and intense centers shading off toward ill-defined edges."[62] Our primal "visceral space-sense," in short, is clearly "not about edges, bound-aries, outlines."[63] Furthermore, as evident from our use of common contours in drawings,[64] not to mention the critical optical fact that we are almost constantly moving,[65] even what we see are actually blurred-edge essences that visually fade into one another. The fact that it takes congenitally blind persons who gain sight following surgery a long time before they can actually perceive bounded "things"[66] suggests that even visual contours are something we *learn* to see.

The transition from any supposedly discrete "thing" we men-tally carve out of ecological continuums (a forest, a mountain, a desert) to its surroundings is more gradual than abrupt and usually involves a zone rather than a sharp line.[67] As we look at coastlines, for example, we see that they actually connect land and water at least as much as they separate them from each other.[68] The absence of clear-cut dividing lines obviously generates ambiguity. When shop interiors and exteriors or sidewalk and street literally interpenetrate one another,[69] our conventional either/or logic is clearly inadequate. Nor can we sustain a "neat" compartmentalization of space as roads suddenly narrow, practically transforming three- into two-lane traf-fics in a rather chaotic manner. Just as ambiguous in the way it actually negotiates inside and outside is the door, the quintessential embodiment of the half-open.[70] Even the notion (on which rests our initial experience of an insular self) that our body is a closed system sharply cut off from everything else is defied by the fact that the air we constantly breathe is part of *both* the self and its environment.[71]

The fact that "framed" experiential realms like art or play are never really totally cut off from their unframed surroundings generates somewhat similar ambiguity. A typical case in point is the ambiguous "slide"[72] we experience as we gradually drift from being wide awake to being sound asleep or out of ordinary reality into the world of make-believe. Moreover, framed events also "spill over" the frames that are supposed to contain them, thereby generating inevitably ambiguous situations.[73] Thus, for example, we sometimes mistake the framed for the unframed, like the hundreds of thousands of panic-stricken listeners who mistook Orson Welles's 1938 radio dramatization of *The War of the Worlds* for a real invasion from Mars. At the same time, however, we sometimes also mistake the unframed for the framed. When comedian Dick Shawn died of a heart attack in the middle of a performance, it took his audience a while before they realized that it was not part of the show,[74] not unlike the spectators at a Halloween costume party who mistook a real murder for a mere gag.[75] Moreover, we cannot always tell parody from plagiarism or clinical from erotic massage, and when Daddy yawns in the middle of reading what Piglet said to Pooh, it may not always be absolutely clear to his child whether it is Daddy or Piglet who is yawning.

Nor are the supposedly discrete temporal blocks we mentally carve out of historical continuums (day and night, childhood and adulthood) really separated from one another by actual gaps. In actuality, they "flow" into each other, essentially connected by borderline ("liminal"[76]) intermediate periods such as twilight and adolescence. As actual mixtures of the essences they connect,[77] such temporal bridges are inevitably ambiguous. That explains why we often feel in limbo when we commute between home and work[78] as well as the ambiguous sense of ownership we experience between the time we sign an agreement to buy a house and the time we actually close the deal. Just as ambiguous are "liminal persons" who are structurally as well as existentially caught in the interstitial cracks betwixt and between several status categories to neither of which they fully belong[79]—newborns who are yet to be circumcised or baptized, students between high school and college, new recruits who are no longer civilians but have yet to be sworn in as full-fledged soldiers, fiancés, presidents-elect, prisoners on parole, and patients in terminal coma.

Just as ambiguous are immigrants, converts, slaves,[80] parvenus, and products of "mixed" marriages. Lying on the proverbial margins of several different social categories, such "marginal" persons[81] are living proof that social life is indeed organized in a web of cross-cutting networks rather than confined to insular groups.[82] After all, even a group such as "family" is never fully insular. Not only do we normally transgress its boundaries when we marry; such lines are fuzzy anyway, as they actually entail an entire twilight zone inhabited by borderline individuals whose membership is ambiguous— distant "wakes-and-weddings" relatives, live-in housekeepers, pets we include even in our family photo albums, next-door neighbors, dead members who are psychologically still present.[83] It is not at all clear, for example, whether my third cousin is part of my family and should thus be invited to family reunions and avoided as a sexual partner. (Genetically speaking, of course, we are all cousins to some degree.) The delineation of other clusters of social identity is just as problematic. Thus, for example, despite the rough clustering of white-collar, blue-collar, and agricultural occupations,[84] social classes are about as discrete as families.[85] So are generations, social movements, and subcultures. In fact, even "cultures" and "societies" are not really discrete. Intermarriage has always existed even among Jews[86] and Gypsies, whereas pidgins and creoles attest to the non-insular nature of speech communities. (Even languages like Basque include at least some nonindigenous words.) Color lines are just as fuzzy. Since "races" are never in a state of perfect reproductive isolation, they do not constitute discrete gene pools. As a result, not a single gene that is present in all members of one race and none of another has yet been identified.[87] The differences between the sexes are also just a matter of degree, as even the distributions of purely physiological male and female features are rarely bipolar. While men's voices are usually deeper than women's, and the female body is, on the average, less muscular and hairy than the male's, many women nonetheless do have a deeper voice or a more muscular and hairy body than many men. In fact, even the distinction between human and animal is repeatedly blurred by philosophers and natural scientists who claim that "there are no leaps in nature,"[88] essentially backing Aristotle's notion of a great "chain of being" connecting all classes of living things (as well as living and "lifeless" things[89]) through a continuous gradation of differences rather than sharp-cut divisions.[90] After all, "about 99 percent of our genes are identical to [those of] chimpanzees, so that the remaining 1 percent accounts for all the differences between us. . . . [T]he greater distances by which we stand apart from the gorilla, the orangutan, and the remaining species of living apes and monkeys . . . are only a matter of degree."[91]

In short, instead of well-defined islands unequivocally separated from each other by substantial gaps, the world normally presents itself in the form of blurred-edge essences distinguished from one another only by "insensible gradations."[92] Analytic thinking, there-fore, is clearly not the only mode by which we process reality. In fact, even most of the concepts we use to organize our experience are not clear-cut and sharply delineated but, rather, vague[93] and often modified by such "hedges" as "largely," "sort of," "quite," "almost," or "more or less."[94] (Until recently, such an ability to process fuzzy categories and negotiate subtle nuances actually dis-tinguished our thinking from that of machines.)[95] As we can see in the illustration here (in marked contrast to the one on p. 26), mem-bership in categories is basically a matter of degree and the transition from member to nonmember gradual rather than abrupt.[96] We there-fore normally process them not in terms of their outlines, but, rather, in terms of their most central, prototypical instances (the "clearest cases"),[97] and as we move away from the latter we get progressively more distant from their core essence through a gradual "fadeout."[98] The fact that the orbits of such mental fields ("light" and "dark," "soft" and "loud," "winter" and "spring") usually overlap[99] obvi-ously makes ambiguity an inevitable presence in our lives.

The Social Construction of Discontinuity

Breaking up reality into discrete islands of meaning is, thus, an inevitably arbitrary act. The very existence of dividing lines (not to mention their location) is a matter of convention. It is by pure con-vention, for example, that we regard Danish and Norwegian as two separate languages yet Galician as a mere dialect of Portu-guese. It is likewise by sheer convention that we draw a line be-tween heroin and other lethal substances such as alcohol and tobacco (not to mention its own chemical cousins, which we use as pain-killers or as controlled substitutes for heroin itself).[100] It is mere convention that similarly leads us to regard cooking or laun-dering as "service" occupations and fishermen or raftsmen as less skilled than assembly-line workers or parking-lot attendants.[101]

Perceiving reality in terms of fuzzy essences with blurred edges

Just as arbitrary is the way in which we carve supposedly discrete species out of the continuum of living forms,[102] separate the masculine from the feminine,[103] cut up continuous stretches of land into separate continents (Europe and Asia, North and Central America), or divide the world into time zones.[104] Nor are there any natural divides separating childhood from adulthood, winter from spring, or one day from the next (both my children, indeed, used to refer to the morning before their last afternoon nap as "yesterday"),[105] and if we attribute distinctive qualities to decades ("the Roaring Twenties") or centuries ("nineteenth-century architecture"),[106] it is only because we happen to count by tens. Had we used nine, instead, as the basis of our counting system, we would have undoubtedly discovered the historical significance of 9- , 81- , and 729-year cycles and generated fin-de-siècle and millenary frenzy around the years 1944 and 2187. We probably would also have experienced our midlife crisis at the age of thirty-six!

It is we ourselves who create categories and force reality into supposedly insular compartments.[107] Mental divides as well as the "things" they delineate are pure artifacts that have no basis whatsoever in reality.[108] A category, after all, is "a group of things [yet] things do not present themselves . . . grouped in such a way. . . . [Nor is their resemblance] enough to explain how we are led to group . . . them together in a sort of ideal sphere, enclosed by definite limits."[109] Classification is an artificial process of concept formation rather than of discovering clusters that already exist.[110] Entities such as "vitamins," "politicians," "art," and "crime" certainly do not exist "out there." The way we construct them resembles the way painters and photographers create pictures by mentally isolating supposedly discrete slices of reality from their immediate surroundings.[111] In the real world, there are no divides separating one insular "thing" from another. The "introduction of closure into the real" is a purely mental act.[112]

And yet, while boundaries and mental fields may not exist "out there," neither are they generated solely by our own mind. The discontinuities we experience are neither natural nor universal, yet they are not entirely personal either. We may not all classify reality in a precisely identical manner, yet we certainly do cut it up into rather similar mental chunks with pretty similar outlines. It is indeed a mind that organizes reality in accordance with a specific logic, yet it is usually a group mind using an unmistakably social logic (and therefore also producing an unmistakably social order).[113] When we cut up the world, we usually do it not as humans or as individuals, but rather as members of societies.

The logic of classification is something we must learn. Socialization involves learning not only society's norms but also its distinctive classificatory schemas. Being socialized or acculturated entails knowing not only how to behave, but also how to perceive reality in a socially appropriate way. An anthropologist who studies another culture, for example, must learn "to see the world as it is constituted for the people themselves, to assimilate their distinctive categories. . . . [H]e may have to abandon the distinction between the natural and the supernatural, relocate the line between life and death, accept a common nature in mankind and animals."[114] Along similar lines, by the time she is three, a child has already internalized the conventional outlines of the category "birthday present" enough to know that, if someone suggests that she bring lima beans as a present, he must be kidding.

Whenever we classify things, we always attend some of their distinctive features[115] in order to note similarities and contrasts among them while ignoring all the rest as irrelevant.[116] The length of a film, for example, or whether it is in color or in black and white is quite irrelevant to the way it is rated, whereas the color of a dress is totally irrelevant to where it is displayed in a department store. What to stress among what is typically a "plethora of viable alternatives" is largely a social decision,[117] and being socialized entails knowing which features are salient for differentiating items from one another and which ones ought to be ignored as irrelevant.[118] It involves learning, for example, that, whereas adding cheese makes a hamburger a "cheeseburger,"[119] adding lettuce does not make it a "lettuceburger," and that it is the kind of meat and not the condiment that goes with it that gives a sandwich its distinctive identity. It likewise involves learning that the sex of the person for whom they are designed is probably the most distinctive feature of clothes (in department stores men's shirts are more likely to be displayed alongside men's pajamas than alongside women's blouses), and that the way it is spelled may help us locate an eggplant in a dictionary but not in a supermarket. Similarly, we learn that in order to find a book in a bookstore we must attend its substantive focus and the first letters of its author's last name (and ignore, for example, the color of its cover), yet that in order to find it in a book exhibit we must first know who published it. (We also learn that bookstores regard readers' ages as a critical feature of books, thus displaying children's books on dogs alongside children's books on boats rather than alongside general books on dogs.) We likewise learn that, in supermarkets, low-sodium soup is located near the low-sugar pineapple slices ("diet food"), marzipan near the anchovy paste ("gourmet food"), and canned corn near the canned pears (rather than by the fresh or frozen corn). And so we learn that, for the purpose of applying the incest taboo, brotherhood "counts" as a measure of proximity to oneself, whereas having the same blood type is irrelevant.[120]

Separating the relevant (figure) from the irrelevant (ground) is not a spontaneous act. Classifying is a normative process, and it is society that leads us to perceive things as similar to or different from one another through unmistakably social *"rules* of irrelevance"[121] that specify which differences are salient for differentiating entities from one another and which ones are only negligible differences among variants of a single entity. Ignoring differences which "make no difference" involves some social pressure to disregard them. Though we often notice them, we learn to ignore them as irrelevant, just as we inhibit our perception of its ground in order to perceive the figure.[122] Along the same lines, ignoring the stutter or deformity of another is not a spontaneous act but rather a social display of tact.[123] It is rules of irrelevance that likewise lead judges, professors, and doctors to display "affective neutrality"[124] and acquit innocent defendants, reward good students, and do their best to save patients' lives even when they personally despise them. They also lead bureaucrats who screen applications to exclude applicants' sex or race from their official considerations even if they are personally attentive to it.

The social construction of discontinuity is accomplished largely through language:

> We dissect nature along lines laid down by our native languages. The categories . . . we isolate from the world of phenomena we do not find there because they stare every observer in the face. . . . [T]he world is presented in a kaleidoscopic flux of impressions which has to be organized by our minds—and this means largely by the linguistic systems in our minds. We cut nature up . . . as we do, largely because we are parties to an agreement to organize it in this way—an agreement that . . . is codified in the patterns of our language. . . . [W]e cannot talk at all except by subscribing to the organization and classification of data which the agreement decrees.[125]

Not only does language allow us to detach mental entities from their surroundings and assign them fixed, decontextualized meanings, it also enables us to transform experiential continuums into discontinuous categories ("long" and "short," "hot" and "cold"). As we assign them separate labels, we come to perceive mental essences such as "professionals," "criminals," or "the poor" as if they were indeed discrete.[126] It is language that allows us to carve out of a continuous voice range the discrete categories "alto" and "soprano," distinguish "herbs" (basil, dill) from leaves we would never allow on our table, define vague discomfort in seemingly sharp categories such as "headache" or "nausea," and perceive after-shave lotion as actually different from eau de toilette or cologne. At the same time, it is our ability to assign them a common label that also allows us to lump things together in our mind.[127] Only the concept "classical," for example, makes Ravel's music similar to Vivaldi's, and only the concept "alcoholic" makes wine seem "closer" to vodka than to grape juice.

Since it is the very basis of social reality,[128] we often forget that language rests on mere convention and regard such mental entities, which are our own creation, as if they were real. "The trouble," the Eleatic Stranger reminds Young Socrates,

> began at the moment when you [said] that there are two classes of living creature, one of them being mankind, and the other the rest of the animals lumped together. . . . [B]ecause you were able to give the common name "animals" to what was left, namely to all creatures other than man, you thought that these creatures do in actual fact make up one class. . . . [Yet cranes too might] classify the race of cranes as being distinct from all other creatures: the rest they might well lump together, men included, giving them the common appellation of "the beasts." So let us try to be on the watch against mistakes of that kind.[129]

By the same token, as we divide a single continuous process into several conceptual parts ("cause" and "effect,"[130] "life" and "death"[131]), we often commit the fallacy of misplaced concreteness and regard such purely mental constructs as if they were actually separate. We likewise reify the mental divide separating "white-collar" from "manual" labor[132] as well as the purely mental outlines of such entities as races, classes,[133] families, and nations. Like the dwellers of Plato's proverbial cave, we are prisoners of our own minds, mistaking mere social conceptions for actual experiential perceptions.

It is society that helps us carve discrete islands of meaning out of our experience. Only English speakers, for example, can "hear" the gaps between the separate words in "perhapstheyshould-havetrieditearlier," which everyone else hears as a single chain of sound. Along similar lines, while people who hear jazz for the first time can never understand why a seemingly continuous stretch of music is occasionally interrupted by bursts of applause, jazz connoisseurs can actually "hear" the purely mental divides separating piano, bass, or drum "solos" from mere "accompaniment." Being a member of society entails "seeing" the world through special mental lenses. It is these lenses, which we acquire only through socialization, that allow us to perceive "things." The proverbial Martian cannot see the mental partitions separating Catholics from Protestants, classical from popular music, or the funny from the crude. Like the contours of constellations, we "see" such fine lines only when we learn that we should expect them there. As real as they may feel to us, boundaries are mere figments of our minds. Only the socialized can "see" them. To all cultural outsiders they are totally invisible.

Only through such "glasses" can entities be "seen." As soon as we remove them, boundaries practically disappear and the "things" they delineate fade away. What we then experience is as continuous as is Europe or the Middle East when seen from space or in ancient maps, or our own neighborhood when fog or heavy snow covers curbs and property lines, practically transforming familiar milieus into a visually undifferentiated flux. This is the way reality must appear to the unsocialized—a boundless, unbroken world with no lines. That is the world we would have inhabited were it not for society.

5

The Fuzzy Mind

The problem is that the structure of any language cannot grasp the nature of unity consciousness any more than a fork could grasp the ocean.[1]

The Ocean

Discernible only through society's mental glasses, islands of meaning are invisible to anyone not wearing them. That means practically every single one of us before we become socialized and thereby acquire such mental "tickets" to social reality.

In the beginning, claims Freud, "the ego includes everything, later it separates off an external world from itself. Our present ego-feeling is . . . only a shrunken residue of a much more inclusive—indeed, an all-embracing—feeling."[2] Our first experiences, before we are even born, are those of dwellers of an essentially undifferentiated environment. In the placental world, an "interpenetrating mix-up" of fetus and amniotic fluid,[3] there is no distinction between subject and object. Yet such fusion of self and environment does not end with birth. Before it can actually differentiate itself from its surroundings and develop a separate, distinct identity, the infant is, experientially speaking, "symbiotically" bound to its mother.[4] With its body practically molded into hers in an almost perfect fit (and in a relaxed manner that sharply contrasts with the muscular tightness so characteristic of rigidity),[5] it has no clear sense yet of itself as an insular entity unambiguously detached from its surroundings. Self and world are still a single experiential whole.

As we all spend our first, prenatal months in an everpresent sea of undifferentiated fluid, the experience understandably brings to mind the image of a fish in the sea (whereas the opposite image of a fish out of water, by contrast, suggests uprootedness).[6] Indeed, ever since Freud,[7] our earliest experience has often been described as an "oceanic" experience, evoking the sensation of lying in the midst of an infinite expanse of wavy, vague watery essences gradually flowing-fading into one another. Such fluid experience of reality is the distinctive hallmark of the infant's mind in particular and of an entire mind-set that sharply contrasts with rigidity in general. (No wonder the rigid mind abhors fluidity. Proto-Nazi propaganda abounded with alarming metaphors of streams, oceans, and floods, and a firm boundary in the form of a dam was a popular image of what might save Germany from drowning.)[8] The world we inhabit as infants is the world before the third day of the Creation—a boundless, monotonous, continuous ocean uninterrupted yet by the insular mental entities that we only later learn to "see."

Not differentiating subject from object is but one aspect of infants' (as well as young children's) fluid experience of reality and is inseparable, for example, from their inability to think analytically. The problem they have perceiving discrete insular entities is manifested in their inability to differentiate themselves from their surroundings as well as in their obvious difficulty in overcoming context. Such difficulty is quite evident from the problem they have detaching overlapping figures from each other or isolating "camouflaged" entities from the complex configurations in which they are visually embedded.[9] It is also evident from the problem they have thinking in a "focused" manner, which clearly presupposes an ability to separate the relevant from the irrelevant.

Nor do young children seem to appreciate conventional closure, spatial or temporal. Thus, for example, when they draw, they often use both sides of the paper for the same picture.[10] By the same token, not till they learn to attend social signals such as clearing the throat or saying "Amen" can they actually discern the mental contours of conventional segments of religious services.[11] Nor do they seem to need rites of passage, as evident from the remarkable ease with which they enter and exit social encounters, sometimes separated from one another by long stretches of virtually no contact, without any of the greeting and farewell rituals we have come to regard as natural.

They also do not seem to notice the conventional mental divides separating different experiential realms from one another. As a result, they cannot appreciate humor or irony or tell ordinary television programs from commercials (a problem obviously exacerbated by advertisers' practice of using characters from programs in the commercials interrupting those selfsame programs). As evident from the way they experience Santa Claus or the tooth fairy, they also cannot fully distinguish "reality" from the worlds of dream, fiction, fantasy, or make-believe.[12] (Pretending that he is an eagle, my son claims that his "eagleness" is apparent even to the birds around him.) They certainly do not trust the ability of frames to prevent things from transgressing their limits. In their rather fluid world, there is no guarantee that ghosts and monsters, for example, can indeed be safely confined to the fairy-tale or cartoon world. When they were little, both my children felt somewhat reassured by notes my wife and I posted around their beds warning witches not to enter their room, as if such mere figments could indeed step out of the fictional frames in which they belong and literally enter their lives.

As their world is clearly not as compartmentalized as the world of adults, children are oblivious to the distinctions we make and have trouble fitting their experience into our conventional categories.[13] Unaware, for example, of the mental divides separating the animate from the inanimate and humans from animals,[14] they kiss and talk to plastic dolls and can much more easily identify with a fawn (Bambi) than with the dangerous creature it fears, man. (No wonder only in children's zoos are visitors allowed actual contact with animals.) Nor do they abhor the anomalous (as I learned from my son's initial fascination with bats) or find the intermediate revolting. As evident from the tremendous success of Mickey Mouse, Porky Pig, or the Berenstain Bears, they clearly love human-animal composites. They are initially also quite fascinated by snot, spittle, feces, and other such ambiguous links between the self and the world.

The fluid world of children is preserved almost intact in mythical thought, which typically leaves what we normally separate in our ordinary thinking practically undifferentiated.[15] In mythical thought, inside and outside, self and world, life and death all blend into each other, and the merely representational realms of dreams or symbols are not framed as separate from the "real" world.[16] An animist ensoulment of practically everything likewise ignores the conventional mental divides separating humans from animals[17] as well as the animate from the "inanimate."

Such fluidity also characterizes the world of the mystic, who basically regards all mental entities as but different aspects of an indivisible cosmic "oneness."[18] In sharp contrast to the conventional analytic perception of discrete "things," mysticism renounces the very idea of "classifying and dissecting,"[19] promoting instead a holistic view of reality whereby everything flows into everything. (Such fusion of what we normally regard as separate is aptly captured in the way Chinese mystics have traditionally depicted the yin and yang aspects of the universe as literally interpenetrating each other.) Understandably hostile to language, it regards the equation of discrete mental entities with real "things" as a mere illusion.[20] Thus, for example, as evident from the way Buddhism, Cabalism, and Taoism promote androgyny,[21] mysticism defies the conventional distinction between masculinity and femininity. By the same token, it is oblivious to all political borders and group divisions and ignores even the conventional existential divide separating man from a transcendent God. The immanent Buddha, claim Zen masters, exists in every single one of us.[22] The quest for such "mystic union" with the divine likewise pervades both the Cabalist and Hasidic versions of Judaism.[23]

An overwhelmingly fuzzy world where everything seems to blend with practically everything else is also the hallmark of madness. Like infants, psychotics have trouble detaching discrete entities from the contexts within which they are embedded. Thus, for example, they have difficulty differentiating figures from their surrounding ground and, being constantly bombarded by an undifferentiated stream of stimuli, have trouble attending anything in a focused manner.[24] As evident from the way they hang on to the concrete as well as their highly overinclusive manner of applying concepts, they are also quite oblivious to the outlines of our categories,[25] as a result of which they have trouble keeping conventional entities mentally separate from one another. Like infants, they also seem to be unaware of the fine lines that keep different experiential realms separate from one another. As a result, they confuse reality with their own dreams or fantasies about it, and the merely figurative or symbolic with the actual.[26] They likewise tend to take everything literally and have difficulty appreciating tongue-in-cheek humor or irony. Unlike the rest of us, they also have trouble framing the voices they "hear" inside their head as mere thoughts, experiencing such purely internal talk as emanating from outside their body.

This kind of difficulty differentiating inner from outer experience is but one aspect of a fundamental fusion of self and environment. As evident from their fluctuating body image,[27] the fragmented contours of the figures they draw,[28] and the way they consistently underestimate their distance from objects around them,[29] psychotics have trouble experiencing the self as an insular entity, unambiguously detached from its immediate surroundings. They basically live in a "twilight state of existence," uncertain where they themselves end and the rest of the world begins.[30] Unable to tell what is inside and what is outside the self, they are often unclear whether things emanate from inside or outside their body[31] and may ascribe to others actions conventionally believed to emanate from within one's own self. Given the hazy boundaries of their self, [32] no wonder they experience it as highly penetrable, as manifested in the common delusion that others can actually read and even control their thoughts.[33]

Children normally outgrow their oceanic experience as part of the process of individuation, and the psychotic "regression" to such feelings of fusion with the world is usually the result of an incomplete separation from one's mother.[34] This link between individuation and the mental ability to differentiate[35] also sheds some light on the psychology of women. Probably because they are of the same sex, girls typically separate from their mothers much more slowly than boys and thus tend to experience themselves as less detached from their environment.[36] That, as well as the fact that women, working at home, have traditionally led a far less compartmentalized life than men, who normally experience a sharp split between the home and work worlds,[37] results in their tendency to experience reality in a somewhat more fluid manner than do men. Females, for example, are less skillful than males in isolating entities from their surrounding context.[38] As evident from their preference for openness in graphic design as well as play,[39] they are clearly also less obsessed with closure.

The "regression" to the infant's fluid world prior to the emergence of discrete entities is also manifested in a pronounced preference for open, unbroken spaces over bounded, compartmentalized ones. In sharp contrast to the analytic style of perceiving insular "things" separated from one another by empty gaps, some people tend to focus precisely on those essentially continuous gaps, as evident from their strong attraction to sailing, skiing, hang gliding, or motorcycling in the country.[40] It is likewise manifested in a difficulty to isolate "camouflaged" entities from the context in which they are embedded or to experience the contours of one's own body as definite and firm.[41]

Children normally separate from their mothers with the help of some pacifier, security blanket, or stuffed animal. Such "transitional objects"[42] are clear agents of continuity. Literally constituting a bridge between the self and the world, they help the child to feel connected at the same time that it experiences its most devastating separation. Embodying its fantasies of connectedness,[43] dolls and teddy bears allow the child to separate from its mother yet still be experientially embedded in an ever-present familiar environment. As intermediaries between "me" and "not me," they help establish an ambiguous, transitional zone between the self and the world, allowing the child to feel both separate and connected at the same time.[44]

As evident from the fact that adults, too, quite literally cling to transitional objects (cigarettes, chewing gum, munchies, Walkmen),[45] the experience of a distinct, separate selfhood is usually offset by a strong need to feel attached to something.[46] Even as adults we never fully let go of our primal maternal environment and stubbornly hold onto fantasies of merging with her again.[47]

Residues of the infant's original experience of reality thus always remain in the deep layers of the adult self.[48] Even when we no longer perceive it as an undifferentiated ocean, the world is nonetheless still dotted with experiential "lakes." The mind that helps us process such pockets of fluidity is a pronouncedly fuzzy mind that blurs distinctions and disregards boundaries. Fascinated by ambiguity, it connects as well as blends essences that are conventionally separate. Such a mind is the antithesis of the rigid mind.

Letting Go

The most common nonpsychotic manifestation of the fuzzy mind in adulthood is the experience of "flow,"[49] whereby we essentially relinquish our selfhood for a while and practically blend with the world. Such "regression" to our primal oceanic experience occurs quite often when we sleep,[50] yet it also characterizes our normal drift from wakefulness to sleep as well as various states of being in mental limbo, such as when we lie on the beach with our eyes closed, practically floating in a daydream. Furthermore, even our wakeful life is dotted with numerous moments of "unmindful," absent-minded reverie, typically characterized by an inability to concentrate fully in a focused manner, quite literally manifested by a wide, "blank," unfocused stare.[51]

We often attain such mental fluidity quite intentionally, as through meditation, where we deliberately let go of our ordinary discriminating capacities[52] and enter a state of mental free-floating where everything seems to blend with everything. When meditating, we abandon the conventional distinction between figures and grounds and, along with it, the habit of ignoring the "empty" gaps between discrete "things."[53] We likewise "thaw" the "frozen" mental walls of entities to a point where we can spiritually merge with them.[54] Such fluid experience of space, where outside practically blends with inside, in fact culminates in the obliteration of the very distinction between subject and object (that is, in the virtual dissolution of the self) as we relax our muscles, concentrate on experiencing an uninterrupted flow between self and environment through breathing, allow our consciousness to transgress the limits of our body, and mentally blend with the cosmos.[55] No wonder meditation plays such a central role in mysticism. Defying the separateness of the self and attaining a state of consciousness in which it practically "melts" away is the mystic's utmost goal when meditating.[56]

Such a fluid mental state can also be reached with the help of psychedelic and other drugs. Thus, for example, under the influence of mescaline, even normally rigid "things" such as our own body "flow" into their surroundings.[57] In a similar fashion, even alcohol undermines our normal ability to maintain distance between self and surrounding objects (as well as to remain within the confines of a bounded lane when we drive).

Opening Up

As we might expect, the rigid mind abhors drugs. Nor does it typically tolerate too much sleep or daydreaming. Not surprisingly, it also objects to physical contact, particularly in its ultimate, sexual form.

Physical contact defies the conventional image of the self as a discrete, separate, insular entity. Even a mere handshake literally locks individuals in each other's grip (and is therefore indeed used to

ritually represent the onset of their relationship, or at least a brief
periodic "contact" between them), and lovers often express their
attachment to each other by intertwining their fingers.[58] They express their rejection of the notion of a detached, sealed-off self even
more emphatically by opening their arms to, or actually embracing,
each other, thereby displaying their willingness to overcome their
physical separateness and literally merge with each other.[59]

Open lips, not to mention open legs, are even more suggestive
icons of "opening up" to others. Indeed, sex is the ultimate state in
which the boundaries between separate selves literally melt away.
(As we reach orgasm we recapture for a brief moment our primal
oceanic experience.[60] Not surprisingly, we often close then our eyes,
thereby relinquishing our usual grip on the highly analytic sense of
vision and staying with the far more vague sensations we experience
through hearing, smell, and taste.) During intercourse, we literally
close the gap that normally separates us from others.[61] Since gaps
between them make entities seem discrete, eliminating the actual
physical gaps between lovers necessarily blurs their body contours,
thereby obliterating the selves they symbolically envelop. That is the
essence of the biblical image of cleaving to each other—an image also
used to express the mystic union with God[62]—to the point of being,
quite literally, "one flesh."[63]

The insular self also dissolves in love: "At the height of being in
love the boundary between ego and object threatens to melt away.
Against all evidence of his senses, a man who is in love declares that
'I' and 'you' are one, and is prepared to behave as if it were a fact."[64]
Essentially blending two selves in a union aptly described as "two
hearts beating as one,"[65] love is the utmost expression of our need to
offset our insular separateness by some feeling of connectedness and
to recapture our primal oceanic experience by spiritually merging
with others. (People whose early surroundings are inhospitable,
however, often have difficulty falling in love.) It is basically antithetical to privacy (as evident from lovers' wish to be always together) as well as to other tokens of individuality—private property,
territoriality, secrecy. Sharing one's personal possessions, space, or
information about oneself is clearly one of the most common forms
of displaying love (as well as intimacy).[66]

Love and sex connect individuals as well as social groups. As
demonstrated by numerous Romeos and Juliets throughout history,
they practically ignore limits and can easily overcome the widest
social chasms. Nothing defies social barriers between races, classes,

or religions more forcefully than does intermarriage. As evident from the existence of both pethood[67] and bestiality,[68] love and sex also blur the conventional distinction between human and animal, and Philip Roth's Alexander Portnoy reminds us that sexual desire also has no regard for the mental divide separating the animate from the inanimate.[69] In ignoring society's most fundamental boundaries,[70] sex poses a major threat to the social order. No wonder it is so abhorred by the rigid mind.

Ritual Fluidity

We also blend with our social surroundings when we sing in a choir, participate in communal worship, or march in a parade. While social life usually emphasizes differences in rank or function, such situations, generally known as "communitas," specifically play down such differences and instead highlight interpersonal commonality.[71] Like breathing and moving "in sync"[72] during intercourse, when we sing, pray, or march in unison we practically relinquish our individuality and allow our distinctive voice or body to literally merge with others'.

As evident from the ubiquitous presence of standard uniforms in them, "communitas" is usually situated within ritual occasions (military ceremonies, religious services, commencements). A typical case in point are initiation rites, which entail a pronounced institutionalized effort to play down individuality by holding in abeyance attributes that normally distinguish persons from each other. Initiates are thus sometimes stripped of both status (rank, property) and identity (name, family ties)—that is, of anything that would normally distinguish them from their fellow initiates.[73]

In order to dramatize the ambiguity inherent in transience, initiates are sometimes also perceived as *both* male and female, human and animal, live and dead.[74] In that, they resemble other pronouncedly ambiguous figures whose specific ritual function is to mediate among normally separate categories and domains. As evident from the assortment of masks and costumes they wear, shamans, for example, clearly blur fundamental conventional distinctions—between human and animal, male and female, young and old.[75] The pervasive presence of masks and costumes in ritual also implies a highly fluid conception of identity.

Ritual also promotes other institutionalized forms of transgression—eating food that is ordinarily considered taboo, engaging in sexual contacts that are normally prohibited (such as with animals[76]), entering drug-induced states of hallucinatory trance or ecstasy. Not surprisingly, it is typically situated around interstitial cracks (such as points of transition) in social structures, a sort of institutionalized "time out" when the social order is temporarily suspended.

Playful Promiscuity

Ritual also features status reversal, which basically mocks the social order by exposing the conventional basis of social distinctions.[77] Nowhere is this more evident than in carnival, which practically suspends all hierarchical distinctions and also promotes a fluid conception of identity in general (as manifested, for example, in transvestism). It also blurs many other conventional distinctions, such as those between man and animal (as manifested in masquerading).[78]

It is the application of an unmistakably playful frame of mind that allows such symbolic obliteration of the social order. A pretty "safe" frame for containing otherwise unacceptable transgressions, play is a perfect vehicle for challenging conventional classificatory schemata.[79]

Play highlights the fluidity of essence in general and identity in particular. Magicians' hat tricks, playful tasks such as turning a tracing of one's hand into a turkey, and visual or vocal impressions of others are practically all experiments with metamorphosis. Transgressing one's own identity by playfully transforming oneself into somebody else is also a main feature of play environments such as the costume party (or the transvestite show), where we basically mock national, gender, professional, and other conventional social barriers through cross-dressing and masquerading. Such mental promiscuity is also prominently featured in the circus. In marked contrast to the museum or the zoo, which promote the rigid compartmentalization of nature, this utterly playful environment, where animals are dressed, walk upright, ride bicycles, and eat at a table,[80] confounds even the distinction between man and beast. It is also in the circus or the fair that anomalous freaks of nature used to be displayed.[81]

Through play, we also defy finitude. Consider, for example, the Beatles' album *Sgt. Pepper's Lonely Hearts Club Band,* deliberately cut in such a way that on manual record players it would play on and on ad infinitum;[82] or the verse,

> *Pete and Repeat sat on a boat. Pete fell off. Who was left?*
> *Repeat.*
> *OK. Pete and Repeat sat on a boat. . . .*

We likewise defy conventional divides, practically molding out of given mental archipelagos altogether new islands of meaning. Thus, for example, by regrouping the letters forming the seemingly Latin sign "ORE STABIT FORTI SAR AREP LACET ORESTAT," we literally transform it into the English sign "O rest a bit for 'tis a rare place to rest at."[83] Along similar lines, by regrouping the constituent words forming the seemingly nonsensical verse

> *Every lady in the land*
> *Has twenty nails on each hand*
> *Five and twenty on hands and feet*
> *This is true without deceit*

we highlight the conventional basis of clustering words in phrases and show that it is actually a playful distortion of the verse,

> *Every lady in the land*
> *has twenty nails. On each hand*
> *five, and twenty on hands and feet.*
> *This is true without deceit.*[84]

By the same token, by ignoring the spaces between—and thereby regrouping the syllables forming—the words in the following sentences, we may unveil the otherwise concealed names of a river, a flower, and a woman:

> When the speaker beGAN GESticulating the audience roared with laughter.

> The itinerary of the congressmen included JaPAN, SYria, India, and Java.

> On the desk of a certain country schoolteacher IS A BELL which she uses for signalling class periods.[85]

Ambiguity is a critical element in such word puzzles. The letters
GES, for example, constitute not only the first syllable of the word
gesticulating but also the last syllable of the concealed word *Ganges.*
Along similar lines, in the following verse, the very same word is
used both to end one sentence and to begin another:

> *Lulu had a steamboat*
> *The steamboat had a bell*
> *Lulu went to heaven*
> *The steamboat went to—*
> *HELLO, operator, give me number nine*
> *If you disconnect me,*
> *I'll kick you in the —*
> *BEHIND the refrigerator*
> *Lies a broken glass*
> *Lulu fell down*
> *And broke her big fat—*
> *ASK me no more questions,*
> *I'll tell you no more lies,*
> *That's what Lulu told me*
> *Just before she died.*[86]

Somewhat similar, in this regard, are "knock-knock" jokes, the very
essence of which lies in the way they highlight the ambiguous nature
of constituent elements that can be perceived in more than one context of meaning:

> *Knock, Knock.*
> *Who's there?*
> *Isadore.*
> *Isadore who?*
> *Isadore [Is the door] locked? I can't get in.*
>
> *Knock, Knock.*
> *Who's there?*
> *Wendy.*
> *Wendy who?*
> *Wendy [When do you] want to come out and play?*
>
> *Knock, Knock.*
> *Who's there?*
> *Howell.*

Howell who?
Howell [How will] you have your pizza, plain or with sausage?[87]

It is the idea that the same figure can be perceived against more than one mental ground that makes puns, riddles,[88] cards (a five of hearts can be used as a five in one series and as a heart in another), and other play forms of multiple meaning so appealing to the fuzzy mind. In connecting contexts that are normally separate from each other, such ambiguous mental bridges basically defy the very notion of discrete islands of meaning.

Riddles, nonsense verses, and circus shows are typically associated with children. All in all, the world of play is perceived as a child's world and adults normally experience it as a form of "regression." This need not surprise us. After all, play does capture our primal fluid experience of the world and allows us to perceive reality in a manner which the rigid adult's mind rarely does.

Comic Transgression

Transgressing conventional boundaries is also a major feature of humor,[89] a special form of play that occupies a very similar role in our life.

Like other forms of play, humor promotes mental promiscuity by connecting realms of meaning that are usually separate from one another.[90] The comic use of colloquial language in a formal literary text, for example, defies the common distinction between "high" and popular culture.[91] Through the use of multiple meaning, jokes, like puns, likewise fuse normally unrelated contexts,[92] mentally transporting us from one to another. Thus, for example, the following answer to the question: "Why did the Pope meet Kurt Waldheim?", "Because Klaus Barbie was unavailable,"[93] basically defies the conventional mental separation of the categories "heads of state" and "Nazi criminals" from each other, suggesting that they are not necessarily incompatible. Consider also the joke about the woman who refuses to be evacuated by boat or helicopter from a flooded area because God, in her dream, promised to save her. When she finally drowns, God explains that he did send a boat and a helicopter to rescue her, but to no avail. The essence of the joke, of course, lies in the totally unexpected, blasphemous mental fusion of human and divine means of salvation.

Frames are among the boundaries most commonly transgressed in humor.[94] Thus, for example, in Pierre Etaix's film *Le Grand Amour,* as the protagonist, reconstructing in his mind a scene from his youth, tries to recall where exactly in a restaurant he was sitting, we see him mentally pursuing several possible versions of the same scene until an angry waiter finally asks him to please make up his mind where he wants to sit. Along similar lines, in Luis Buñuel's *The Discreet Charm of the Bourgeoisie,* a man wakes up from a dream and proceeds to go straight to the party about which he just dreamed. Both scenes, it then turns out, were only part of a dream of one of the other characters in them! The frame in which characters are anchored is just as ambiguous in Lewis Carroll's *Through the Looking-Glass:*

> "He's dreaming now," said Tweedledee: "and what do you think he's dreaming about?"
> Alice said "Nobody can guess that."
> "Why, about *you!*" Tweedledee exclaimed, clapping his hands triumphantly. "And if he left off dreaming about you, where do you suppose you'd be?"
> "Where I am now, of course," said Alice.
> "Not you!" Tweedledee retorted contemptuously. "You'd be nowhere. Why, you're only a sort of thing in his dream!"
> "If that there King was to wake," added Tweedledum, "you'd go out—bang!—just like a candle!"
>
> .   .   .   .
>
> He shouted this so loud that Alice couldn't help saying "Hush! You'll be waking him, I'm afraid, if you make so much noise."
> "Well, it's no use *your* talking about waking him," said Tweedledum, "when you're only one of the things in his dream. You know very well you're not real."
> "I *am* real!" said Alice, and began to cry.
> "You won't make yourself a bit realer by crying," Tweedledee remarked: "there's nothing to cry about."
> "If I wasn't real," Alice said—half laughing through her tears, it all seemed so ridiculous—"I shouldn't be able to cry."
> "I hope you don't suppose those are *real* tears?" Tweedledum interrupted in a tone of great contempt.[95]

The mental brackets surrounding the entire story, of course, are just as open to comic transgression, as we see in Jonathan Gefen's children's story about a man who lives in a world where everything is green until one day he spots a blue man: "The green man stopped his green car and asked the blue man: 'Hey, blue man, what are you

doing here?' 'Me?' said the blue man, 'I am from another story.' "[96]
In a similar fashion, having just told a joke about a lost brick, a
comedian tells another joke about two passengers who, in a fight,
end up throwing each other's dog and pipe off a train. Noting that
when the train arrives at the next stop the dog is already waiting
there, he then asks his audience to guess what he is carrying in his
mouth. When some say "the pipe," he announces, "No, the brick
from the previous joke!" Similar mental brackets are farcically transgressed by the Saul Steinberg cartoon character who chips up the
outline of the cartoon itself,[97] the villain in Mel Brooks's *Blazing
Saddles* who hails a cab and asks the driver to take him out of the
film, or the devil in William Dieterle's film *The Devil and Daniel
Webster,* who, with a pointed finger (just like Uncle Sam on James
M. Flagg's "I Want *You* for U.S. Army" poster) and a puckish wink,
targets the viewer as his next victim. Conventional frame limits are
likewise breached when the orchestra rises and the conductor takes
his bow before the piece is actually completed (as in Schadrin's First
Concerto for Orchestra),[98] when the commercials interrupting a television program are part of the program itself (as in *Saturday Night
Live*),[99] or when a stand-up comic incorporates hecklers' comments
(or even trips by members of the audience to the bathroom) into his
show.[100]

Humor also defies the insular, sealed-off self created by the rigid
mind. Comic depictions of the body, for example, highlight the way
it transgresses its limits and blends with its surroundings.[101] They
feature specifically those organs

> through which the world enters the body or . . . through which the
> body itself goes out to meet the world. . . . [T]he emphasis is on
> the apertures or the convexities, or on various ramifications and
> offshoots: the open mouth, the genital organs, the breasts, the phal-
> lus, the potbelly, the nose . . . those parts of the grotesque body in
> which it outgrows its own self. . . . [N]ext is the anus. All these
> convexities and orifices have a common characteristic; it is within
> them that the confines between . . . the body and the world are
> overcome.[102]

The comic mind is likewise fascinated by corporeal processes that
highlight the open nature of the body—eating, defecating, copulat-
ing, farting, sneezing.[103]

The thick wall normally separating the rich from the poor practically melts away as Charlie Chaplin, the prototypical trickster,[104]

steps out of a Rolls-Royce in a hilarious scene from *City Lights* and
beats an absolutely stunned tramp to a cigar butt lying on the sidewalk. As manifested in numerous jokes, limericks, and lampoons,
humor virtually respects no boundary. Generally perceived as non-
serious and thus pretty harmless, it constitutes the perfect medium
for transgressions that in almost any other context would be considered totally unacceptable:

> *First farmer:* Did you hear about this fellow Kinsey, that's
>   been going around saying things against us farmers?
> *Second farmer:* What's he been saying?
> *First farmer:* He says us farmers go around fucking sheep—
>   and goats—and chickens—and snakes—
> *Second farmer:* Snakes?[105]

Fluidity in Art

Like humor, art, too, makes transgressions of boundaries more
palatable. Even those of us who revere society's moral limits nonetheless tolerate and perhaps even enjoy robbery and murder when
they take place in a book or on the screen. The way art legitimates
transgression is likewise demonstrated by the remarkable success of
plays such as Jean Poiret's *La Cage aux Folles* and Harvey Fierstein's
Torch Song Trilogy, which depict homosexuals in a sympathetic manner.

Art is a stylized form of fantasy. A mental type of adventure,[106]
in which limits tend to lose their tight grip on our mind, fantasy, like
humor, respects no boundary (which is precisely what makes it at
the same time so attractive yet so feared by the rigid mind). Even
those of us who never venture into illicit love affairs or forbidden
sexual territory nonetheless explore such transgressions in our personal[107] as well as collective (Oedipus and his mother, Leda and the
swan) fantasies. Fantasy likewise blurs the conventional distinction
between live and inanimate (Walt Disney's *Silly Symphonies*) and
mocks the very notion of insularity (in George Dunning's animated
film *Yellow Submarine,* a voracious figure literally sucks up the very
ground within which it is situated). Typically abhorred by the rigid
mind, blends and mixtures, too, haunt our imagination in the form
of mythical composites of animals (griffins, chimeras) or humans
and animals (satyrs, mermaids, angels, or the combinations of hu-

mans and rams, jackals, scarabs, and birds that adorn ancient Egyptian walls). Science fiction, fairy tale, and other forms of fantasy also promote a fluid conception of essence by featuring transformations of ordinary persons into superhuman (Superman, Batman),[108] animal (werewolves, the Frog Prince), and other (Cinderella, Mr. Hyde) unrecognizable versions of themselves as well as of inanimate (Pinocchio) or dead (Sleeping Beauty) beings into live ones. Such a fluid conception of essence is likewise promoted through kinetic art.

Art also promotes unconventional mixtures and combinations. Artistic "promiscuity" is prominently featured, for example, in the arts of collage, assemblage, and photomontage[109] and is likewise manifested in culinary art (in assorted appetizer platters)[110] as well as in music (in stylistic mélanges such as Astor Piazzolla's blend of chamber music and tango, Pee Wee Hunt's Dixieland versions of *Carmen* and *Rigoletto,* or Claude Bolling's suites featuring classical instrumentalists accompanied by jazz rhythm sections). Fusions of live and animated film (Robert Zemeckis's *Who Framed Roger Rabbit?*) and multimedia potpourris of slides, music, lecture, and dance[111] likewise remind us that the lines between "media" are drawn by critics who, "for purposes of convenient classification, attempt to impose a pattern on what is largely a fluid situation."[112] The fuzzy mind also generates musical pastiches wherein several pieces, sewn together by segues such as the ones used in piano bars or on late Beatles albums,[113] literally flow into one another, forming a single continuous acoustic thread.

The quest for fluidity also underlies the artist's attempt to defy the conventional partitioning of reality into entities by blurring the very distinction between figure and ground. As evident, for example, from the fact that we rarely recognize spaces between buildings,[114] we normally regard the ground against which we perceive "things" as empty, a void.[115] Artists, however, often attend such "negative" spaces and use them dynamically in painting and sculpture.[116] Moreover, they often eliminate gaps altogether by superimposing several separate figures on each other[117] or "gluing" them together by using a common contour line.[118] Consider, in this regard, the remarkable attempts of Maurits Escher to fill up visual fields without leaving any "empty" space.[119] By designing spaces that function as each other's ground, so that those that constitute the ground for one set of figures also constitute a second set of figures against the latter as ground (as in *Mosaic II*[120]), he basically managed to create a world with practically no gaps. In demonstrating how the same space can be perceived as both figure and ground, such "optical puns"[121] clearly defy the routine differentiation of "things" from nonthings.

The very same principle underlies polyphony, which blurs the conventional distinction between "solo" and "accompaniment" by featuring simultaneously several "voices" that attract our attention with equal force.[122] Consider, for example, the "dialogues" between flute and bassoon in Heitor Villa-Lobos's *Bachiana Brasileira* No. 6 or between trumpet and saxophone in Chet Baker's and Gerry Mulligan's *My Funny Valentine* and *Moonlight in Vermont,* not to mention the intricate contrapuntal "multilogues" in Bach's Brandenburg Concertos Nos. 2, 3, and 5 or *Musical Offering.* The fact that each of the voices we hear in these pieces can be ambiguously perceived as both "figure" and "ground" inevitably blurs their distinctive "outlines" and precludes their experience as discrete melodic islands.

©1957 M. C. Escher/Cordon Art, Baarn, Holland

MOSAIC II. Optical puns: The same space is perceived as both figure and ground, "thing" and "nonthing"

Art also plays up on the visual vagueness of essence. Both kinetic and op art,[123] for example, mock the very notion of solid entities with rigid contours. So do works such as Escher's *Still Life and Street* or *Metamorphosis II,* in which a desk and a street, or a town and a chessboard, literally flow into each other in a way that leaves unanswered the question where one ends and the other begins. (A similar effect is created acoustically when a melody is successively taken up by different instruments with no break whatsoever in tone color.)[124] Utilizing a somewhat unfocused style of looking as part of their quest for new ways of seeing the familiar,[125] artists may also produce works characterized by a pronouncedly hazy ambience. Instead of well-articulated figures with sharp contours, Turner's (*Procession of*

©1937 M. C. Escher/Cordon Art, Baarn, Holland

STILL LIFE AND STREET. The boundlessness of entities: Desk and street "flowing" into one another

Boats, Figures in a Pink Atmosphere) and Seurat's (*At the "Concert Européen," The Cat*) works, for example, feature blurred patches fading into one another as if seen through heavy fog. Such renunciation of contours also characterizes harmony, where separate voices lose their distinctive tonal color and are perceived as an undifferentiated blend (like a curry that includes a mixture of onion, garlic, tomato, chilis, ginger, cumin, coriander, fenugreek, and turmeric). Note, for example, the "thick" sonic texture of orchestral or choral pieces such as Sibelius's *Finlandia* or Verdi's Requiem. Such texture is also produced by the tonal fusion of only two or three voices (as in the Beatles' *If I Fell, Nowhere Man,* and *Because*) or even by a single voice, either chordally (as in Liszt's Piano Sonata or Bud Powell's *Ruby, My Dear*) or through overdubbing (as exemplified by John Lennon's "multitracked" voice on *I Should Have Known Better* or *Sun King*). As we listen to such music, we often close our eyes, further curtailing our ability to discriminate between distinct entities. Letting ourselves "drown" in such ocean of sound, we briefly recapture our primal oceanic experience.

Frames, too, are transgressed in art. In Crockett Johnson's book *Harold and the Purple Crayon*[126] as well as in Wolfgang Peterson's film *The Neverending Story* (or Robert Stevenson's *Mary Poppins*), characters practically "enter" pictures and books. By the same token, in David McPhail's *The Magical Drawings of Moony B. Finch*[127] and Woody Allen's *The Purple Rose of Cairo,* they literally jump out of drawings and movies into real life. In Escher's *Reptiles* a lizard likewise crawls out of a drawing and in Magritte's *Common Sense* still-life objects are placed *on top of* a blank, framed canvas.

Nor does art shy away from frame ambiguity. When we watch Alain Resnais's film *Last Year at Marienbad,* we are never quite sure whether we are watching the narrator's present reality, fantasy, or memory. By the same token, in Magritte's *Human Condition I, Les Promenades d'Euclide,* or *The Fair Captive,* it is totally unclear whether we are looking at an actual landscape through a transparent glass or at a mere painting of it. Both interpretations are equally plausible. (In fact, in his *Evening Falls* and *The Door to Freedom,* the view we see through a shattered window is even reproduced on the broken glass around it!) In Escher's art, it is likewise possible for a man to be part of a picture at which he is looking (*Print Gallery*)[128] and for two hands to paradoxically draw each other (*Drawing Hands*).

The world of art also features castrati (in opera), husky-voiced

Georges-Pierre Seurat. *At the "Concert Européen."* (c. 1887). Conté crayon, 12¼ × 9⅜". COLLECTION, THE MUSEUM OF MODERN ART, NEW YORK. Lillie P. Bliss Collection. Photo copyright © April 23, 1991 The Museum of Modern Art, New York

Blurred vision: Figures without contours gradually fading into one another

LES PROMENADES D'EUCLIDE. An ambiguous frame: An actual street
seen through a window of a mere painting of it?

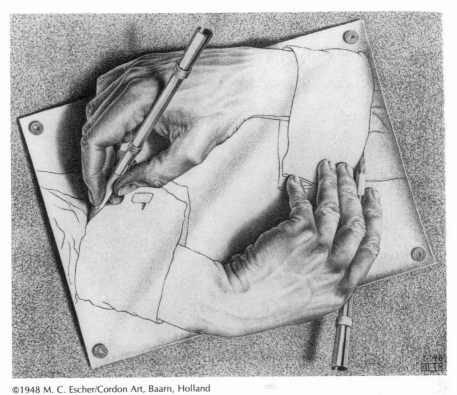

DRAWING HANDS. Playing with frames: Which hand is real and which merely representational?

women wearing high hats and ties (in cabarets), and other pronouncedly ambiguous performers. Moreover, only in that world are explicit symbols of androgyny (Michael Jackson, David Bowie) idolized by people who would never allow the fusion of conventional notions of masculinity and femininity anywhere else. No wonder artists are often seen by the rigid mind as the embodiment of transgression.

The Ethics of Fluidity

Fluidity is not just a fact. It is also an ideal and, as such, has a significant moral dimension. It is a moral objection to social divisions, for example, that inspires liberal immigration legislation to open national borders and has led communal movements such as the kibbutz to try and destroy the insular family. Similar moral concerns underlie the communal objection—as articulated by both Rousseau and Marx[129]—to private property, the foremost symbolic represen- tation of the insular self.

Marx, of course, repudiated not only private property and the family, but also religion, the state, and the class system, practically advocating the elimination of any barrier between human beings and each other. Hence his appeal to proponents of racial desegregation, who object to racial barriers, as well as to those who champion equal job opportunity and defy gender distinctions. His dream of a trans- national society likewise appeals to pacifists.[130]

Cosmopolitanism, of course, was introduced long before Marx by the Stoics, who, in accordance with their general taste for con- tinuums and mixtures,[131] resented all political borders. Rather than be an Athenian or a Corinthian, taught Epictetus, one ought to regard oneself as a citizen of the world.[132] Such ideas were also promoted by Paul: "There is no distinction between Jew and Greek; the same Lord is Lord of all."[133] "[Christ] has made us both one, and has broken down the dividing wall. . . . [creating] one new man in place of the two."[134] In order to obliterate the very distinction be- tween Jew and Gentile, Paul urged Jews to abandon all ritual markers (dietary laws, circumcision, Sabbath observance) designed to pre- serve Jewish distinctiveness and allowed them even to marry Gentiles.[135]

Both Paul's and Epictetus's were highly universalistic[136] ethics, yet even universalism entails some tacit assumptions about the ho- rizons of the "universe" involved. Though their moral horizons were certainly wider than most of their contemporaries', the Stoics and the early Christians nonetheless confined their "universalism" to hu- mans only. Expanding such horizons even further to also include nonhuman life within one's sphere of moral concern has been a foremost objective of ethicists such as Albert Schweitzer:

> [Ethics] must widen the circle from the narrowest limits of the family first to include the clan, then the tribe, then the nation and finally all mankind. But even [there] it cannot stop. By reason of the quite universal idea, which is as elastic as one pleases, of par- ticipation in one common nature, it is compelled to declare the unity of mankind with all created beings. . . . Ethics consist in responsibility toward all that lives—responsibility which has be- come so wide as to be limitless.[137]

To found an ethical world-view on ethics which are only concerned with our fellow-man [is] the fault of too narrow a conception of ethics. . . . Only when ethics embrace the whole Universe is an ethical world-view really possible. . . . Ethics are boundless in their domain [and] are concerned with all living things.[138]

[The truly ethical person] goes out of his way to avoid injuring anything living. . . . [He] is careful not to crush any insect as he walks. If he works by lamplight . . . he prefers to keep the window shut and to breathe stifling air, rather than to see insect after insect fall on his table with singed and sinking wings. If he goes into the street after a rainstorm and sees a worm which has strayed there, he . . . helps it back from the deadly paving stones into the lush grass. Should he pass by an insect which has fallen into a pool, he spares the time to reach it a leaf or stalk on which it may clamber and save itself.[139]

In the West, the cradle of rat poison and insecticides, few but Saint Francis of Assisi[140] and a handful of animal-rights activists would even be bothered by such concerns. In the East, however, where *all* life is viewed as a single unity, they are part of a long ethical tradition.[141] After all, within the context of the doctrine of transmigration, the very distinction between human and animal—two birth states that every soul assumes numerous times in different incarnations[142]—is rather trivial. Whereas Judeo-Christianity is morally indifferent to the killing of animals, the ultimate manifestation of the Indian Jainist ethic of nonviolence (*ahimsa*)—in fact, the very first vow taken by Jain monks—is a commitment to refrain from harming any living creature, be it human or vermin.[143] The foremost expression of such commitment is vegetarianism, yet Jains also avoid digging, swimming, and even fanning themselves. In order to protect even microorganisms, they likewise carefully dust stools before sitting on them and wear special mouth cloths so as not to inhale them.[144]

Yet ethics may require an even broader expansion of our moral horizons. The truly ethical person, insists Schweitzer, also "tears no leaf from its tree, breaks off no flower."[145] Such moral sensitivity culminates in the "land ethic," which, in an effort to protect the land from human expansion through pollution, deforestation, and exhaustion of natural resources, includes the entire "environment" within our sphere of moral concern.[146] Along with the mystic's, the environmentalist's view of the world is probably the closest approximation of the infant's primal oceanic experience.

Fluidity and Modernity

Like its rigid counterpart, the fuzzy mind manifests itself more prominently in some cultural environments than others. Racial ambiguity, for example, is accepted far more readily by Brazilians or Hawaiians than by Japanese,[147] and the Malay definition of territory is much vaguer than that of the Germans.[148] Nor do all cultures avoid lexical ambiguity or perceive individuals as separable from their social surroundings.[149]

Cultures that cherish fluidity usually manifest it in more than one domain. The ubiquitous presence of ambiguity in Eskimo art, for example, also resonates in their rather fuzzy notions of family (as manifested in residential and adoption arrangements), rules, and gender.[150] Americans' aversion to boundaries is likewise manifested in their ethnic "melting pot" ideology as well as in the cultural eclecticism underlying American architecture and cuisine.[151] By the same token, it is not a coincidence that the Navajo, whose clan structure is pretty fuzzy, also revere hermaphrodites and avoid closure in their design,[152] or that the Central African Lele, who routinely practice intermarriage, also venerate an exceptionally ambiguous animal such as the pangolin—a scaly, tree-dwelling anteater.[153] Nor is it a coincidence that the early Christians, who abolished the distinction between Gentile and Jew, also produced, in marked contrast to Jews, an ambiguous blend of man and God in the form of Jesus.

Yet attitudes toward ambiguity vary even within the same culture across time and the fuzzy mind has clearly achieved more prominence in some historical periods than others. Consider, for instance, the Renaissance. Its pronouncedly transgressive and promiscuous spirit is manifested in the irreverent writings of Rabelais[154] as well as in the paintings of Bosch, which feature ambiguous composites of humans and birds, pigs, beetles, and fish.[155] It was also during the Renaissance that the art of polyphony reached its florescence, as in the music of Palestrina.

The fuzzy mind has gained a similar cultural prominence since the late nineteenth century.[156] Fluidity, we shall now see, is a hallmark of modernity.

Like its rigid counterpart, the fuzzy mind often manifests itself in architecture (porches[157] and balconies, for example, clearly blur the distinction between indoor and outdoor), and the modern bent for fluidity is indeed quite evident in modern design. Modernism has produced fireplaces that gradually "emerge" from the surrounding room (as in Frank Lloyd Wright's Falling Water) as well as dioramas in which three-dimensional habitats recede imperceptibly into flat backdrops (as in the American Museum of Natural History in New York City). Such visual flow is also created by glass, the modern architectural use of which has evolved from the glass-covered shopping arcades and exhibition palaces of the nineteenth century[158] to the glazed office buildings, skylights, picture windows, and sunrooms of today. In allowing them to visually interpenetrate each other, glass clearly blurs the distinction between inside and outside.[159]

Yet even transparent partitions hinder full visual flow: "In a car you're always in a compartment, and because you're used to it you don't realize that through the car window everything you see is just more TV. You're a passive observer and it is all moving by you boringly in a frame. On a [motorcycle] the frame is gone. . . . You're *in* the scene, not just watching it. . . ."[160] It is precisely such concern for visual flow that has led to the invention of the contact lens and inspired modern "open" design,[161] whose foremost manifestation is Wright's "integral" architecture, based on the principle of "continuity."[162] The fluid quality of Wright's design is a result of a conscious effort to treat much of the interior of the house as a single undifferentiated space: "Dwellings [used to be] cut up . . . [I]nteriors consisted of boxes . . . called *rooms* . . . I could see little sense in this . . . [s]o I declared the whole lower floor as one room."[163] Such superfluity of walls—one of the most remarkable achievements of modern architecture[164]—is manifested in the transformation of kitchens and dining rooms into integrated blends of vaguely defined work and eating "areas."[165] It also underlies the concept of the split-level house as well as modern ideas of remodeling such as removing interior walls and ceilings. A fluid conception of the relations between interior and exterior[166] has likewise inspired the idea of buildings with no walls, a classic example of which is Alexandre Gustave Eiffel's famous tower in Paris.[167]

The modern bent for fluidity is also manifested in art. Like modern physics, which has abandoned the distinction between matter and void, modern art blurs the distinction between "positive" (figure) and "negative" (ground) space, basically rejecting the traditional perception of the space between objects as empty.[168] Cubist experiments with multiperspectival representation have likewise altered our perception of the contours that supposedly delineate objects,[169] whereas modern poetry and literature have similarly questioned the necessity of punctuation. E. E. Cummings, for example, often ignored the conventional spaces between words, generating word strings such as "eyeswhichneversmile."[170] (He would also mock punctuation by spreading a word across several lines separated from one another by wide gaps.)[171] Joyce's classic experiment with the idea of a continuous stream of consciousness in *Ulysses* likewise concludes with a thirty-six-page passage virtually uninterrupted by a single period or comma.[172]

Modern art has also tried to blur the distinction between art and life by letting the artistic and the "real" literally interpenetrate each other. That has entailed, for example, an attempt to blur the conventional distinction between artistic and "real" time. Such temporal fusion of art and life is manifested in poems that begin in the middle of a word within parentheses and books that begin on page 9 in the middle of a sentence.[173] It is likewise manifested in the use of fade-ins, whereby musical pieces emerge almost imperceptibly from the silence preceding them (Debussy's *Prélude à l'Après-Midi d'un Faune*, the Beatles' *Eight Days a Week*), and fade-outs, whereby they slowly disappear into the void that follows them. Consider also, in this regard, poems that end in the middle of a sentence,[174] musical pieces that end before the final resolution of the tonic,[175] and theatrical performances that continue throughout the intermission.[176] The ultimate expression of the attempt temporally to integrate art and life, however, is the "happening," a distinctively modern art form that makes artistic time practically boundless.[177]

The mental frame separating art from life has also been breached by the similar modernist attempt to blur the conventional distinction between artistic and "real" space.[178] Thus, for example, in *A Woman with Chrysanthemums*, basically defying the traditional convention of placing the "action" at the center of the picture, as far away as possible from its nonartistic surroundings, Degas purposely highlights through the woman's gaze what would have been included in the picture had it not been interrupted by the frame.[179] Furthermore, nothing emphasizes the intrusive nature of the frame more dramatically than a cut-off head (in *Horse and Jockey*) or face (in *Ballet Dancers in Butterfly Costumes* or in Toulouse-Lautrec's *Tête-à-tête Supper*). Mondrian creates the same effect with deliberately truncated geometrical figures that seem to extend beyond, and thus be completed in our mind only outside, the artistic frame (as in *Diamond Painting in Red, Yellow, and Blue*),[180] and so does Seurat by continuing the picture on the frame itself.

The Metropolitan Museum of Art, Bequest of Mrs. H. O. Havemeyer, 1929. The H. O. Havemeyer Collection. (29.100.128)

A WOMAN WITH CHRYSANTHEMUMS. Defying boundaries: A woman
looks through the frame separating art from life

The attempt to integrate artistic and "real" space has naturally led to the modern concept of "environmental" art. As evident from modern sculpture and urban grafitti[181] as well as from the environmental theater (in which the stage literally interpenetrates the house and the traditional gap between performers and audience is practically obliterated),[182] such art is perceived as inseparable from its nonartistic surroundings. The pinnacle of environmental art is the "environment," which, like the "happening," represents the ultimate expression of the modern effort to integrate art and life. In marked contrast to paintings, which are confined to a frame conceived as a window through which observers peep into an altogether separate world,[183] "environments" are practically unframed,[184] and observers are therefore literally situated *within* them!

The attempt to integrate art and life has also entailed an effort to blur the traditional distinction between artistic and "real" objects.[185]

Diamond Painting in Red, Yellow, and Blue; Piet MONDRIAN; National
Gallery of Art, Washington; Gift of Herbert and Nannette Rothschild

Mental transgression of the frame separating artistic
from "real" space

Ever since Braque and Picasso first used actual newspaper scraps in
their collages, modern artists (for example, Kurt Schwitters, Marcel
Duchamp, Jean Dubuffet) have included in their art objects ranging
from tickets and candy wrappers to light bulbs, shoes, and parts of
automobiles.[186] In an effort to make their art more "real," Dada
performers would likewise read on stage recent articles from the
newspaper.[187] Modern artists have also stretched the artistic frame to
include actual events that would have occurred even without their
intervention, thereby producing pieces of sculpture that embody natural processes such as the melting of blocks of ice, musical pieces
featuring sounds of birds, and shows that consist of simply watching
the street.[188] They have also encouraged contact between what is
inside and what is normally outside the artistic frame, as evident
from the attempt of modern theater to include actual interaction
between the performers and the audience as part of the performance[189] (as, for example, in Joseph Heller's *We Bombed in New
Haven,* where actors actually step out of their characters and casually
talk to the audience[190]).

Such fusion of art and life obviously generates considerable ambiguity. In a modernist "environment" which basically confounds the artistic and the nonartistic, one can never be absolutely sure what is meant to be experienced as art and what just happens to be there. By the same token, I recall watching a performance of the Merce Cunningham company and trying to figure out whether some of the sounds I was hearing were part of the John Cage music to which the company was dancing or actual sirens on the street outside.

Such ambiguity is often produced quite deliberately. Thus, for example, in Karlheinz Stockhausen's *Hymnen,* sounds of static that we would normally regard as mere noise are actually part of the piece itself.[191] Consider also John Barth's *Giles Goat-Boy, or the Revised New Syllabus.* It opens with a "Publisher's Disclaimer" in which the editor in chief recounts a debate within the press whether to publish the book and even encloses four negative reactions of editors to it. In a "Cover-Letter to the Editors and Publisher," Barth then describes how he actually got the complete manuscript from one Stoker Giles. The manuscript itself, the taped autobiography of Giles's father, is followed by a short "Posttape" presumably written by the same author, yet in a "Postscript to the Posttape" Barth then claims that it was authored by some impostor and notes that even its type differs from that of the manuscript itself. The book ends with a "Footnote to the Postscript to the Posttape" in which the editor notes that the type of the "Postscript" differs from that of the "Cover-Letter"![192]

Such deliberate confusion of art and life is a prominent feature of modern theater. Thus, for example, in *We Bombed in New Haven,* the curtain is raised "prematurely," thereby exposing the supposedly embarrassed actors to the audience as if they are still not ready.[193] Just as baffling is the actors' rebellion against the director in Pirandello's *Tonight We Improvise:*

> *Dr. Hinkfuss:* [A]s the audience must already have guessed, this rebellion among the actors was faked, agreed on in advance between them and me, in order to make the performance seem more authentic. (. . . the actors stop and stare at him . . . in various poses of astonishment. . . .) Faked, too, this astonishment.
>
> *The leading actor* (trembling with indignation): A dirty trick! The audience must not believe a word of it. My protest was not in any way faked. (. . . strides off angrily.)

> *Dr. Hinkfuss* (. . .): Acting, acting, all acting, even this
> outburst. I should perhaps, after all, have conceded
> something to the ego of an actor like Mr.——, in-
> deed one of the best on the stage today.
>
> . . . .
>
> *The character actress:* You really want to make people be-
> lieve that this emergence of our roles was agreed on
> between us ahead of time?
> *Dr. Hinkfuss:* Just ask the audience if they think we are not
> at this moment really improvising?
> (The gentleman in the orchestra, four others in the orches-
> tra, and the gentleman in the balcony start applaud-
> ing. They stop at once if the real audience does not
> contagiously follow their example.)
> *The character actress:* But yes, of course, we are really im-
> provising now. We're out of our roles and we're im-
> provising. . . .
> *Dr. Hinkfuss:* All right, then—keep it up, keep it up.*[194]

Television, too, helps blur the distinction between framed and
unframed reality. Whereas going to the movies necessarily entails
leaving one's ordinary surroundings, soap operas are in fact spatially
inseparable from the rest of one's life.[195] In homes where television
is on most of the time, they are also temporally integrated into one's
"real" life and, unlike the experience of going out in the evening to
see a show, may not even interrupt its regular flow.

By offering a continuous stream of programs ranging from science and religion to art, sports, politics, and sex, television also
defies the traditional separateness of these "domains." Furthermore,
by ignoring conventional divides among traditionally separate stocks
of knowledge, it also brings historically segregated "communities of
discourse" (men and women, children and adults, different social
classes) into a single common mental orbit.[196] By juxtaposing professional experts and mere witnesses, it also softens traditional status
barriers.[197]

The modern world is generally averse to status distinctions and
other social barriers. This aversion is manifested in the ideologies of
both romantic love and racial integration as well as in an "integrative" philosophy of management that downplays hierarchical and

departmental divisions within organizations,[198] and a "community" mental health system that defies the traditional segregation of the mentally ill from the rest of society.[199] It is also manifested in the feminist effort to "degenderize" society and in the gay movement, both of which reflect an underlying commitment to androgyny and a rejection of the traditional view of masculinity and femininity as mutually exclusive.[200]

Modernity also entails the obliteration of traditional islands of group identity. In an age of global communication (newspaper, television, computer) networks, insular cultures are becoming increasingly obsolete. The very notion of a "pure" culture seems somewhat pointless when Jews eat egg rolls, Brazilians wear Levis, Koreans play soccer, and Tunisians listen to jazz.[201] As the world moves toward greater integration of historically insulated political and economic systems, that is also true of nation-states. Markets are by and large indifferent to social distinctions,[202] and the proliferation of a market economy as well as the development of global markets have certainly made such distinctions less significant, as societies are becoming increasingly interdependent politically as well as economically. In a world of multinational corporations, national borders may soon be history.

Multinational corporations and global communication networks are distinctively modern phenomena. So are feminism, integrative management, interdisciplinary scholarship,[203] and the work of Cage, Magritte, Cummings, and Barth. Nor is it a coincidence that Dada, cubism, the cabaret, and the collage are all products of the same generation (the one that also produced Debussy, Pirandello, and Mondrian) or that the "happening," the gay movement, unisex fashion, the "open school" (with its movable walls, flexible schedules, unstructured curriculum, and flexible age-grouping),[204] "open marriage," and Eastern mysticism all flourished in America around the same time. The historical coincidence of such a wide variety of cultural phenomena suggests that they are more closely interrelated than might appear at first glance. Indeed, they are all expressions of all-embracing attempts to blur distinctions and obliterate barriers. The very same attitude toward boundaries underlies the holistic critique of the medical compartmentalization of our body into supposedly insular systems, the animal-rights movement, community mental health, environmental art, and poststructuralism. They are but different manifestations of the fuzzy mind, all products of the same basic modern effort to destroy the ossified order promoted by the rigid mind.

Ours is an age of "declassification,"[205] of blurred distinctions. It is an age that brings together musical styles as different from one another as ragtime (*Good Day Sunshine*), rock (*Doctor Robert*), big band (*Got to Get You into My Life*), pop (*Here, There and Everywhere*), chamber (*Eleanor Rigby*), Indian (*Love You To*), children (*Yellow Submarine*), and electronic (*Tomorrow Never Knows*) music in a single album (the Beatles' *Revolver*). It is an age of

> philosophical inquiries looking like literary criticism (. . . Cavell on Beckett or Thoreau, Sartre on Flaubert), scientific discussions looking like belles-lettres *morceaux* (Lewis Thomas, Loren Eiseley), baroque fantasies presented as deadpan empirical observations (Borges, Barthelme) . . . parables posing as ethnographies (Castaneda), theoretical treatises set out as travelogues (Lévi-Strauss), ideological arguments cast as historiographical inquiries (Edward Said), epistemological studies constructed like political tracts (Paul Feyerabend). . . . [O]ne waits only for quantum theory in verse or biography in algebra.[206]

What we are seeing today, then, "is not just another redrawing of the cultural map—the moving a few disputed borders . . . but an alteration of the principles of mapping. Something is happening to the way we think about the way we think."[207]

6

The Flexible Mind

To want to get rid of [rigidity] does not mean advocating a wishy-washy formlessness but forms which may be just as definite at any one moment but not so permanent; something that can assume a variety of different shapes or change from one to another and back again. One would then become interested not in the static nature of things but in the range of their potential natures. . . . Enough rigidity to give context, meaning and security. Enough flexibility to give change, improvement, adventure and hope.[1]

The rigid mind typically envisions a highly compartmentalized world made up of sharply delineated insular entities separated from one another by great divides. The fuzzy mind, by contrast, invokes a world made up of vague essences fading gradually into one another. Instead of mental ghettos, it features mental twilight zones. Instead of clear-cut distinctions, it highlights ambiguity.

Both mind-sets entail certain costs as well as certain advantages. Examining what we gain and what we lose by seeing the world through each of them may help us identify yet a third mode of experiencing reality that might combine the best each of them can offer us.

Transgression and Creativity

Islands of meaning are generated by analytic thinking, which presupposes a mental scalpel that allows us to carve "things" out of their context.[2] Such a scalpel, however, inevitably violates the integrity of our experience. "When analytic thought, the knife, is applied to experience, something is always killed in the process."[3]

What is usually killed in the process is context. By searching for laws that are independent of context and relying on highly decontextualized laboratory research and statistics, science, for example, ignores the fact that meaning is inherently grounded in particular contexts.[4] Our analytic ability to decontextualize is admittedly a great intellectual achievement[5] (we could not have developed algebra, geometry, or formal logic, for instance, without it), yet it clearly also entails some "context blindness."[6] Being able to focus, for example, inevitably presupposes wearing mental blinders. As such, it entails a tunnel vision and, since tunnels are necessarily narrow, narrow-mindedness as well.

No wonder there is a great deal of rigidity surrounding personal and collective identity crises. The need for clear-cut distinctions may very well be generated by insecurity.[7] After all, denying ambiguity instead of acknowledging its inevitability is rather defensive: "Experience is continuous, whereas categories are discrete, so that boundaries [are] established between categories by *repressing* what lies between them."[8] It is the fear of ambiguity that gives rise to the outlines that allow us to keep the things we draw separate from one another.[9] No wonder people who are exceptionally good at differentiating figures from grounds often abhor the unclean.[10]

The purist urge to compartmentalize reality and avoid mental promiscuity belies an awareness that the gaps separating entities from one another are mere figments of our mind. There would be no need for the incest taboo were it not for our deep fear that we might indeed blend with our familial surroundings, and only the recognition that races are mere mental constructs gives rise to the antimiscegenation laws that protect their separateness. Genderizing reality is likewise motivated by the realization, so vividly dramatized by transvestites, that the great divide separating the masculine from the feminine is largely mental. And only the knowledge that we are much closer to animals than we would like to admit makes us so obsessed with our human separateness.[11]

Romantic fantasies about the ideal mate or perfect love certainly help the rigid deny the ubiquitous presence of imperfection all around them.[12] Fantasizing about "monstrous" composites, however, may actually be a much healthier way to confront the inevitability of ambiguity. The ambiguous image of Tarzan, for example, clearly helps us cope with the Darwinian redefinition of our identity vis-à-vis apes, just as the image of the minotaur helped our ancestors face up to the dramatic change in their perception of cattle following domestication: "[Cattle became] part of the continuum of the human family. The diminished differences between people and cattle . . . created tensions. . . . [T]he man-bull figures [keep] man and cattle sufficiently separate in cultures where they live too close together. The image confronts ambivalence directly, as it were, by embodying it."[13] In much the same way, the ambiguous image of Frankenstein's monster helps us come to grips with the way modern technology blurs the distinction between humans and inanimate objects.[14] Fantasizing about androgyny may likewise help us confront the current redefinition of masculinity and femininity.[15]

By practically "freezing" reality, rigidity certainly inhibits change. Innovation is inherently antithetical to boundaries.[16] It "rejoices in mongrelisation and fears the . . . pure. Melange, hotchpotch . . . is how newness enters the world."[17] Transgressing boundaries is a hallmark of creativity, which almost by definition presupposes not accepting any structure as a given, and mature artists indeed avoid the neatly circumscribed.[18] Creativity usually flourishes on verges.[19] In art as in humor, in science as in cooking, it entails defying existing divisions and connecting the separate.[20] Creative artists ignore the conventional distinctions between painting and sculpture (the collage) or classical music and jazz (Jacques Loussier's interpretations of Bach). Creative scholars likewise defy the parochialism of insular academic disciplines[21] and fill the intellectual gaps among them,[22] thus contributing at once to anthropology, psychiatry, and communication (Gregory Bateson), to public administration as well as to computer science (Herbert Simon).

We normally regard those who transgress boundaries as deviants, yet they might also be seen as innovators[23] who could show us how to break away from the ossified mental cages in which we often lock ourselves and realize our creative potential. As a defensive effort to deny the inevitability of ambiguity, rigidity certainly makes us more dogmatic and less imaginative. As such, it clearly prevents us from fully realizing such potential.

Boundaries and Order

Even creativity, however, presupposes boundaries that one can transgress. Without some order that can be symbolically destroyed, for example, there could be no humor. By the same token, even the pronouncedly irregular phrasing of the bossa nova[24] nonetheless presupposes the highly regular samba beat. We need structures in order to defy them.

From the moment we are born and first detached from our immediate environment we experience our self as an island surrounded by void.[25] Such insularity inevitably entails a fundamental sense of loneliness[26] that accounts for much of our suffering and may even lead to suicide.[27] And yet, at least some detachment from our surroundings is necessary for our psychological well-being. Psychotics' experience of the self as highly penetrable is hardly enviable. Nor is agoraphobics' fear of the open. Many other psychological problems are likewise the result of not having fully separated ourselves from our parents.

Such separateness is critical to the development of selfhood. By literally insulating us from the world, our skin certainly protects us from blending with (either being penetrated by or spilling over into) our surroundings.[28] By symbolically promoting our separateness, private property[29] (having our own toys) and privacy (the right to keep secrets from our parents[30] and close the door to our room) likewise enhance our ability to develop a distinct identity.

Boundaries similarly protect groups from blending with their social surroundings. A firm boundary that makes it absolutely clear who is included in a group as it separates them from nonmembers certainly helps members develop a distinct collective identity.[31] That accounts for the somewhat vague identity of "fuzzy" communities or families of missing persons.[32] It also explains why groups are particularly protective of their boundaries during major identity crises.[33] Insularity clearly promotes a sense of identity. It is restricted access that helps neighborhoods retain their distinctive character[34] and strict endogamy that has preserved Jews and Gypsies for so long.

By the same token, it is boundaries that allow us to perceive any "thing" at all.[35] As evident from our inability to notice objects that blend with their surroundings,[36] fusion entails mental dissolution. In order to focus on anything, we must perceive some discontinuity between that which we attend and that which we ignore. Without it, it is practically impossible to differentiate any mental figure from its surrounding ground (which is why even calendars that display the days of an entire month in a single row without breaking them up into weekly segments nonetheless often depict Sunday in a distinctive color[37]). It is boundaries, therefore, that allow us—visually as well as mentally—to "grasp" any entity at all.

It is our basic need for order and deep fear of chaos that make us draw lines. A world with no lines is a chaotic world,[38] which is why we have symbolically set aside the first three days of the Creation just for making distinctions. Classifying certainly makes our environment more predictable. Only in the highly compartmentalized world of the supermarket, the encyclopedia, or the *Yellow Pages* do we always know where to find things, and

By providing closure, boundaries make us feel more secure. That is why river and lake shorelines are of such great help in cities like Boston and Chicago[39] and why leaving the above paragraph in the middle of a sentence is so unsettling.[40] The tranquilizing effect of boundaries also accounts for what we miss in unframed cave paintings[41] as well as for the wide appeal of the town square, "the purest expression of man's fight against being lost in a gelatinous world."[42] Boundaries also protect us from the endless anguish generated by open-endedness. Deadlines, for instance, help even perfectionists complete assignments. By closing our libidinal and possessional horizons, moral limits likewise help protect us from our own passions and ambitions, which are inherently insatiable. A world with no limits is a world of perpetual misery.[43]

Boundaries also make our world less monotonous. Whereas soups and harmony highlight the sensual appeal of fusion, it is the aesthetics of contrast that make cliffs and beaches so attractive.[44] By the same token, though we certainly derive much pleasure from fluid design,[45] dividing an undifferentiated space into several rooms clearly adds some variety to our life.[46] So do the distinction we draw between weekdays and weekends[47] and the rigid work schedules that allow us to have both a public and a private life.[48] With increasing computerization, more of us will be working at home, which will clearly add to our life an integrity that in our rigid bureaucratic existence we currently lack. It can also make it, however, much more monotonous and one-dimensional.

Mental Plasticity

It is ironic that we should regard boundaries, the quintessential antithesis of ambiguity, with such ambivalence. Yet the same lines that promote tunnel vision and narrow-mindedness by forcing reality into ossified pigeonholes also provide us with a sense of order and security.

We do not really have to choose between rigidity and fluidity. Thus, for example, we need to feel connected *as well as* separate and distinct.[49] By overdefining our self we clearly risk detachment and loneliness, yet by underdefining it as fused with others' we likewise risk having no identity. Rigid and porous selves are equally pathological[50] and overindividuation and underindividuation can both lead to suicide.[51]

Even our own musculature presents a compromise between a stiff structure that cannot bend and a formless puddle that cannot stand. A similarly delicate balance between rigidity and fluidity also underlies our vision of the ego as a happy medium between an utterly restrictive superego and a totally unbridled id as well as our experience of spaces marked off by half walls and light screens as both private and public.[52] It is the way in which moderate liberalism combines boundedness and boundlessness that likewise attracts those who detest both the rigid world of conservatives and the fuzzy world of radicals, and it is the compromise they offer between the ocean and the bathtub that makes lakes so appealing to both the claustrophobic and the agoraphobic.

Striking a happy medium through balance and moderation, however, is not the only way to integrate structure and flow. A somewhat different option is presented by the Japanese portable (*biyo-bu, tsuitate*) and sliding (*fusuma, shoji*) screens[53] that allow users to combine several rooms into one by simply removing or opening them or to carve out of a single undifferentiated space several separate rooms by simply closing them. It is the provisional nature of these partitions (as well as of the accordion wall, the door,[54] the convertible car top, and the Venetian blind) that allows such a blend of boundedness and boundlessness. In marked contrast to walls, they are all products of a highly flexible mind.

Flexibility entails the ability to be both rigid and fuzzy. Flexible people notice structures yet feel comfortable destroying them from time to time. Analytically focused at some times, they are quite sensitive to context at others. They may likewise step occasionally "out of their skin"[55] yet, unlike psychotics, can fully restore their selfhood when they so wish. In fact, it is precisely their ability to be rigid that allows them also to be fuzzy.[56] After all, one must have a pretty solid self to which one can always return in order to be able to step out of it periodically when fantasizing or meditating.

Having a brain that allows both analytic and synthetic thinking,[57] we need not really choose between structure and flow and can allow both the rigid and the fuzzy mind to operate in a complementary fashion.[58] Creative people, in fact, use both mind-sets, thereby vacillating between being rigid and fuzzy.[59] Such mental mobility allows them to replace one mental structure with another. It is the creative person who can reassemble "BEE RCONTA INSAL COHOL" as "BEER CONTAINS ALCOHOL" or the rapidly repeated "LAME DUCK" as "ACCLAIMED."[60] It is the creative artist,[61] observer,[62] and detective[63] who can likewise reverse conventional figure-ground configurations and attend precisely what we normally ignore.

The flexible mind defies our conventional rigid conception of classification by recognizing that any entity can be situated in more than one mental context. (*Cow,* for example, can be grouped together with both *cat* and *corn* as a word that begins with *c,* only with *cat* as a word that denotes an animal, and only with *corn* as a word that denotes an edible object.) Recognizing the inherently open *potential* of essence,[64] it avoids freezing entities in any one mental context by assigning them fixed meanings, treating them instead like algebraic symbols that can assume practically any value.[65] By avoiding closure,[66] it thus promotes a rather plastic notion of meaning. It is such flexibility that underlies symbolic systems such as language[67] and money and allows us to use our knowledge in different contexts.[68]

Children often assign several meanings to the same entity. In their make-believe world, in which they so casually shed their ordinary identity and assume in rapid succession several other personas, an object can be practically anything.[69] It is this plastic notion of essence that accounts for the tremendous popularity of toys such as the multiform "transformer" as well as for the wide appeal of Play-Doh, from which one can literally mold an infinite number of entities.[70] Such open-mindedness is usually over, however, as soon as we leave the world of childhood. By the time we start taking "multiple-choice" intelligence and aptitude tests, it becomes quite clear that multiple meaning is in fact no longer acceptable.

There is no reason why this should be so—why entities should have only one fixed meaning. There is no reason why one should not be able to strum a toy alligator as if it were a guitar and use one's socks as mittens, as my son did so casually when he was four. By the same token, we should be able to use a beer can for drinking as well as for fixing a motorcycle,[71] like the Eskimos who thaw and eat in the spring the very same frozen fish they used for a sled during the winter.[72]

The world can be so much richer than the rigid mind with its either/or logic would allow us to realize. That, however, requires elastic boundaries that would not preclude multiple ways of carving up the world into "things." We must therefore stop reifying the lines we draw and remember that the entities they help define are, after all, only figments of our own mind.

Flexibility need not entail giving up structure altogether. It does imply, however, dynamic,[73] elastic mental structures. Such structures would allow us to break away from the mental cages in which we so often lock ourselves, yet still avoid chaos. With them, we can be creative as well as secure.

Notes

Preface

1. See also Avner Falk, "Border Symbolism," *Psychoanalytic Quarterly* 43 (1974):650.
2. Eviatar Zerubavel, *Patterns of Time in Hospital Life* (Chicago: University of Chicago Press, 1979), pp. 5–32, 91–104.
3. Eviatar Zerubavel, *Hidden Rhythms* (Chicago: University of Chicago Press, 1981), pp. 101–66.
4. Eviatar Zerubavel, *The Seven-Day Circle* (New York: Free Press, 1985), pp. 107–29.

Introduction *In the Beginning*

1. Genesis 1:1–5.
2. Ibid., 6–10.
3. See, for example, Paul Seligman, *The Apeiron of Anaximander* (London: Athlone Press, 1962).
4. Gyorgy Kepes, *Language of Vision* (Chicago: Paul Theobald, 1951 [1944]), p. 45; Wolfgang Köhler, *Gestalt Psychology* (New York: New American Library, 1947), pp. 84, 93.
5. See also Ferdinand de Saussure, *Course in General Linguistics* (New York: Philosophical Library, 1959 [1915]), pp. 116–22; Michel Foucault, *The Order of Things* (New York: Vintage, 1973 [1966]), p. 144.
6. Paul Starr, "Social Categories and Claims in the Liberal State," in Mary Douglas, ed., *How Classification Works* (Edinburgh: Edinburgh University Press, forthcoming).
7. Emile Durkheim and Marcel Mauss, *Primitive Classification* (Chicago: University of Chicago Press, 1963 [1903]), p. 4. See also Karl W. Deutsch, "Autonomy and Boundaries according to Communications Theory," in Roy R. Grinker, ed., *Toward a Unified Theory of Human Behavior* (New York: Basic Books, 1956), pp. 278–79; Anatol Rapoport, "Statistical Boundaries," in *Toward a Unified Theory of Human Behavior,* p. 308. In Hebrew, the words for *classifying* (*sivug*) and *boundary* (*syag*) indeed derive from the same root.
8. Kenneth Burke, *A Grammar of Motives* (Berkeley: University of California Press, 1969 [1945]), p. 24. See also Gottlob Frege, "Logic in Mathematics," in *Posthumous Writings* (Chicago: University of Chicago Press, 1979 [1914]), pp. 155,

123

179, 195, 229, 241; Joan Weiner, "The Philosopher Behind the Last Logicist," in Crispin Wright, ed., *Frege—Tradition and Influence* (Oxford: Basil Blackwell, 1984), p. 72n.

9. Don Handelman, "The Ritual Clown: Attributes and Affinities." *Anthropos* 76 (1981):340.

10. Gustav Ichheiser, *Appearances and Realities* (San Francisco: Jossey-Bass, 1970), p. 8.

11. See also Henning Henningsen, *Crossing the Equator* (Copenhagen: Munksgaard, 1961), pp. 99–101.

12. Ken Kesey, *One Flew Over the Cuckoo's Nest* (New York: Viking, 1964), p. 190. See also Luis Buñuel's film *The Exterminating Angel.* It likewise took more than seven years to break Vladimir Kuts's 1957 five thousand-meter world record, yet only a year after it was finally broken, this seemingly unbreakable barrier was bettered by six runners in fourteen different races! (*World Sports International Athletics Annual—1966* [London: World Sports, 1966], p. 54. See also Cordner Nelson and Roberto Quercetani, *The Milers* [Los Altos, Calif.: Tafnews, 1985], pp. 200–211).

Chapter 1 *Islands of Meaning*

1. Jean Jacques Rousseau, "A Discourse on the Origin of Inequality," in *The Social Contract and Discourses* (New York: E. P. Dutton, 1950 [1754]), p. 234.

2. On "typification," see Alfred Schutz and Thomas Luckmann, *The Structures of the Life-World* (Evanston, Ill.: Northwestern University Press, 1973), pp. 77, 229–41; Peter L. Berger and Thomas Luckmann, *The Social Construction of Reality* (Garden City, N.Y.: Anchor, 1967), pp. 31, 54–58.

3. George G. Simpson, *Principles of Animal Taxonomy* (New York: Columbia University Press, 1961), p. 2.

4. See also Betty Edwards, *Drawing on the Artist Within* (New York: Simon & Schuster, 1986), pp. 167–71.

5. See, for example, Charles O. Frake, "The Diagnosis of Disease among the Subanun of Mindanao," *American Anthropologist* 63 (1961):113–32.

6. Carolyn M. Bloomer, *Principles of Visual Perception* (New York: Van Nostrand Reinhold, 1976), p. 49. On "monster adjustment" see also Imre Lakatos, *Proofs and Refutations* (Cambridge, England: Cambridge University Press, 1976), p. 30; David Bloor, "Polyhedra and the Abominations of Leviticus: Cognitive Styles in Mathematics," in Mary Douglas, ed., *Essays in the Sociology of Perception* (London: Routledge & Kegan Paul, 1982), p. 200. See also Harold Garfinkel, "Common Sense Knowledge of Social Structures: The Documentary Method of Interpretation in Lay and Professional Fact Finding," in *Studies in Ethnomethodology* (Englewood Cliffs, N.J.: Prentice-Hall, 1967 [1962]), pp. 79–94.

7. Suzanne J. Kessler and Wendy McKenna, *Gender* (New York: John Wiley, 1978), pp. 142–53.

8. See also Mary W. Helms, *Ulysses' Sail* (Princeton: Princeton University Press, 1988), pp. 172–82.

9. Herman A. Witkin et al., *Psychological Differentiation* (Potomac, Md.: Lawrence Erlbaum Associates, 1974 [1962]), pp. 10, 14, 35, 57–58, 80.

10. Edgar Rubin, *Visuell Wahrgenommene Figuren* (Copenhagen: Gyldendal, 1921 [1915]).

11. Yi-Fu Tuan, *Segmented Worlds and Self* (Minneapolis: University of Minnesota Press, 1982), pp. 118, 132–33. See also Köhler, *Gestalt Psychology*, pp. 80–81.

12. See also Robert C. Tryon, *Identification of Social Areas by Cluster Analysis* (Berkeley: University of California Press, 1955), p. 71.

13. Barry Schwartz, "The Social Psychology of Privacy, " *American Journal of Sociology* 78 (1968):747.

14. Charles A. Ferguson, "Diglossia," *Word* 15 (1959):325–40.

15. Stanley J. Tambiah, "Animals Are Good to Think and Good to Prohibit," *Ethnology* 8 (1969): 423–59; Pierre Bourdieu, "The Berber House," in Mary Douglas, ed., *Rules and Meanings* (Harmondsworth, England: Penguin, 1973 [1971]), pp. 98–110.

16. Robert Hertz, "The Pre-eminence of the Right Hand: A Study in Religious Polarity," in Rodney Needham, ed., *Right and Left* (Chicago: University of Chicago Press, 1973 [1909]); Barry Schwartz, *Vertical Classification* (Chicago: University of Chicago Press, 1981).

17. Kurt Lewin, *Principles of Topological Psychology* (New York: McGraw-Hill, 1936), p. 44.

18. Helms, *Ulysses' Sail*, pp. 22–31.

19. Gerald D. Suttles, *The Social Order of the Slum* (Chicago: University of Chicago Press, 1968), pp. 13–38, 225; Albert Hunter, *Symbolic Communities* (Chicago: University of Chicago Press, 1982 [1974]), pp. 84, 88.

20. See also Schwartz, "The Social Psychology of Privacy," pp. 747–49.

21. Virginia Woolf, *A Room of One's Own* (San Diego: Harcourt Brace Jovanovich, 1957 [1929]), p. 110. See also pp. 4, 109; Christopher Alexander et al., *A Pattern Language* (New York: Oxford University Press, 1977), pp. 669–71.

22. On such segmentation of everyday life, see Kenneth L. Pike, *Language in Relation to a Unified Theory of the Structure of Human Behavior* (The Hague: Mouton, 1967 [1954]), pp. 73–82; Roger G. Barker and Herbert F. Wright, *Midwest and Its Children* (Hamden, Conn.: Archon, 1971 [1955]), pp. 225–73; Roger G. Barker, ed., *The Stream of Behavior* (New York: Appleton-Century-Crofts, 1963).

23. Zerubavel, *The Seven-Day Circle*, pp. 121–29. See also pp. 102–6 and Zerubavel, *Patterns of Time in Hospital Life*, pp. 98–101. That is why nurses can take four-day blocks off only if no more than two of these days are within "the same" week (*Patterns of Time in Hospital Life*, p. 21; *The Seven-Day Circle*, pp. 128–29).

24. See also Barbara H. Smith, *Poetic Closure* (Chicago: University of Chicago Press, 1968), pp. 2–4.

25. Zerubavel, *Patterns of Time in Hospital Life*, pp. 31–32.

26. Zerubavel, *Hidden Rhythms*, pp. 101–37; Zerubavel, *The Seven-Day Circle*, pp. 118–20.

27. Zerubavel, *Hidden Rhythms*, pp. 138–66.

28. Yael Zerubavel, "The Last Stand: On the Transformation of Symbols in Modern Israeli Culture," (Ph.D. diss., University of Pennsylvania, 1980), pp. 301–21; Yael Zerubavel, "Collective Memory and Historical Metaphors: Masada and the Holocaust as National Israeli Symbols" (paper presented at the meetings of the Association for Jewish Studies, Boston, December 1987).

29. See also Roy Turner, "Some Formal Properties of Therapy Talk," in David Sudnow, ed., *Studies in Social Interaction* (New York: Free Press, 1972), pp. 367–96.

30. Alfred Schutz, "On Multiple Realities," in *Collected Papers* (The Hague: Martinus Nijhoff, 1973 [1945]), vol. 1, pp. 230–31. See also William James, *The Principles of Psychology* (Cambridge: Harvard University Press, 1983 [1890]), pp. 920–23.

31. See also Gregory Bateson, "A Theory of Play and Fantasy," in *Steps to an Ecology of Mind* (New York: Ballantine, 1972 [1955]), pp. 187–88; Marion Milner, *The Suppressed Madness of Sane Men* (London: Tavistock, 1987), pp. 80–81, 225–26.

32. Georg Simmel, "The Handle," in Kurt H. Wolff, ed., *Georg Simmel, 1858–1918* (Columbus: Ohio State University Press, 1959 [1911]), p. 267.

33. Bateson, "A Theory of Play and Fantasy," pp. 184–92; Erving Goffman, *Frame Analysis* (New York: Harper Colophon, 1974).

34. See also Goffman, ibid., pp. 496–559; Erving Goffman, *Forms of Talk* (Philadelphia: University of Pennsylvania Press, 1981), pp. 144–57, 173–86, 226–327.

35. Schutz, "On Multiple Realities," p. 233; Goffman, *Forms of Talk*, pp. 251–69.

36. Gregory Bateson, *Mind and Nature* (New York: E. P. Dutton, 1979), p. 125.

37. See also Georg Simmel, "Sociability: An Example of Pure, or Formal Sociology," in Kurt H. Wolff, ed., *The Sociology of Georg Simmel* (New York: Free Press, 1950 [1917]), pp. 47–53.

38. Goffman, *Frame Analysis*, pp. 77–78; Murray S. Davis, *Smut* (Chicago: University of Chicago Press, 1983), pp. 216–19.

39. Joan P. Emerson, "Behavior in Private Places: Sustaining Definitions of Reality in Gynecological Examinations," in Hans P. Dreitzel, ed., *Recent Sociology No. 2* (London: Macmillan, 1970), pp. 74–97; Davis, *Smut*, pp. 219–24.

40. Goffman, *Frame Analysis*, p. 412.

41. Rudolf Arnheim, *Art and Visual Perception* (Berkeley: University of California Press, 1967 [1954]), p. 231; Edward T. Cone, *Musical Form and Musical Performance* (New York: W. W. Norton, 1968), p. 15; Meyer Schapiro, "On Some Problems in the Semiotics of Visual Art: Field and Vehicle in Image-Signs," *Semiotica* 1 (1969):224; Boris Uspensky, *A Poetics of Composition* (Berkeley: University of California Press, 1973), p. 143; Rudolf Arnheim, *The Power of the Center* (Berkeley: University of California Press, 1982), pp. 50–52, 63.

42. Schutz, "On Multiple Realities," pp. 230–33.

43. Bateson, "A Theory of Play and Fantasy," p. 187.

44. Goffman, *Frame Analysis*, pp. 201–46.

45. Davis, *Smut*, pp. 29–30.

46. Michel Butor, "The Book as Object," in *Inventory* (New York: Simon & Schuster, 1968), pp. 50–51; Goffman, *Frame Analysis*, pp. 227–30. See also Erving Goffman, *Behavior in Public Places* (New York: Free Press, 1963), pp. 43, 50–53; Goffman, *Frame Analysis*, p. 220.

47. Goffman, *Frame Analysis*, pp. 224–25; Goffman, *Forms of Talk*, pp. 131–40.

48. See, for example, Erving Goffman, *Encounters* (Indianapolis: Bobbs-Merrill, 1961), pp. 65–66; Harland G. Bloland, "Opportunities, Traps, and Sanctuaries: A Frame Analysis of Learned Societies," *Urban Life* 11 (1982):87ff.

49. See also Goffman, *Encounters*, pp. 63–64.

50. Erving Goffman, *The Presentation of Self in Everyday Life* (Garden City, N.Y.: Anchor, 1959), pp. 151–53; Goffman, *Behavior in Public Places,* p. 84; Goffman, *Frame Analysis,* p.207.

51. Our assumption, however, may be false. Traveling in Europe and speaking together in Hebrew, my wife and I were once surprised on a bus by the woman sitting in front of us, who turned and asked us in Hebrew something about the weather. It was a subtle hint designed to remind us that "nonpersons" may interact with us in a far more "focused" way than we realize.

52. Heinz Werner, *Comparative Psychology of Mental Development* (New York: International Universities Press, 1957 [1940]), pp. 452–53; Witkin et al., *Psychological Differentiation,* p. 5; Herman A. Witkin, "Psychological Differentiation and Forms of Pathology," *Journal of Abnormal Psychology* 70 (1965):319.

53. Victor Tausk, "On the Origin of the 'Influencing Machine' in Schizophrenia," in Robert Fliess, ed., *The Psychoanalytic Reader* (New York: International Universities Press, 1948 [1919]), vol. 1, p. 68; Witkin et al., *Psychological Differentiation,* p. 14; Witkin, "Psychological Differentiation and Forms of Pathology," pp. 320–21.

54. Sigmund Freud, *Civilization and Its Discontents* (New York: W. W. Norton, 1962 [1930]), p. 13.

55. Tausk, "On the Origin of the 'Influencing Machine.' "

56. Paul Federn, "The Ego as Subject and Object in Narcissism," in *Ego Psychology and the Psychoses* (London: Imago Publishing Co., 1953 [1928]), p. 285.

57. Paul Federn, "Ego Psychological Aspect of Schizophrenia," in *Ego Psychology and the Psychoses,* p. 225. See also Tausk, "On the Origin of the 'Influencing Machine,' " p. 69; Jean Piaget, *The Construction of Reality in the Child* (New York: Basic Books, 1954), p. 281; Ernst Prelinger, "Extension and Structure of the Self," *Journal of Psychology* 47 *(1959):13–23;* Witkin et al., *Psychological Differentiation,* p. 134.

58. Nancy Chodorow, *The Reproduction of Mothering* (Berkeley: University of California Press, 1978), p. 68. See also Otto Fenichel, *The Psychoanalytic Theory of Neurosis* (New York: W. W. Norton, 1945), pp. 35–36.

59. Margaret S. Mahler and Kitty La Perriere, "Mother-Child Interaction during Separation-Individuation," in Margaret S. Mahler, *Separation-Individuation* (New York: Jason Aronson, 1979 [1965]), p. 36; Margaret S. Mahler, "On the First Three Subphases of the Separation–Individuation Process," in *Separation–Individuation,* pp. 121–22; Margaret S. Mahler et al., *The Psychological Birth of the Human Infant* (New York: Basic Books, 1975), pp. 52–54, 63.

60. Arthur Koestler, *The Act of Creation* (New York: Macmillan, 1964), p. 292.

61. Donald T. Campbell, "Common Fate, Similarity, and Other Indices of the Status of Aggregates of Persons as Social Entities," *Behavioral Science* 3 (1958): 17–18. See also Reuben Hill, *Families Under Stress* (Westport, Conn.: Greenwood, 1971 [1949]), pp. 3–5; Fredrik Barth, *Ethnic Groups and Boundaries* (Boston: Little, Brown, 1969), p. 9.

62. See, for example, Kurt Koffka, *Principles of Gestalt Psychology* (New York: Harbinger, 1935), p. 665; Hill, *Families Under Stress,* pp. 3–5; Kai T. Erikson, *Wayward Puritans* (New York: John Wiley, 1966), pp. 11, 13, 196; Richard Handler, *Nationalism and the Politics of Culture in Quebec* (Madison: University of Wisconsin Press, 1988).

63. Mark Krain, "A Definition of Dyadic Boundaries and an Empirical Study of Boundary Establishment in Courtship," *International Journal of Sociology of the Family* 7 (1977): 120. See also Erving Goffman, *Relations in Public* (New York: Harper Colophon, 1972), pp. 19–23.

64. Sigmund Freud, *The Ego and the Id* (New York: W. W. Norton, 1962 [1923]), p. 16; Stanley R. Palombo and Hilde Bruch, "Falling Apart: The Verbalization of Ego Failure," *Psychiatry* 27 (1964):250, 252, 256.

65. Mahler and La Perriere, "Mother-Child Interaction," p. 36; Margaret S. Mahler, "On Human Symbiosis and the Vicissitudes of Individuation," in *Separation–Individuation*, pp. 85–86; Mahler, "On the First Three Subphases," pp. 124–25; Mahler et al., *The Psychological Birth of the Human Infant*, p. 72; Louise J. Kaplan, *Oneness and Separateness* (New York: Touchstone, 1978), pp. 191–98.

66. See, for example, James, *Principles of Psychology*, pp. 280–83.

67. Kaplan, *Oneness and Separateness*, p. 200.

68. Werner, *Comparative Psychology of Mental Development*, p. 452.

69. Georg Simmel, "The Secret and the Secret Society," in Kurt H. Wolff, ed., *The Sociology of Georg Simmel* (New York: Free Press, 1950 [1908]), pp. 321–22; Goffman, *Relations in Public*, pp. 38–39; Eviatar Zerubavel, "Personal Information and Social Life," *Symbolic Interaction* 5 (1982):102–5.

70. See also Lewin, *Principles of Topological Psychology*; Maria A. Rickers-Ovsiankina, "Social Accessibility in Three Age Groups," *Psychological Reports* 2 (1956):283–94; Maria A. Rickers-Ovsiankina and Arnold A. Kusmin, "Individual Differences in Social Accessibility," *Psychological Reports* 4 (1958):391–406; Prelinger, "Extension and Structure of the Self."

71. Irwin Altman and Dalmas A. Taylor, *Social Penetration* (New York: Holt, Rinehart and Winston, 1973).

72. Max Weber, *Economy and Society* (Berkeley: University of California Press, 1978 [1925]), pp. 43–46; Campbell, "Common Fate," p. 22.

73. Arnold Van Gennep, *The Rites of Passage* (Chicago: University of Chicago Press, 1960 [1908]), pp. 103, 113.

74. Pitirim A. Sorokin, *Social and Cultural Mobility* (New York: Free Press, 1964 [1927]), p. 133. See also pp. 1–10; Pierre Bourdieu, "The Social Space and the Genesis of Groups," *Theory and Society* 14 (1985):723–44.

75. Georg Simmel, "The Stranger," in Kurt H. Wolff, ed., *The Sociology of Georg Simmel* (New York: Free Press, 1950 [1908]), pp. 402–8; Robert E. Park, "The Concept of Social Distance," *Journal of Applied Sociology* 8 (1924):339–44.

76. See, for example, Ward H. Goodenough, "Yankee Kinship Terminology: A Problem in Componential Analysis," in Stephen A. Tyler, ed., *Cognitive Anthropology* (New York: Holt, Rinehart and Winston, 1969 [1965]), pp. 269–71; David M. Schneider, *American Kinship* (Chicago: University of Chicago Press, 1980), pp. 23, 73.

77. Eliot Freidson, *Doctoring Together* (Chicago: University of Chicago Press, 1980 [1975]), pp. 69–85; Carol L. Kronus, "The Evolution of Occupational Power: An Historical Study of Task Boundaries between Physicians and Pharmacists," *Sociology of Work and Occupations* 3 (1976):3–37; Andrew Abbott, *The System of Professions* (Chicago: University of Chicago Press, 1988).

78. Margaret Mead, "Crossing Boundaries in Social Science Communications," *Social Science Information* 8 (1969):7.

79. Erikson, *Wayward Puritans,* p. 10.
80. Ibid., p. 12.
81. "Next: R-Rated Record Albums?" *Newsweek,* August 26, 1985, p. 69.
82. "Botha Goes Slow," *Newsweek,* August 26, 1985, p. 27.
83. Elihu Katz and Daniel Dayan, "Contests, Conquests, Coronations: On Media Events and Their Heroes," in Carl F. Graumann and Serge Moscovici, eds., *Changing Conceptions of Leadership* (New York: Springer-Verlag, 1986), p. 139.
84. *Newsday,* January 30, 1986, Part 2, p. 19.
85. Mark Johnson, *The Body in the Mind* (Chicago: University of Chicago Press, 1987).
86. Fred Attneave, "Dimensions of Similarity." *American Journal of Psychology* 63 (1950):516–56; Charles E. Osgood et al., *The Measurement of Meaning* (Urbana: University of Illinois Press, 1957), pp. 86, 89–97; Foucault, *The Order of Things,* pp. xviii–xix, xxii; Richard Beals et al, "Foundations of Multidimensional Scaling," *Psychological Review* 75 (1968):132; Samuel Fillenbaum and Amnon Rapoport, *Structures in the Subjective Lexicon* (New York: Academic Press, 1971), p. 4; J. Douglas Carroll and Myron Wish, "Multidimensional Perceptual Models and Measurement Methods," in Edward C. Carterette and Morton P. Friedman, eds., *Handbook of Perception, vol. 2: Psychophysical Judgment and Measurement* (New York: Academic Press, 1974), pp. 425–26; Eugene Hunn, "Toward a Perceptual Model of Folk Biological Classification," *American Ethnologist* 3 (1976): 515; Robert Darnton, *The Great Cat Massacre and Other Episodes in French Cultural History* (New York: Vintage, 1985), p. 192; Frederick L. Bates and Walter G. Peacock, "Conceptualizing Social Structure: The Misuse of Classification in Structural Modeling," *American Sociological Review* 54 (1989):569n.
87. Anthony F. Wallace and John Atkins, "The Meaning of Kinship Terms," *American Anthropologist* 62 (1960):67.
88. The Hebrew words for *fence (gader)* and *definition (hagdara)* indeed derive from the same root.
89. Max Wertheimer, "Untersuchungen zur Lehre von der Gestalt," *Psycholo. Forsch.* 4 (1923):301–50.
90. See also Werner, *Comparative Psychology of Mental Development,* pp. 222–25.
91. See, for example, Attneave, "Dimensions of Similarity"; Osgood et al., *The Measurement of Meaning,* pp. 89–97; Warren S. Torgerson, *Theory and Methods of Scaling* (New York: John Wiley, 1958), pp. 250, 260ff; Werner S. Landecker, "Class Boundaries," *American Sociological Review* 25 (1960):873; Roger N. Shepard, "The Analysis of Proximities: Multidimensional Scaling with an Unknown Distance Function," *Psychometrika* 27 (1962): 126; R. E. Bonner, "On Some Clustering Techniques," *IBM Journal of Research and Development* 8 (1964):22–32; Warren S. Torgerson, "Multidimensional Scaling of Similarity," *Psychometrika* 30 (1965): 379–93; Peter M. Blau and Otis D. Duncan, *The American Occupational Structure* (New York: John Wiley, 1967), pp. 67–75, 152–61; Beals et al., "Foundations of Multidimensional Scaling," p. 127; Jack B. Arnold, "A Multidimensional Scaling Study of Semantic Distance," *Journal of Experimental Psychology* 90 (1971):349–72; Fillenbaum and Rapoport, *Structures in the Subjective Lexicon;* Abraham A. Moles, *Théorie des Objets* (Paris: Éditions Universitaires, 1972), pp. 59–61, 74; Stephen K. Reed, "Pattern Recognition and Categorization," *Cognitive Psychology* 3 (1972): 382–407; Peter H.A. Sneath and

Robert R. Sokal, *Numerical Taxonomy* (San Francisco: W. H. Freeman, 1973), p. 119; Carroll and Wish, "Multidimensional Perceptual Models," p. 393; Robert R. Sokal, "Classification: Purposes, Principles, Progress, Prospects," *Science* 185 (1974): 1119; Victor Turner, "Metaphors of Anti-Structure in Religious Culture," in *Dramas, Fields, and Metaphors* (Ithaca: Cornell University Press, 1975 [1974]), p. 294; Alfonso Caramazza et al., "Subjective Structures and Operations in Semantic Memory," *Journal of Verbal Learning and Verbal Behavior* 15 (1976): 103–17; Hunn, "Toward a Perceptual Model," p. 515; Carol L. Krumhansl, "Concerning the Applicability of Geometric Models to Similarity Data: The Interrelationship between Similarity and Spatial Density," *Psychological Review* 85 (1978): 445–63; Edward E. Smith and Douglas L. Medin, *Categories and Concepts* (Cambridge: Harvard University Press, 1981), p. 105.

92. See, for example, Kurt Goldstein and Martin Scheerer, "Abstract and Concrete Behavior: An Experimental Study with Special Tests." *Psychological Monographs* 53 (1941), #2, pp. 59–60, 75–82, 103–7, 128.

93. Foucault, *The Order of Things,* p. 136.

94. Köhler, *Gestalt Psychology,* p. 93; Federn, "Ego Psychological Aspect of Schizophrenia," p. 222; Talcott Parsons, *The Social System* (New York: Free Press, 1964 [1951]), p. 482; Campbell, "Common Fate," pp. 18–20; Bonner, "On Some Clustering Techniques," p. 22; Smith, *Poetic Closure,* pp. 23–24; Robert R. Sokal, "Clustering and Classification: Background and Current Directions," in J. Van Ryzin, ed., *Classification and Clustering* (New York: Academic Press, 1977), p. 7; Smith and Medin, *Categories and Concepts,* pp. 110–11.

95. See also Jerome S. Bruner et al., *A Study of Thinking* (New York: John Wiley, 1956), pp. 2–4; Stephen C. Johnson, "Hierarchical Clustering Systems," *Psychometrika* 32 (1967): 242; Yehudi A. Cohen, "Social Boundary Systems," *Current Anthropology* 10 (1969):109–11.

96. Foucault, *The Order of Things,* p. 140.

97. On "allomorphs," see Pike, *Language in Relation to a Unified Theory,* pp. 164, 176–77, 206; Dwight Bolinger, *Aspects of Language* (New York: Harcourt, Brace & World, 1968), pp. 58–63. On their functional phonological analogues, "allophones," see Roman Jakobson, *Six Lectures on Sound and Meaning* (Cambridge: MIT Press, 1978 [1942]), pp. 28–33; Pike, *Language in Relation to a Unified Theory,* pp. 44–46, 325–28; Mario Pei, *Glossary of Linguistic Terminology* (New York: Columbia University Press, 1966), p. 10; Bolinger, *Aspects of Language,* pp. 43–44.

98. See Ray L. Birdwhistell, *Kinesics and Context* (Philadelphia: University of Pennsylvania Press, 1970), pp. 166, 193–95, 229.

99. Murray S. Davis, *Intimate Relations* (New York: Free Press, 1973), pp. 76–77.

100. Umberto Eco, *A Theory of Semiotics* (Bloomington: Indiana University Press, 1976), p. 77.

101. See also Zerubavel, *Patterns of Time in Hospital Life,* p. 4.

102. See also Y. Zerubavel, "The Last Stand," p. 309.

103. Henri Tajfel, *Human Groups and Social Categories* (Cambridge, England: Cambridge University Press, 1981), pp. 115–16, 121, 133, 243.

104. See also Richard Williams, *Hierarchical Structures and Social Value* (Cambridge, England: Cambridge University Press, 1990).

105. Howard F. Stein, *Developmental Time, Cultural Space* (Norman: University of Oklahoma Press, 1987), p. 6.

106. Berger and Luckmann, *The Social Construction of Reality*, pp. 30–34, 54–58; Schutz and Luckmann, *The Structures of the Life-World*, pp. 73–79, 238–41.

107. Van Gennep, *The Rites of Passage*.

108. Henningsen, *Crossing the Equator*.

109. Marshall Sahlins, *Culture and Practical Reason* (Chicago: University of Chicago Press, 1976), pp. 181–82n.

110. Van Gennep, *The Rites of Passage*, pp. 65–88.

111. Ibid., pp. 50–64, 146–65; Robert Hertz, "A Contribution to the Study of the Collective Representation of Death," in *Death and the Right Hand* (Aberdeen, Scotland: Cohen and West, 1960 [1907]), pp. 80–86; Michael C. Kearl, *Endings* (New York: Oxford University Press, 1989), p. 95.

112. Y. Zerubavel, "Collective Memory and Historical Metaphors."

113. Goffman, *Relations in Public*, pp. 73–94; Davis, *Intimate Relations*, pp. 56ff; Stuart Albert and William Jones, "The Temporal Transition from Being Together to Being Alone: The Significance and Structure of Children's Bedtime Stories," in Bernard S. Gorman and Alden E. Wessman, eds., *The Personal Experience of Time* (New York: Plenum, 1977), p. 131. See also Emanuel A. Schegloff and Harvey Sacks, "Opening up Closings," *Semiotica* 8 (1973):289–327; Stuart Albert and Suzanne Kessler, "Processes for Ending Social Encounters: The Conceptual Archaeology of a Temporal Place," *Journal for the Theory of Social Behavior* 6 (1976):147–70; Goffman, *Forms of Talk*, p. 130.

114. See also John Carey, "Temporal and Spatial Transitions in American Fiction Films," *Studies in the Anthropology of Visual Communication* 1 (1974):45.

115. Pike, *Language in Relation to a Unified Theory*, p. 76.

116. On ways of invoking or suspending the theatrical frame before the introduction of the curtain, see William Beare, *The Roman Stage* (London: Methuen, 1964), p. 179; Elizabeth Burns, *Theatricality* (New York: Harper Torchbooks, 1973), p. 41.

117. Michel Butor, "On Fairy Tales," in *Inventory* (New York: Simon & Schuster, 1968 [1960]), p. 213.

118. For a general discussion of "metamessages," see Gregory Bateson et al., "Toward a Theory of Schizophrenia," in *Steps to an Ecology of Mind* (New York: Ballantine, 1972 [1956]), p. 222; Bateson, "A Theory of Play and Fantasy."

119. Smith, *Poetic Closure*, pp. 24–25. See also pp. 50–95, 98–150, 158–66, 172–86.

120. Cone, *Musical Form and Musical Performance*, p. 13.

121. Jan-Peter Blom and John J. Gumperz, "Social Meaning in Linguistic Structure: Code-Switching in Norway," in John J. Gumperz and Dell Hymes, eds., *Directions in Sociolinguistics* (New York: Holt, Rinehart and Winston, 1972), pp. 425–26; John J. Gumperz, *Discourse Strategies* (Cambridge, England: Cambridge University Press, 1982), p. 76.

122. Goffman, *Forms of Talk*, p. 176.

123. Holly Giffin, "The Coordination of Meaning in the Creation of a Shared Make-Believe Reality," in Inge Bretherton, ed., *Symbolic Play* (Orlando, Fla.: Academic Press, 1984), p. 86.

124. Erikson, *Wayward Puritans*, p. 11.

125. Ibid., pp. 11–13.

126. Ibid., p. 13.
127. Butor, "The Book as Object," pp. 54–55.
128. H. Clay Trumbull, *The Threshold Covenant* (New York: Charles Scribner's Sons, 1906), pp. 3–12, 25–28, 66–68.
129. Vered Vinitzky-Seroussi, "Classification of Special Days and Specific People" (paper presented at the annual meeting of the Midwest Modern Language Association, Kansas City, November 1990). See also Esther Lavie, "Age as an Indicator for Reference in the Construction of Social Contexts" (Ph.D. diss., Tel-Aviv University, 1987), pp. 242–81.

Chapter 2 *The Great Divide*

1. Neil Armstrong, July 20, 1969.
2. Fillenbaum and Rapoport, *Structures in the Subjective Lexicon,* p. 12; Amnon Rapoport and Samuel Fillenbaum, "An Experimental Study of Semantic Structures," in A. Kimball Romney et al. eds., *Multidimensional Scaling* (New York: Seminar Press, 1972), vol. 2, pp. 105–14; Roger N. Shepard, "Representation of Structure in Similarity Data: Problems and Prospects," *Psychometrika* 39 (1974):412; Caramazza et al., "Subjective Structures and Operations"; Hunn, "Toward A Perceptual Model," pp. 515–16, 519; Sokal, "Classification," p. 1116; Roger N. Shepard and Phipps Arabie, "Additive Clustering: Representation of Similarities as Combinations of Discrete Overlapping Properties," *Psychological Review* 86 (1979): 87–123; Anthony Wilden, *The Rules Are No Game* (London: Routledge & Kegan Paul, 1987), pp. 93, 222–23.
3. Sneath and Sokal, *Numerical Taxonomy,* p. 198; Sokal, "Classification," p. 1120; Hunn, "Toward a Perceptual Model," p. 519; Sokal, "Clustering and Classification," p. 7.
4. Edward T. Hall, *The Hidden Dimension* (Garden City, N.Y.: Anchor, 1969 [1966]), pp. 113–64; Robert Sommer, *Personal Space* (Englewood Cliffs, N.J.: Prentice-Hall, 1969), pp. 26–57.
5. See, for example, Wystan H. Auden, "Prologue: The Birth of Architecture," in *About the House* (New York: Random House, 1965), p. 4.
6. Werner, *Comparative Psychology of Mental Development,* p. 386.
7. See also C. P. Snow, *The Two Cultures and A Second Look* (London: Cambridge University Press, 1969 [1959]), pp. 4, 16–17, 69; Karl W. Deutsch, *Nationalism and Social Communication* (Cambridge: MIT Press, 1966), pp. 36–55; George Hackett, "The Canonization of Ollie," *Newsweek,* December 22, 1986, p. 26.
8. Trumbull, *The Threshold Covenant,* pp. 177–78.
9. See also Alexander et al., *A Pattern Language,* pp. 717–18, 847–51, 858–59, 893–95.
10. See, for example, the discussion of "ordered metric scales" in Clyde H. Coombs, "Psychological Scaling without a Unit of Measurement," *Psychological Review* 57 (1950):145–58.
11. See, for example, Albert and Jones, "The Temporal Transition," p. 114.
12. William F. Fry, *Sweet Madness* (Palo Alto, Calif.: Pacific, 1968 [1963]), p. 143n.
13. Jack Goody, *The Domestication of the Savage Mind* (Cambridge, England: Cambridge University Press, 1977), pp. 80–81, 108, 111.
14. See, for example, Stéphane Mallarmé, *A Tomb for Anatole* (San Francisco: North

Point, 1983 [1961]), pp. 106, 131. See also Jackson Mac Low, *Representative Works 1938–1985* (New York: Roof, 1986) pp. 53, 62–70, 106–27; Stephen Kern, *The Culture of Time and Space 1880–1918* (Cambridge: Harvard University Press, 1983), pp. 172–74. For a similar attempt to graphically capture the actual phrasing of spoken discourse, see also Dennis Tedlock's translation of Zuni narrative poetry in *Finding the Center* (New York: Dial Press, 1972).

15. Kern, ibid., p. 175.
16. See, for example, Jean-Luc Godard's film *The Married Woman*.
17. Van Gennep, *The Rites of Passage*, p. 11.
18. Julie M. Gricar, "How Thick Is Blood?: The Social Construction and Cultural Configuration of Kinship," (Ph.D. diss., Columbia University, 1991).
19. See also Terence S. Turner, "Transformation, Hierarchy and Transcendence: A Reformulation of Van Gennep's Model of the Structure of Rites of Passage," in Sally F. Moore and Barbara G. Myerhoff, eds., *Secular Ritual* (Amsterdam: Van Gorcum, 1977), pp. 56–57.
20. Van Gennep, *The Rites of Passage*, pp. 75–76.
21. See also ibid., p. 130.
22. Kearl, *Endings*, pp. 346–47.
23. Orlando Patterson, *Slavery and Social Death* (Cambridge, England: Cambridge University Press, 1982), pp. 54–58.
24. Zerubavel, *Hidden Rhythms*, pp. 75–76, 82–95, 99; Eviatar Zerubavel, "Easter and Passover: On Calendars and Group Identity," *American Sociological Review* 47 (1982):284–89; Zerubavel, *The Seven-Day Circle*, pp. 20–23, 26, 28–43.
25. Amnon Rubinstein, *To Be a Free People* (Tel-Aviv: Schocken, 1977), p. 104.
26. On the centrality of leaps to a discontinuous experience of reality, see also Richard Sorabji, *Time, Creation, and the Continuum* (Ithaca: Cornell University Press, 1983), pp. 52–61, 384–93.
27. For a classic statement, see Jean Piaget and Bärbel Inhelder, *The Child's Conception of Space* (New York: W. W. Norton, 1967 [1948]).
28. Stephen M. Kosslyn et al., "Cognitive Maps in Children and Men," *Child Development* 45 (1974):707–16; Richard C. Sherman et al., "Movement and Structure As Determinants of Spatial Representation," *Journal of Nonverbal Behavior* 4 (1979):27–39; Gary T. Allen, "A Developmental Perspective on the Effects of 'Subdividing' Macrospatial Experience," *Journal of Experimental Psychology: Human Learning and Memory* 7 (1981):120–32; Ruth H. Maki, "Why Do Categorization Effects Occur in Comparative Judgment Tasks?" *Memory and Cognition* 10 (1982):254, 260–63; Linda P. Acredolo and Lyn T. Boulter, "Effects of Hierarchical Organization on Children's Judgments of Distance and Direction," *Journal of Experimental Child Psychology* 37 (1984): 409–25. See also Perry W. Thorndyke, "Distance Estimation from Cognitive Maps," *Cognitive Psychology* 13 (1981):526–50.
29. "Psalms and Salutations," *Newsweek*, April 28, 1986, p. 84.
30. Wertheimer, "Untersuchungen zur Lehre von der Gestalt."
31. Roger M. Downs and David Stea, *Maps in Minds* (New York: Harper & Row, 1977), pp. 142–43.
32. See also Hall, *The Hidden Dimension*, p. 140.
33. See, for example, Sorokin, *Social and Cultural Mobility*, p. 3; Leopold von Wiese and Howard Becker, *Systematic Sociology* (New York: John Wiley, 1932), p. 242;

Pitirim A. Sorokin, *Sociocultural Causality, Space, Time* (New York: Russell & Russell, 1964 [1943]), pp. 151–52; Snow, *The Two Cultures*, p. 2.

34. Zerubavel, *The Seven-Day Circle*, p. 128. See also Asher Koriat et al., "An Inquiry into the Process of Temporal Orientation," *Acta Psychologica* 40 (1976):67.

35. See, for example, Saul Steinberg's humorous cartoon depiction of the mental river separating March from April in Harold Rosenberg, *Saul Steinberg* (New York: Alfred A. Knopf, 1978), p. 132.

36. Maurice Halbwachs, *The Collective Memory* (New York: Harper Colophon, 1980 [1950]), p. 101.

37. Janet Harris, *The Prime of Ms. America* (New York: G. P. Putnam's Sons, 1975), p. 72.

38. See, for example, Donald T. Campbell, "Enhancement of Contrast as Composite Habit," *Journal of Abnormal and Social Psychology* 53 (1956):350–55; Simpson, *Principles of Animal Taxonomy*, p. 117; Blau and Duncan, *The American Occupational Structure*, pp. 72, 421; Robert A. LeVine and Donald T. Campbell, *Ethnocentrism* (New York: John Wiley, 1972), p. 222; Tajfel, *Human Groups and Social Categories*, pp. 115, 133.

39. Peter Singer, *Animal Liberation* (New York: Discus, 1977), p. xv.

40. Daniel F. Chambliss, "The Mundanity of Excellence: An Ethnographic Report on Stratification and Olympic Swimmers," *Sociological Theory* 7 (1989):75.

41. Harry Hershfield, *Harry Hershfield Joke Book* (New York: Ballantine, 1964), p. 128.

42. Werner, *Comparative Psychology of Mental Development*, pp. 186–87. See also David Cleveland, *The April Rabbits* (New York: Scholastic Books Services, 1978).

43. Stanley Brandes, *Forty* (Knoxville: University of Tennessee Press, 1985). See also Lavie, "Age as an Indicator," pp. 285–86.

44. Georg Lukács, *History and Class Consciousness* (Cambridge: MIT Press, 1971 [1923]), pp. 83–92; Berger and Luckmann, *The Social Construction of Reality*, pp. 89, 134–35.

45. Emile Durkheim, *The Rules of Sociological Method* (New York: Free Press, 1982 [1895]), pp. 50–59, 69–72.

46. Deutsch, *Nationalism and Social Communication*, p. 18. See also C. B. Fawcett, *Frontiers* (Oxford: Oxford University Press, 1918), p. 34.

47. Zerubavel, *Patterns of Time in Hospital Life*, pp. 32–33.

48. Jeanne Kidd, "The Classification of Cars" (unpublished paper, 1988).

49. See also Lawrence Wright, *Clockwork Man* (London: Elek, 1968), pp. 189–90.

50. Zerubavel, *Patterns of Time in Hospital Life*, pp. 5–6, 10–11.

Chapter 3 *The Rigid Mind*

1. Deuteronomy 22:9–11.

2. On the fundamental difference between the digital and analog modes of processing information, see Anthony Wilden, *System and Structure* (London: Tavistock, 1972), pp. 159, 186, 191–93; Wilden, *The Rules Are No Game*, pp. 222–26.

3. Davis, *Smut*, pp. 15–17, 21–26.

4. Julia Kristeva, *Powers of Horror* (New York: Columbia University Press, 1982 [1980]), p. 4.
5. Michel Foucault, *Madness and Civilization* (New York: Vintage, 1973 [1961]), p. 109.
6. Bruce Lincoln, *Discourse and the Construction of Society* (New York: Oxford University Press, 1989), p. 166. See also Edmund Leach, "Anthropological Aspects of Language: Animal Categories and Verbal Abuse," in Eric H. Lenneberg, ed., *New Directions in the Study of Language* (Cambridge: MIT Press, 1964), p. 39.
7. Mary Douglas, *Purity and Danger* (New York: Praeger, 1966), p. 39.
8. Trumbull, *The Threshold Covenant*, pp. 14–20, 71–82; James G. Frazer, *Folk-Lore in the Old Testament* (London: Macmillan, 1918), vol. 3, pp. 11–13.
9. Hans P. Duerr, *Dreamtime* (London: Basil Blackwell, 1985 [1978]), pp. 46, 243–44.
10. See also Douglas, *Purity and Danger,* pp. 95–96.
11. Ibid., p. 5; Leach, "Anthropological Aspects of Language," p. 39.
12. Trumbull, *The Threshold Covenant,* pp. 10–13; Frazer, *Folk-Lore in the Old Testament,* vol. 3, pp. 1–6.
13. See, for example, Victor Turner, "Betwixt and Between: The Liminal Period in *Rites de Passage,*" in *The Forest of Symbols* (Ithaca: Cornell University Press, 1970 [1964]), pp. 93–111.
14. Lakatos, *Proofs and Refutations,* p. 30; Michael Thompson, *Rubbish Theory* (Oxford: Oxford University Press, 1979), pp. 131ff.; Bloor, "Polyhedra and the Abominations of Leviticus," p. 200.
15. Winthrop D. Jordan, *White over Black* (Chapel Hill: University of North Carolina Press, 1968), pp. 167–78; Joel Williamson, *New People* (New York: Free Press, 1980).
16. Jean-Paul Sartre, *Existential Psychoanalysis* (Chicago: Henry Regnery, 1966 [1943]), pp. 133–43.
17. Darnton, *The Great Cat Massacre,* p. 193.
18. Ibid.; Paul Shepard, *Thinking Animals* (New York: Viking, 1978), p. 100.
19. Shepard, ibid., p. 76.
20. Douglas, *Purity and Danger,* pp. 35–36.
21. Ibid., passim.
22. Ibid., p. 121; Leach, "Anthropological Aspects of Language," p. 38.
23. Paul Schilder, *The Image and Appearance of the Human Body* (New York: International Universities Press, 1950 [1935]), pp. 188, 213.
24. Mikhail Bakhtin, *Rabelais and His World* (Cambridge: MIT Press, 1968 [1965]), p. 29. Emphasis added.
25. Ibid., p. 320. Emphasis added. See also Klaus Theweleit, *Male Fantasies* (Minneapolis: University of Minnesota Press, 1987 [1977]), p. 244. The self is conventionally portrayed as a discrete chunk in space as well as in time. Threatened by anything that might suggest that the individual's life is not discrete, the rigid mind has traditionally avoided in art not only open wounds and gaping orifices but also pregnancy and death throes (Bakhtin, ibid., p. 29).
26. Bakhtin, ibid., p. 322n.
27. Norbert Elias, *The Civilizing Process* (New York: Urizen, 1978 [1939]), pp. 143–60.

28. Davis, *Smut,* pp. 123–24. See also pp. 98–99, 116–18, 122–23.
29. Ibid., p. 116.
30. See also Georg Simmel, "Conflict," in *Conflict and the Web of Group Affiliations* (New York: Free Press, 1964 [1908]), p. 29; Charles H. Cooley, *Human Nature and the Social Order* (New York: Schocken, 1964 [1922]), pp. 182, 194; Koffka, *Principles of Gestalt Psychology,* p. 328; Piaget, *The Construction of Reality in the Child,* p. 233.
31. Leach, "Anthropological Aspects of Language," pp. 40–44; Sahlins, *Culture and Practical Reason,* pp. 171–75.
32. Douglas, *Purity and Danger,* p. 35.
33. See also Leach, "Anthropological Aspects of Language," pp. 43–44.
34. Davis, *Smut,* pp. 134–41, 146–49.
35. Singer, *Animal Liberation,* p. 198. Emphasis added.
36. Sasha R. Weitman, "Intimacies: Notes toward a Theory of Social Inclusion and Exclusion," *Archives Européennes de Sociologie* 11 (1970):358–59. See also Georg Simmel, "Quantitative Aspects of the Group," in Kurt H. Wolff, ed., *The Sociology of Georg Simmel* (New York: Free Press, 1950 [1908]), pp. 126–27; Krain, "A Definition of Dyadic Boundaries," p. 120.
37. See also Cohen, "Social Boundary Systems," p. 107.
38. Hill, *Families under Stress,* pp. 3–5.
39. Cooley, *Human Nature and the Social Order,* p. 210.
40. Campbell, "Enhancement of Contrast"; LeVine and Campbell, *Ethnocentrism,* p. 222; Tajfel, *Human Groups and Social Categories,* pp. 115, 133; Michèle Lamont, "The Making of Inequality: Cultural and Moral Exclusion in the French and the American Middle Class" (paper presented at the meetings of the American Sociological Association, San Francisco, August 1989).
41. Pierre Bourdieu, *Distinction* (Cambridge: Harvard University Press, 1984 [1979]).
42. Hunter, *Symbolic Communities,* p. 85. See also pp. 84, 111, 181.
43. William G. Sumner, *Folkways* (New York: New American Library, 1960 [1906]), p. 27.
44. Simmel, "Conflict," pp. 91, 96–99; Lewis A. Coser, *The Functions of Social Conflict* (New York: Free Press, 1964 [1956]), pp. 33–38, 87–110.
45. Simmel, ibid., pp. 97–98.
46. Ibid., p. 98.
47. George Orwell, *Nineteen Eighty Four* (New York: New American Library, 1961 [1949]).
48. J. H. Hutton, *Caste in India* (Bombay: Oxford University Press, 1963), pp. 79–80.
49. Gilbert T. Stephenson, *Race Distinctions in American Law* (New York: D. Appleton, 1910), pp. 154–99, 207–33, 272; Bertram W. Doyle, *The Etiquette of Race Relations in the South* (New York: Schocken, 1971 [1937]), pp. 39, 139, 146–52.
50. Bourdieu, *Distinction,* p. 481.
51. Ibid., passim.
52. See also Thorstein Veblen, *The Theory of the Leisure Class* (New York: Macmillan, 1899); Jodi E. Brodsky, "Intellectual Snobbery: A Socio-Historical Perspective," (Ph.D. diss., Columbia University, 1987).
53. Weber, *Economy and Society,* pp. 43–44, 342–43; Frank Parkin, *Marxism and Class*

Theory (New York: Columbia University Press, 1979), pp. 44–71; Raymond Murphy, *Social Closure* (Oxford: Oxford University Press, 1988).

54. John K. Hemphill and Charles M. Westie, "The Measurement of Group Dimensions," *Journal of Psychology* 29 (1950):327.

55. Abbott, *The System of Professions*. See also Randall Collins, *The Credential Society* (New York: Academic Press, 1979), pp. 131–81.

56. On the latter, see Kronus, "The Evolution of Occupational Power." See, however, Thomas F. Gieryn, "Boundary-Work and the Demarcation of Science from Non-Science: Strains and Interests in Professional Ideologies of Scientists," *American Sociological Review* 48 (1983):791–92.

57. Sorokin, *Social and Cultural Mobility*, p. 137.

58. Louis L. Snyder, ed., *Hitler's Third Reich* (Chicago: Nelson-Hall, 1981), pp. 213–14.

59. Stephenson, *Race Distinctions in American Law*, pp. 78–83; Williamson, *New People*. See also Doyle, *The Etiquette of Race Relations in the South*, p. 64.

60. Virginia R. Domínguez, *White by Definition* (New Brunswick, N.J.: Rutgers University Press, 1986), pp. 268–69.

61. Robert K. Merton, "Intermarriage and the Social Structure: Fact and Theory," *Psychiatry* 4 (1941):368.

62. Genesis 1:26–28.

63. Singer, *Animal Liberation*, pp. 199–208.

64. Erasmus, "On Good Manners for Boys," in *Collected Works* (Toronto: University of Toronto Press, 1985 [1530]), vol. 25, pp. 276, 282, 284.

65. Keith Thomas, *Man and the Natural World* (New York: Pantheon, 1983), p. 38.

66. Leslie Fiedler, *Freaks* (New York: Simon & Schuster, 1978), p. 24; Darnton, *The Great Cat Massacre*, p. 193.

67. E. E. Evans-Pritchard, *Nuer Religion* (London: Oxford University Press, 1956), pp. 84–85; Douglas, *Purity and Danger*, p. 39.

68. Thomas, *Man and the Natural World*, p. 39.

69. Foucault, *Madness and Civilization*, pp. 68–76.

70. Shepard, *Thinking Animals*, pp. 103, 106.

71. Edward O. Wilson, *Biophilia* (Cambridge: Harvard University Press, 1984), pp. 127, 129.

72. Shepard, *Thinking Animals*, p. 103.

73. Alan Dundes, *Cracking Jokes* (Berkeley: Ten Speed, 1987), p. viii.

74. Shepard, *Thinking Animals*, pp. 103–4.

75. Rabindranath Tagore, *The Home and the World* (London: Macmillan, 1971 [1919]). See also Hanna Papanek and Gail Minault, eds., *Separate Worlds* (Delhi: Chanakya, 1982).

76. On the use of this image in feminist discourse, see Linda K. Kerber, "Separate Spheres, Female Worlds, Woman's Place: The Rhetoric of Women's History," *Journal of American History* 75 (1988):9–39.

77. Kessler and McKenna, *Gender*, pp. 161–67.

78. Sahlins, *Culture and Practical Reason*, pp. 182–83, 190–95.

79. Raymond Firth, *Symbols—Public and Private* (Ithaca: Cornell University Press, 1973), pp. 265–83, 298.

80. Fiedler, *Freaks*, pp. 32–33, 179. See also Kessler and McKenna, *Gender*, pp. 142–53.

81. Janice G. Raymond, *The Transsexual Empire* (Boston: Beacon, 1979), pp. 114–15.

82. Harold Garfinkel, "Passing and the Managed Achievement of Sex Status in an 'Intersexed' Person," in *Studies in Ethnomethodology* (Englewood Cliffs, N.J.: Prentice-Hall, 1967), p. 125.

83. Christie Davies, "Sexual Taboos and Social Boundaries," *American Journal of Sociology* 87 (1982):1036.

84. Alfred C. Kinsey et al., *Sexual Behavior in the Human Male* (Philadelphia: W. B. Saunders, 1948), pp. 636–37.

85. Richard Green, *Sexual Identity Conflict in Children and Adults* (New York: Basic Books, 1974), p. 302; Raymond, *The Transsexual Empire,* pp. xviii, 46, 115; Margrit Eichler, "Sex Change Operations: The Last Bulwark of the Double Standard," in Laurel Richardson and Verta Taylor, eds., *Feminist Frontiers* (New York: Random House, 1989 [1980]), pp. 281–90.

86. Bernard Landis, *Ego Boundaries* (New York: International Universities Press, 1970 [Monograph no. 24 (vol. 6, no. 4) in Psychological Issues series]), pp. 70–76.

87. See, for example, Seymour Fisher and Sidney E. Cleveland, *Body Image and Personality* (New York: Dover, 1968), p. 55.

88. Didier Anzieu, *The Skin Ego* (New Haven: Yale University Press, 1989 [1985]), p. 20.

89. Selma H. Fraiberg, *The Magic Years* (New York: Charles Scribner's Sons, 1959), p. 130.

90. See also Kaplan, *Oneness and Separateness,* pp. 56–57.

91. Else Frenkel-Brunswik, "Comprehensive Scores and Summary of Interview Results," in T. W. Adorno et al., *The Authoritarian Personality* (New York: Harper, 1950), pp. 480–82.

92. See, for example, Fisher and Cleveland, *Body Image and Personality,* p. 55.

93. Else Frenkel-Brunswik, "Intolerance of Ambiguity as an Emotional and Perceptual Personality Variable," *Journal of Personality* 18 (1949):115; Else Frenkel-Brunswik, "Dynamic and Cognitive Personality Organization as Seen through the Interviews," in T. W. Adorno et al., *The Authoritarian Personality* (New York: Harper, 1950), p. 463; Maurice Merleau-Ponty, "The Child's Relations with Others," in *The Primacy of Perception* (Evanston, Ill.: Northwestern University Press, 1964 [1960]), pp. 101–2, 105; Michael P. Rogin, *Ronald Reagan, the Movie* (Berkeley: University of California Press, 1987), pp. 290–92.

94. See, for example, Frenkel-Brunswik, "Dynamic and Cognitive Personality Organization," pp. 443, 451; Daniel J. Levinson, "The Study of Ethnocentric Ideology," in T. W. Adorno et al., *The Authoritarian Personality* (New York: Harper, 1950), p. 150; Seymour Fisher, "Patterns of Personality Rigidity and Some of Their Determinants," *Psychological Monographs* 64 (1950):1–47; Jack Block and Jeanne Block, "An Investigation of the Relationship between Intolerance of Ambiguity and Ethnocentrism," *Journal of Personality* 19 (1950–51):310; Merleau-Ponty, "The Child's Relations with Others," p. 102; Milton Rokeach, *The Open and Closed Mind* (New York: Basic Books, 1960).

95. See, for example, Frenkel-Brunswik, "Intolerance of Ambiguity," p. 128.

96. Maurice Merleau-Ponty, *Phenomenology of Perception* (New York: Humanities Press, 1962), p. 283.

97. See also the discussion of "ocnophilia" in Michael Balint, *Thrills and Regressions* (New York: International Universities Press, 1959), pp. 53, 124.

98. See also Zerubavel, *Hidden Rhythms,* pp. 44–54.

99. See also Kaplan, *Oneness and Separateness,* pp. 218–19.

100. Ibid., p. 102.

101. In a state of intoxication, the distinction between self and environment is often blurred. See Michael Balint, *The Basic Fault* (London: Tavistock, 1968), p. 56.

102. Witkin et al., *Psychological Differentiation,* pp. 10, 14, 35, 57–58, 80; Samuel Messick and John W. French, "Dimensions of Cognitive Closure," *Multivariate Behavioral Research* 10 (1975):5.

103. Balint, *The Basic Fault,* p. 67; Jean Liedloff, *The Continuum Concept* (New York: Alfred A. Knopf, 1977), pp. 58–65; Morris Berman, *Coming to Our Senses* (New York: Simon & Schuster, 1989), p. 27.

104. Bruno Bettelheim, *The Empty Fortress* (New York: Free Press, 1967), p. 277. See also pp. 109–12, 161–64, 174, 178.

105. Ibid., pp. 421–22. See also Helen B. Lewis, *Psychic War in Men and Women* (New York: New York University Press, 1976), pp. 290–91.

106. Chodorow, *The Reproduction of Mothering,* p. 169. See also pp. 109–10, 166–68; Carol Gilligan, *In a Different Voice* (Cambridge: Harvard University Press, 1982), pp. 7–9.

107. Witkin et al., *Psychological Differentiation,* pp. 214–15; Eleanor E. Maccoby and Carol N. Jacklin, *The Psychology of Sex Differences* (Stanford, Calif.: Stanford University Press, 1974), pp. 97, 101–5. See also Robert Kegan, *The Evolving Self* (Cambridge: Harvard University Press, 1982), p. 208.

108. Kate Franck and Ephraim Rosen, "A Projective Test of Masculinity and Femininity," *Journal of Consulting Psychology* 13 (1949):251–52.

109. Sidney M. Jourard, "Some Lethal Aspects of the Male Role," *Journal of Existential Psychiatry* 7 (1962):334.

110. See, for example, Berman, *Coming to Our Senses,* p. 27.

111. Ludwik Fleck, *Genesis and Development of a Scientific Fact* (Chicago: University of Chicago Press, 1981 [1935]), pp. 38–51, 98–111; Karl Mannheim, *Ideology and Utopia* (New York: Harvest, 1936), pp. 26–33.

112. See, for example, Michèle Lamont, "The Power-Culture Link in A Comparative Perspective," *Comparative Social Research* 11 (1989):137–39.

113. Rosabeth M. Kanter, *Commitment and Community* (Cambridge: Harvard University Press, 1972), p. 170.

114. Stein, *Developmental Time, Cultural Space,* pp. 109, 117.

115. Davies, "Sexual Taboos and Social Boundaries," pp. 1036–37.

116. Paul DiMaggio, "Cultural Entrepreneurship in Nineteenth-Century Boston: The Creation of an Organizational Base for High Culture in America," *Media, Culture and Society* 4 (1982):33–50; Paul DiMaggio, "Cultural Entrepreneurship in Nineteenth-Century Boston, Part II: The Classification and Framing of American Art," *Media, Culture and Society* 4 (1982):303–22.

117. Davies, "Sexual Taboos and Social Boundaries," pp. 1048–49.

118. Ibid., pp. 1047–55.

119. Ibid., passim.

120. Durkheim and Mauss, *Primitive Classification.*

121. See also Mannheim, *Ideology and Utopia,* p. 266.

122. Mary Douglas, "Self Evidence," in *Implicit Meanings* (London: Routledge & Kegan Paul, 1978), pp. 276–318.
123. Davies, "Sexual Taboos and Social Boundaries," p. 1043.
124. Douglas, *Purity and Danger*, p. 124; Mary Douglas, *Natural Symbols* (New York: Vintage, 1973 [1970]), pp. 98–99.
125. Jamsheed K. Choksy, *Purity and Pollution in Zoroastrianism* (Austin: University of Texas Press, 1989), pp. 80–87, 92.
126. Davies, "Sexual Taboos and Social Boundaries," pp. 1037–38.
127. Anne Sutherland, *Gypsies* (London: Tavistock, 1975), pp. 13, 247–48, 258–59, 270–71; Carol Miller, "American Rom and the Ideology of Defilement," in Farnham Rehfisch, ed., *Gypsies, Tinkers, and Other Travellers* (London: Academic Press, 1975), pp. 45, 50; Judith Okely, *The Traveller-Gypsies* (Cambridge, England: Cambridge University Press, 1983), pp. 85, 154–56.
128. Okely, ibid., p. 83.
129. Sutherland, *Gypsies,* pp. 149–50, 268–69; Carol Silverman, "Pollution and Power: Gypsy Women in America," in Matt T. Salo, ed., *The American Kalderaš* (Hackettstown, N.J.: Gypsy Lore Society North American Chapter Publications, 1981), p. 58.
130. Sutherland, ibid., pp. 258, 264–69; Miller, "American Rom," p. 42; Silverman, ibid., p. 57.
131. Douglas, *Purity and Danger*, pp. 126–27.
132. Miller, "American Rom," p. 42; Silverman, "Pollution and Power," p. 57; Okely, *The Traveller-Gypsies,* pp. 81–85.
133. Miller, ibid.; Okely, ibid., pp. 80–83.
134. Okely, ibid., pp. 91–94.
135. Ibid., pp. 94–95, 101–3.
136. See, for example, Weitman, "Intimacies," p. 364n.; Douglas, "Self-Evidence," p. 304.
137. Mishnah, *Abodah Zarah* 2.2.
138. Ezra 9:12–14, 10:1–17; Nehemiah 9:2, 13:23–30.
139. "Proselytes," in *Encyclopaedia Judaica* (Jerusalem: Keter, 1972), vol. 13, p. 1184.
140. See, for example, Yael Katzir, "Preservation of Jewish Ethnic Identity in Yemen: Segregation and Integration as Boundary Maintenance Mechanisms," *Comparative Studies in Society and History* 24 (1982):274. See also Jacob Katz, *Exclusiveness and Tolerance* (New York: Schocken, 1962), pp. 73–74.
141. Leviticus 11; Deuteronomy 14:3–20; Douglas, *Purity and Danger,* pp. 55–56; Mary Douglas, "Deciphering a Meal," in *Implicit Meanings* (London: Routledge & Kegan Paul, 1978 [1972]), pp. 263–69; Douglas, "Self Evidence," pp. 283–84.
142. Leviticus 20:24–25.
143. Mishnah, *Kilaim* 8.4.
144. Ibid., 8.20. See also Leviticus 19:19; Deuteronomy 22:10.
145. Mishnah, *Ḥullin*.
146. Ibid., 8.1–3.
147. Mishnah, *Kilaim* 2.10. See also Leviticus 19:19; Deuteronomy 22.9.
148. Mishnah, *Kilaim* 9.9. See also Leviticus 19:19; Deuteronomy 22:11.
149. Mishnah, *Erubin* 10.6.
150. Deuteronomy 22.5.

151. Ibid., 27:21; Leviticus 18:23, 20:15–16; Fiedler, *Freaks,* pp. 149–51.
152. Kristeva, *Powers of Horror,* pp. 102–3.
153. Davis, *Smut,* pp. 95ff., 165–72.
154. Stein, *Developmental Time, Cultural Space,* p. 56.
155. Erikson, *Wayward Puritans,* pp. 69, 114, 154; Pat Lauderdale, "Deviance and Moral Boundaries," *American Sociological Review* 41 (1976):660–76; Albert J. Bergesen, "Political Witch Hunts: The Sacred and the Subversive in Cross-National Perspective," *American Sociological Review* 42 (1977): 220–33. See also Berman, *Coming to Our Senses,* p. 80.
156. Davies, "Sexual Taboos and Social Boundaries," pp. 1042–47.
157. Cohen, "Social Boundary Systems," pp. 107–8.
158. Thomas, *Man and the Natural World,* p. 39.
159. Erikson, *Wayward Puritans,* pp. 107, 113, 138–40.
160. Hall, *The Hidden Dimension,* pp. 132–36.
161. Nachman Ben-Yehuda, *Deviance and Moral Boundaries* (Chicago: University of Chicago Press, 1985), pp. 40, 58, 70, 73.
162. Erikson, *Wayward Puritans,* p. 70.
163. Jordan, *White over Black,* pp. 414–26.
164. Williamson, *New People,* pp. 1–2, 74.
165. On linguistic purism, see, for example, Handler, *Nationalism and the Politics of Culture in Quebec,* pp. 162–69.
166. Page DuBois, *Centaurs and Amazons* (Ann Arbor: University of Michigan Press, 1982), pp. 32, 55–56, 61–67.
167. E. P. Evans, *The Criminal Prosecution and Capital Punishment of Animals* (London: William Heinemann, 1906), pp. 316–31; Joseph Needham, *The Grand Titration* (London: George Allen & Unwin, 1969), pp. 328–29.
168. Emile Durkheim, *The Elementary Forms of the Religious Life* (New York: Free Press, 1965 [1912]), p. 52.
169. Ibid., pp. 53–56.
170. See, for example, Zerubavel, *Hidden Rhythms,* p. 107.
171. Durkheim, *The Elementary Forms of the Religious Life,* p. 55.
172. Henri Hubert, "Etude Sommaire de la Représentation du Temps dans la Religion et la Magie," in Henri Hubert and Marcel Mauss, eds., *Mélanges d'Histoire des Religions* (Paris: Félix Alcan and Guillaumin, 1909 [1905]), pp. 201–4; Hertz, "The Pre-eminence of the Right Hand"; Durkheim, *The Elementary Forms of the Religious Life,* pp. 346–47; Edmund Leach, "Two Essays Concerning the Symbolic Representation of Time," in *Rethinking Anthropology* (London: Athlone, 1961), pp. 132–34; Zerubavel, *Hidden Rhythms,* pp. 102–5; Schwartz, *Vertical Classification,* pp. 91–93, 105–6; Zerubavel, *The Seven-Day Circle,* pp. 116–20.
173. Durkheim, *The Elementary Forms of the Religious Life,* pp. 338–45.
174. Exodus 3:5.
175. Zerubavel, *Hidden Rhythms,* pp. 131–32. See also pp. 117–24.
176. See, for example, Choksy, *Purity and Pollution in Zoroastrianism,* pp. 23–77.
177. See, for example, Katz, *Exclusiveness and Tolerance,* p. 73.
178. Joseph H. Hertz, ed., *The Authorized Daily Prayer Book* (New York: Bloch, 1960), p. 749; Zerubavel, *Hidden Rhythms,* pp. 136–37. See also Jacob Mann,

"Genizah Fragments of the Palestinian Order of Service," *Hebrew Union College Annual* 2 (1925):318.

179. Solomon Ganzfried, ed., *The Code of Jewish Law* (New York: Hebrew Publishing Co., 1961), 96.5; Samuel M. Segal, *The Sabbath Book* (New York: Thomas Yoseloff, 1957), p. 132.

180. Weber, *Economy and Society*, pp. 219, 957.

181. Ibid.

182. Zerubavel, *Patterns of Time in Hospital Life*, p. 32; Zerubavel, *Hidden Rhythms*, pp. 153–66.

183. See also Eviatar Zerubavel, "The Language of Time: Toward a Semiotics of Temporality," *Sociological Quarterly* 28 (1987):346, 353.

184. Miwako Kidahashi, "Dual Organization: A Study of a Japanese-Owned Firm in the United States," (Ph.D. diss., Columbia University, 1987), pp. 255–78.

185. Thomas S. Kuhn, *The Structure of Scientific Revolutions* (Chicago: University of Chicago Press, 1970 [1962]).

186. Needham, *The Grand Titration*, pp. 329–30. See also Evans, *The Criminal Prosecution and Capital Punishment of Animals*, pp. 162–64.

187. Duerr, *Dreamtime*, pp. 99, 126.

188. Emile Durkheim, *The Division of Labor in Society* (New York: Free Press, 1984 [1893]), pp. 294–308; Basil Bernstein, "On the Classification and Framing of Educational Knowledge," in *Class, Codes, and Control* (London: Routledge & Kegan Paul, 1971), pp. 202–29.

189. Foucault, *The Order of Things*, pp. 128–32, 137–38; Paul Bouissac, "Circus Performance as Ritual: An Aspect of Animal Acts," in *Circus and Culture* (Bloomington: Indiana University Press, 1976), pp. 110–15; Darnton, *The Great Cat Massacre*, pp. 191–213.

190. See also Susan Stewart, *On Longing* (Baltimore: Johns Hopkins University Press, 1984), pp. 151–66.

191. Goody, *The Domestication of the Savage Mind*, p. 105. Emphasis added.

Chapter 4 *The Social Lens*

1. Denis Diderot, quoted in Darnton, *The Great Cat Massacre*, p. 195.

2. Robert M. Pirsig, *Zen and the Art of Motorcycle Maintenance* (New York: Bantam New Age, 1981 [1974]), p. 66.

3. Ibid.

4. Hall, *The Hidden Dimension*, pp. 131–64.

5. Kurt Lewin, "Some Social-Psychological Differences between the United States and Germany," in *Resolving Social Conflicts* (London: Souvenir, 1973 [1936]), pp. 18–25.

6. Peter Gould and Rodney White, *Mental Maps* (Harmondsworth, England: Penguin, 1974), pp. 182–84.

7. Jakobson, *Six Lectures on Sound and Meaning*, p. 30. See also pp. 28–33, 74–76.

8. Benjamin L. Whorf, "Language, Mind, and Reality," in *Language, Thought, and Reality* (Cambridge: MIT Press, 1956 [1942]), p. 253.

9. Eco, *A Theory of Semiotics*, pp. 76–78; Benjamin L. Whorf, "Science and Linguistics," in *Language, Thought, and Reality*, p. 210; A. R. Radcliffe-Brown, "The Study of Kinship Systems," in *Structure and Function in Primitive Society*

(New York: Free Press, 1965 [1941]), p. 73; Gary Witherspoon, *Language and Art in the Navajo Universe* (Ann Arbor: University of Michigan Press, 1977), p. 121.

10. Whorf, "Science and Linguistics"; Whorf, "Language, Mind, and Reality."

11. John B. Carroll and Joseph B. Casagrande, "The Functions of Language Classifications in Behavior," in Eleanor E. Maccoby et al., eds., *Readings in Social Psychology* (New York: Holt, Rinehart and Winston, 1958), pp. 26–31. See also pp. 22–26.

12. See, for example, Lucien Lévy-Bruhl, *How Natives Think* (New York: Washington Square Press, 1966 [1910])."

13. See, for example, Claude Lévi-Strauss, *The Savage Mind* (Chicago: University of Chicago Press, 1966 [1962]).

14. On allomorphs, allophones, allokines, allophiles, and allochrones, see notes 97–101 of chapter 1.

15. Durkheim and Mauss, *Primitive Classification,* p. 20.

16. See Durkheim, *The Elementary Forms of the Religious Life,* pp. 167–68.

17. Darnton, *The Great Cat Massacre,* p. 192.

18. See Whorf, "Science and Linguistics," p. 210.

19. Tajfel, *Human Groups and Social Categories,* p. 170.

20. Mannheim, *Ideology and Utopia,* pp. 84–87.

21. See, for example, Bärbel Inhelder and Jean Piaget, *The Early Growth of Logic in the Child* (New York: Humanities Press, 1964), pp. 105, 116–17, 169, 282; Jane Thompson, "The Ability of Children of Different Grade Levels to Generalize on Sorting Tests," *Journal of Psychology* 11 (1941):123.

22. Rudolf Arnheim, *Visual Thinking* (Berkeley: University of California Press, 1969), p. 200.

23. Judith M. Gerson and Kathy Peiss, "Boundaries, Negotiation, Consciousness: Reconceptualizing Gender Relations," *Social Problems* 32 (1985):317–31.

24. Williamson, *New People;* Domínguez, *White by Definition.* See also John K. Chance, *Race and Class in Colonial Oaxaca* (Stanford, Calif.: Stanford University Press, 1978), pp. 94–104, 126–43, 155–59.

25. Reginald L. Poole, "The Beginning of the Year in the Middle Ages," *Proceedings of the British Academy* 10 (1921–23):113–37. See also Zerubavel, *Patterns of Time in Hospital Life,* p. 8.

26. Stephen J. Gould, "Taxonomy as Politics: The Harm of False Classification," *Dissent,* Winter 1990, p. 74.

27. Foucault, *The Order of Things,* pp. 264–65.

28. Beare, *The Roman Stage,* p. 238.

29. Singer, *Animal Liberation,* p. 1.

30. In the eighteenth century, the governor of Grenada likewise appointed one superintendent for both blacks and mules. See Jordan, *White over Black,* p. 233.

31. Christopher D. Stone, *Should Trees Have Standing?* (Los Altos, Calif.: William Kaufmann, 1974), pp. 6–7.

32. Evans, *The Criminal Prosecution and Capital Punishment of Animals.*

33. Ibid., pp. 198–99, 175. See also p. 172.

34. Stephenson, *Race Distinctions in American Law,* p. 15. See also Williamson, *New People.*

35. Hunter, *Symbolic Communities,* pp. 84, 181.

36. Werner Sollors, *Beyond Ethnicity* (New York: Oxford University Press, 1986), pp. 71–72.
37. Richard Hogan, "The Frontier as Social Control," *Theory and Society* 14 (1985):35–51.
38. Sandra C. Hinson, "How Feminist and Radical Books Are Classified: An Inter-Bookstore Comparison" (unpublished paper, 1986).
39. "Have Gays Taken over Yale?" *Newsweek,* October 12, 1987, p. 96.
40. Jordan, *White over Black,* pp. 217–39, 491–506.
41. Gould, "Taxonomy as Politics."
42. Viviana A. Zelizer, *Pricing the Priceless Child* (New York: Basic Books, 1985), pp. 58, 75, 84.
43. See also Roy Wallis, ed., *On the Margins of Science* (Keele: University of Keele, 1979 [Sociological Review Monograph #27]); Gieryn, "Boundary-Work and the Demarcation of Science from Non-Science."
44. Y. Zerubavel, "The Last Stand," pp. 196–99.
45. M. Martin Halley and William F. Harvey, "Medical vs. Legal Definitions of Death," *Journal of the American Medical Association* 204 (May 6, 1968):423–25. See also Robert Zussman, *Intensive Care* (Chicago: University of Chicago Press, forthcoming).
46. The attorney of the Missouri Abortion Clinics, as quoted in the *New York Times,* April 27, 1989, p. B13.
47. See, for example, Tertullian, "On the Soul," in vol. 10 of *The Fathers of the Church* (Washington, D.C.: Catholic University of American Press, 1950) 25:5–9, 27:1–3, 37:2.
48. *New York Times,* April 7, 1989, p. 13.
49. Brenda Danet, " 'Baby' or 'Fetus'?: Language and the Construction of Reality in a Manslaughter Trial," *Semiotica* 32 (1980):187–219.
50. Peter G. Brown and Henry Shue, eds., *Boundaries* (Totowa, N.J.: Rowman and Littlefield, 1981), pp. 105.
51. Schwartz, "The Social Psychology of Privacy," pp. 748–49.
52. Goffman, *Frame Analysis,* p. 73.
53. George F. Will, "Lithuania and South Carolina," *Newsweek,* January 29, 1990, p. 80.
54. *Newsweek,* April 9, 1990, p. 32.
55. Singer, *Animal Liberation,* pp. 2, 21.
56. Kinsey et al, *Sexual Behavior in the Human Male,* pp. 639–47.
57. See also Eviatar Zerubavel, "The Standardization of Time: A Sociohistorical Perspective," *American Journal of Sociology* 88 (1982): 14–15, 19.
58. Schutz, "On Multiple Realities," pp. 231–32. See also Davis, *Smut,* p. 74.
59. Sven-Tage Teodorsson, *Anaxagoras' Theory of Matter* (Goteborg, Sweden: Acta Universitatis Gothoburgensis, 1982), p. 99. See also S. Sambursky, *The Physical World of the Greeks* (New York: Macmillan, 1956), pp. 132–57.
60. Arthur O. Lovejoy, *The Great Chain of Being* (Cambridge: Harvard University Press, 1964 [1936]), p. 56.
61. Tuan, *Segmented Worlds and Self,* pp. 126–28.
62. Richard Schechner, *Environmental Theater* (New York: Hawthorn, 1973), p. 15.
63. Ibid., p. 16.
64. Arnheim, *Art and Visual Perception,* pp. 102–3, 216–20.

65. Merleau-Ponty, *Phenomenology of Perception,* p. 329.
66. M. von Senden, *Space and Sight* (London: Methuen, 1960 [1932]).
67. Fawcett, *Frontiers,* pp. 17–19, 24. See also Guillaume de Greef, *La Structure Générale des Sociétés, vol. 3: Théorie des Frontières et des Classes* (Brussels: Larcier, 1908), p. 273.
68. Ken Wilber, *No Boundary* (Boston: New Science Library, 1981 [1979]), pp. 24–25.
69. See, for example, Tuan, *Segmented Worlds and Self,* p. 130.
70. Gaston Bachelard, *The Poetics of Space* (Boston: Beacon, 1969 [1958]), p. 222. See also Georg Simmel, "Brücke und Tür," in *Brücke und Tür* (Stuttgart: K. F. Koehler, 1957 [1909]), pp. 3–4.
71. Balint, *Thrills and Regressions,* p. 66; Balint, *The Basic Fault,* p. 67.
72. Davis, *Smut,* pp. 45–46.
73. Goffman, *Frame Analysis,* pp. 308–21. See also Gary A. Fine, *Shared Fantasy* (Chicago: University of Chicago Press, 1983), pp. 200–3.
74. Personal communication from Murray Davis.
75. Goffman, *Frame Analysis,* pp. 312–13.
76. Van Gennep, *The Rites of Passage.*
77. In Hebrew, the words for *twilight, evening,* and *mixture* all derive from the same root.
78. Christena Nippert-Eng, "Liminality in Everyday Life: Commuting and the Transition between Home and Work" (paper presented at the annual meeting of the American Sociological Association, Atlanta, August 1988).
79. Turner, "Betwixt and Between"; Victor Turner, *The Ritual Process* (Harmondsworth, England: Penguin, 1974 [1969]).
80. Patterson, *Slavery and Social Death,* pp. 38–39, 46–51.
81. Robert E. Park, "Human Migration and the Marginal Man," *American Journal of Sociology* 33 (1928):881–93; Everett V. Stonequist, *The Marginal Man* (New York: Charles Scribner's Sons, 1937). See also Simmel, "The Stranger."
82. Georg Simmel, "The Web of Group Affiliations," in *Conflict and the Web of Group Affiliations* (New York: Free Press, 1964 [1908]), pp. 127–95.
83. David M. Schneider, "American Kin Terms and Terms for Kinsmen: A Critique of Goodenough's Componential Analysis of Yankee Kinship Terminology," in Stephen A. Tyler, ed., *Cognitive Anthropology* (New York: Holt, Rinehart and Winston, 1969 [1965]), p. 290; Carol B. Stack, *All Our Kin* (New York: Harper & Row, 1974), pp. 62–89; Schneider, *American Kinship,* p. 72; Marc Shell, "The Family Pet," *Representations* 15 (1986): 123; Constance Perin, *Belonging in America* (Madison: University of Wisconsin Press, 1988), pp. 26, 107; Gricar, "How Thick Is Blood?" ch. 5.
84. Landecker, "Class Boundaries," pp. 874–75; Blau and Duncan, *The American Occupational Structure,* pp. 59, 65, 78–79, 347.
85. Blau and Duncan, ibid., p. 124.
86. See, for example, Edmund Leach, "The Legitimacy of Solomon: Some Structural Aspects of Old Testament History," *European Journal of Sociology* 7 (1966): 58–101.
87. Stephen J. Gould, "Human Equality Is a Contingent Fact of History," *Natural History* 93 (1984), no. 11:32.
88. Charles Bonnet, quoted in Foucault, *The Order of Things,* p. 147.

89. Aristotle, *The Complete Works* (Princeton: Princeton University Press, 1984): *History of Animals,* book 8, 588b.4–5, 11–13; *Parts of Animals,* book 4, 681.

90. Ibid., *History of Animals,* book 8, 588a.21–588b.3; *Parts of Animals,* book 4, 697a.29–697b.22; John Locke, *An Essay Concerning Human Understanding* (Oxford: Oxford University Press, 1975 [1690]), book 3, chapter 6. 12,23; Lovejoy, *The Great Chain of Being;* Joseph Klaits and Barrie Klaits, eds., *Animals and Man in Historical Perspective* (New York: Harper Torchbooks, 1974), pp. 2–4.

91. Wilson, *Biophilia,* p. 130.

92. Henri Bergson, *Matter and Memory* (London: George Allen & Unwin, 1911 [1908]), p. 278.

93. Ludwig Wittgenstein, *Philosophical Investigations* (New York: Macmillan, 1958 [1953]), part I.68–71.

94. George Lakoff, "Hedges: A Study in Meaning Criteria and the Logic of Fuzzy Concepts," *Journal of Philosophical Logic* 2 (1973):458–508; George Lakoff, *Women, Fire, and Dangerous Things* (Chicago: University of Chicago Press, 1987), pp. 122–25.

95. Lotfi A. Zadeh, "A Fuzzy-Set-Theoretic Interpretation of Linguistic Hedges," *Journal of Cybernetics* 2 (1972), no. 3:4.

96. Ibid.; Lotfi A. Zadeh, "Fuzzy Sets," *Information and Control* 8 (1965):339; Eleanor H. Rosch, "On the Internal Structure of Perceptual and Semantic Categories," in Timothy E. Moore, ed., *Cognitive Development and the Acquisition of Language* (New York: Academic Press, 1973), pp. 112, 130; Paul Kay and Chad K. McDaniel, "The Linguistic Significance of the Meanings of Basic Color Terms," *Language* 54 (1978):610–46; Michael E. McCloskey and Sam Glucksberg, "Natural Categories: Well Defined or Fuzzy Sets?" *Memory and Cognition* 6 (1978):462–72; Linda Coleman and Paul Kay, "Prototype Semantics: The English Word *Lie,*" *Language* 57 (1981):27; Lakoff, *Women, Fire, and Dangerous Things,* pp. 12, 21, 56, 287–88.

97. Bruner et al., *A Study of Thinking,* p. 64; Rosch, "On the Internal Structure of Perceptual and Semantic Categories," pp. 112, 130; Eleanor H. Rosch, "Human Categorization," in Neil Warren, ed., *Studies in Cross-Cultural Psychology* (London: Academic Press, 1977), vol. 1, pp. 13–14, 25–26; Eleanor H. Rosch, "Principles of Categorization," in Eleanor Rosch and Barbara B. Lloyd, eds., *Cognition and Categorization* (Hillside, N.J.: Lawrence Erlbaum Associates, 1978), pp. 35–36. See also Brent Berlin and Paul Kay, *Basic Color Terms* (Berkeley: University of California Press, 1969), p. 13.

98. Schneider, "American Kin Terms and Terms for Kinsmen," p. 290.

99. William Labov, "The Boundaries of Words and Their Meanings," in Charles-James N. Bailey and Roger W. Shuy, eds., *New Ways of Analyzing Variation in English* (Washington, D.C.: Georgetown University Press, 1973), pp. 340–73; Elaine S. Andersen, "Cups and Glasses: Learning That Boundaries Are Vague," *Journal of Child Language* 2 (1975):79–103; Rodney Needham, "Polythetic Classification: Convergence and Consequences," *Man* 10 (1975):349–69.

100. Gould, "Taxonomy as Politics," p. 74.

101. Harry Braverman, *Labor and Monopoly Capital* (New York: Monthly Review Press, 1974), pp. 360–61, 428–30.

102. Locke, *An Essay Concerning Human Understanding,* book 3, chap. 6.27,30,36,37;

Jean-Baptiste Lamarck, *Zoological Philosophy* (New York: Hafner, 1963 [1809]), pp. 20–28; Simpson, *Principles of Animal Taxonomy*, pp. 118–19.

103. Cynthia F. Epstein, *Deceptive Distinctions* (New Haven: Yale University Press, 1988).

104. Zerubavel, "The Standardization of Time," pp. 19–20.

105. See also Zerubavel, *Hidden Rhythms,* pp. 11, 41, 86; Zerubavel, *The Seven-Day Circle,* pp. 11, 139–41.

106. See also Fred Davis, "Decade Labeling: The Play of Collective Memory and Narrative Plot," *Symbolic Interaction* 7 (1984), no. 1:15–24; Hillel Schwartz, *Century's End* (New York: Doubleday, 1990).

107. Kinsey et al., *Sexual Behavior in the Human Male,* p. 639. See also Bergson, *Matter and Memory,* pp. 239–98.

108. Bergson, ibid., p. 259; Jorge Luis Borges, "The Analytical Language of John Wilkins," in *Other Inquisitions, 1937–1952* (Austin: University of Texas Press, 1964 [1952]), p. 104; Edmund Leach, *Culture and Communication* (Cambridge, England: Cambridge University Press, 1976), pp. 33–34.

109. Durkheim and Mauss, *Primitive Classification,* pp. 7–8.

110. Bruner et al., *A Study of Thinking,* p. 232.

111. Arnheim, *The Power of the Center,* p. 42; Ansel Adams, *Camera and Lens* (Hastings-on-Hudson, N.Y.: Morgan & Morgan, 1970), pp. 28–29, 34–37.

112. Wilden, *System and Structure,* p. 204. See also pp. 185, 219.

113. See also Durkheim, *The Elementary Forms of the Religious Life,* pp. 26–33, 479–87.

114. Rodney Needham, "Introduction" to Emile Durkheim and Marcel Mauss, *Primitive Classification* (Chicago: University of Chicago Press, 1973), p. viii.

115. Jakobson, *Six Lectures on Sound and Meaning,* pp. 69–87.

116. Amos Tversky, "Features of Similarity," *Psychological Review* 84 (1977):329.

117. Gould, "Taxonomy as Politics," p. 73.

118. Frake, "The Diagnosis of Disease among the Subanun of Mindanao"; Charles O. Frake, "The Ethnographic Study of Cognitive Systems," in Stephen A. Tyler, ed., *Cognitive Anthropology* (New York: Holt, Rinehart and Winston, 1969 [1962]), pp. 28–41. See also Schutz and Luckmann, *The Structures of the Life-World,* p. 248.

119. Frake, "The Ethnographic Study of Cognitive Systems," p. 36.

120. On how children learn which distinctive features are salient for establishing kinship, see Julie M. Gricar, "Strategies Children Use in the Cognitive Construction of Kinship," *Sociological Studies of Child Development* (forthcoming).

121. Goffman, *Encounters,* pp. 19–26.

122. Bateson, "A Theory of Play and Fantasy," p. 187.

123. See also Goffman, *The Presentation of Self in Everyday Life,* p. 230; Goffman, *Behavior in Public Places,* pp. 83–88.

124. Parsons, *The Social System,* pp. 60, 435, 458–62.

125. Whorf, "Science and Linguistics," pp. 213–14.

126. See also Whorf, "Language, Mind, and Reality," p. 259; Wilber, *No Boundary,* p. 26.

127. See, for example, Locke, *An Essay Concerning Human Understanding,* book 3, chap. 6.39.

128. Emile Durkheim, "The Dualism of Human Nature and Its Social Conditions,"

in Robert N. Bellah, ed., *On Morality and Society* (Chicago: University of Chicago Press, 1973 [1914]), pp. 151–52, 161–62; George H. Mead, *Mind, Self, and Society* (Chicago: University of Chicago Press, 1934), pp. 46–47; Schutz and Luckmann, *The Structures of the Life-World,* pp. 233–35; Berger and Luckmann, *The Social Construction of Reality,* pp. 37–41, 68–69.

129. Plato, *Statesman* (New Haven: Yale University Press, 1952), 263c–263d.
130. Edward De Bono, *The Mechanism of Mind* (Harmondsworth, England: Penguin, 1971 [1969]), p. 197.
131. Danet, " 'Baby' or 'Fetus'?" pp. 187–88. See also Robert S. Morison, "Death: Process or Event?" *Science* 173 (August 20, 1971):694–95.
132. Braverman, *Labor and Monopoly Capital,* pp. 325–26.
133. Bates and Peacock, "Conceptualizing Social Structure," pp. 569–70, 575.

Chapter 5 *The Fuzzy Mind*

1. Wilber, *No Boundary,* p. 55.
2. Freud, *Civilization and Its Discontents,* p. 15. See also Federn, "The Ego as Subject and Object in Narcissism," p. 294; Jean Piaget, *The Child's Conception of the World* (Totowa, N.J.: Helix, 1983 [1929]), pp. 150–54, 159; Werner, *Comparative Psychology of Mental Development,* pp. 361, 440–42; Piaget, *The Construction of Reality in the Child,* pp. 224–27, 233, 240; Balint, *Thrills and Regressions,* p. 67; Edith Jacobson, *The Self and the Object World* (New York: International Universities Press, 1964), p. 47; Mahler, "On Human Symbiosis and the Vicissitudes of Individuation," p. 78; Tuan, *Segmented Worlds and Self,* p. 140.
3. Balint, *The Basic Fault,* p. 66. See also p. 67.
4. Mahler, "On Human Symbiosis and the Vicissitudes of Individuation," p. 78; Mahler, "On the First Three Subphases of the Separation-Individuation Process," p. 121; Mahler et al, *The Psychological Birth of the Human Infant,* pp. 44, 53–54.
5. Kaplan, *Oneness and Separateness,* pp. 100–01, 138.
6. Balint, *The Basic Fault,* p. 66; Stein, *Developmental Time, Cultural Space,* p. 82.
7. Freud, *Civilization and Its Discontents,* pp. 11–12, 15.
8. Theweleit, *Male Fantasies,* pp. 229–31, 245.
9. Lila Ghent, "Perception of Overlapping and Embedded Figures by Children of Different Ages," *American Journal of Psychology* 69 (1956):576–81; Wendy Olesker, "Cognition and the Separation-Individuation Process: A Study of Three Boys at Nursery School," *Psychoanalysis and Contemporary Thought* 1 (1978): 251, 264.
10. Kepes, *Language of Vision,* p. 69.
11. Pike, *Language in Relation to a Unified Theory of the Structure of Human Behavior,* pp. 76–82.
12. Werner, *Comparative Psychology of Mental Development,* pp. 390, 394–402; W. George Scarlett and Dennie Wolf, "When It's Only Make-Believe: The Construction of a Boundary between Fantasy and Reality in Storytelling," *New Directions for Child Development* 6 (1979):29–40; Tuan, *Segmented Worlds and Self,* p. 140.
13. See also Thompson, "The Ability of Children of Different Grade Levels to Generalize on Sorting Tests," p. 122.

14. Sigmund Freud, "One of the Difficulties of Psycho-Analysis," in *Collected Papers* (London: Hogarth, 1925 [1917]), vol. 4, pp. 351–52; Werner, *Comparative Psychology of Mental Development*, p. 442; Harold F. Searles, *The Nonhuman Environment* (New York: International Universities Press, 1960), pp. 57–65.

15. Ernst Cassirer, *The Philosophy of Symbolic Forms, vol. 2: Mythical Thought* (New Haven: Yale University Press, 1955 [1925]), pp. 61ff., 77.

16. Ibid., pp. 36ff., 99, 157ff.; Lévy-Bruhl, *How Natives Think*, pp. 33–36, 42–47, 83–84, 269ff, 303ff.; Arnold H. Modell, *Object Love and Reality* (London: The Hogarth Press, 1969), pp. 11, 20, 31.

17. Cassirer, ibid., pp. 179ff.

18. Karlfried G. Dürckheim, *Zen and Us* (New York: E. P. Dutton, 1987 [1961]), pp. 53–55; Alan Watts, *The Book* (New York: Vintage, 1972 [1966]), pp. 28, 48, 80; Anton Ehrenzweig, *The Hidden Order of Art* (Berkeley: University of California Press, 1967), pp. 294–95; Robert E. Ornstein, *The Psychology of Consciousness* (San Francisco: W. H. Freeman, 1972), pp. 137–38; Tarthang Tulku, *Time, Space, and Knowledge* (Berkeley: Dharma, 1977), p. 17; Wilber, *No Boundary;* Fritjof Capra, *The Tao of Physics* (New York: Bantam, 1984), pp. 116–17.

19. Dürckheim, ibid., p. 49.

20. Capra, *The Tao of Physics*, p. 117.

21. Ibid., pp. 133–34; June Singer, *Androgyny* (Garden City: Anchor, 1976).

22. Dürckheim, *Zen and Us*, p. 48; Kevin Berger and Todd Berger, *Zen Driving* (New York: Ballantine, 1988), p. 8.

23. Gershom Scholem, *The Messianic Idea in Judaism* (New York: Schocken, 1971), pp. 203–27.

24. Werner, *Comparative Psychology of Mental Development*, p. 163; Kurt Goldstein, "Methodological Approach to the Study of Schizophrenic Thought Disorder," in J. S. Kasanin, ed., *Language and Thought in Schizophrenia* (Berkeley: University of California Press, 1944), pp. 32–34; Witkin, "Psychological Differentiation and Forms of Pathology," p. 319; Thomas Freeman et al., *Studies on Psychosis* (New York: International Universities Press, 1966), pp. 72–87, 160–61, 190–91.

25. Marjorie Bolles and Kurt Goldstein, "A Study of the Impairment of 'Abstract Behavior' in Schizophrenic Patients," *Psychiatric Quarterly* 12 (1938): 51–53; Goldstein and Scheerer, "Abstract and Concrete Behavior," pp. 61–74, 87–102, 117–23; Luise J. Zucker, *Ego Structure in Paranoid Schizophrenia* (Springfield, Ill.: Charles C. Thomas, 1958), pp. 42–48; Sidney J. Blatt and Barry A. Ritzler, "Thought Disorder and Boundary Disturbance in Psychosis," *Journal of Consulting and Clinical Psychology* 42 (1974):371; Theodore Lidz and Stephen Fleck, *Schizophrenia and the Family* (New York: International Universities Press, 1985), pp. 424–25.

26. Federn, "The Ego in Schizophrenia," in *Ego Psychology and the Psychoses* (London: Imago Publishing Co., 1953 [1949]), pp. 230, 235; Bateson, "A Theory of Play and Fantasy," pp. 190–92; Bateson et al., "Toward a Theory of Schizophrenia," pp. 205, 209–11; Merleau-Ponty, *Phenomenology of Perception*, p. 287; Harold F. Searles, *Collected Papers on Schizophrenia and Related Subjects* (New York: International Universities Press, 1965), pp. 305, 319, 323–25, 440, 471, 562–65, 583; Sidney Jortner, "An Investigation of Certain Cognitive Aspects of

Schizophrenia," *Journal of Projective Techniques and Personality Assessment* 30 (1966):559–68.

27. Luise J. Zucker, "Evaluating Psychopathology of the Self," *Annals of the New York Academy of Sciences* 96 (1962):849.

28. Ibid., p. 847; Karen Machover, *Personality Projection in the Drawing of the Human Figure* (Springfield, Ill.: Charles C. Thomas, 1949), pp. 133–34, 137–38.

29. Ann Hozier, "On the Breakdown of the Sense of Reality: A Study of Spatial Perception in Schizophrenia," *Journal of Consulting Psychology* 23 (1959):189, 193.

30. Kaplan, *Oneness and Separateness,* p. 16.

31. Freud, *Civilization and Its Discontents,* p. 13; Palombo and Bruch, "Falling Apart," p. 250; Witkin, "Psychological Differentiation and Forms of Pathology," p. 319; Seymour Fisher and Sidney E. Cleveland, "Personality, Body Perception, and Body Image Boundary," in Seymour Wapner and Heinz Werner, eds., *The Body Percept* (New York: Random House, 1965), pp. 52–53; Fisher and Cleveland, *Body Image and Personality,* pp. 16, 238. See also Modell, *Object Love and Reality,* pp. 95, 137.

32. Zucker, *Ego Structure in Paranoid Schizophrenia.*

33. Tausk, "On the Origin of the 'Influencing Machine' in Schizophrenia," pp. 67, 76; Palombo and Bruch, "Falling Apart," p. 248; Searles, *Collected Papers on Schizophrenia and Related Subjects,* pp. 467–68. See also Fisher and Cleveland, *Body Image and Personality,* p. 231; Martha C. Frede et al., "Relationships between Body Image Boundary and Interaction Patterns on the MAPS Test," *Journal of Consulting and Clinical Psychology* 32 (1968):575–78.

34. Tausk, ibid.; Freud, *Civilization and Its Discontents,* p. 13; Goldstein, "Methodological Approach to the Study of Schizophrenic Thought Disorder," pp. 32–34; Fenichel, *The Psychoanalytic Theory of Neurosis,* p. 423; Werner, *Comparative Psychology of Mental Development,* pp. 459, 462–65; Gustav Bychowski, *Psychotherapy of Psychosis* (New York: Grune & Stratton, 1952), pp. 55–56; Witkin et al., *Psychological Differentiation,* pp. 355–56; Zucker, "Evaluating Psychopathology of the Self," p. 844; Jacobson, *The Self and the Object World,* pp. 68–69; Palombo and Bruch, ibid., p. 256; Searles, ibid., pp. 46, 305, 319–25, 525; Freeman et al., *Studies on Psychosis,* p. 73; Gilbert J. Rose, "Body Ego and Reality," *International Journal of Psycho-Analysis* 47 (1966):502–3; Kaplan, *Oneness and Separateness,* p. 16; Lidz and Fleck, *Schizophrenia and the Family,* pp. 372, 414, 424, 430–31.

35. Ruth B. Dyk and Herman A. Witkin, "Family Experiences Related to the Development of Differentiation in Children," *Child Development* 36 (1965):37.

36. Chodorow, *The Reproduction of Mothering,* pp. 93, 109–10, 166–69; Kaplan, *Oneness and Separateness,* p. 221; Gilligan, *In a Different Voice.*

37. See also Joshua Meyrowitz, *No Sense of Place* (New York: Oxford University Press, 1985), p. 207.

38. Witkin et al., *Psychological Differentiation,* pp. 214–15, 218. See also Maccoby and Jacklin, *The Psychology of Sex Differences,* pp. 97, 101–5.

39. Franck and Rosen, "A Projective Test of Masculinity and Femininity," p. 252; Erik H. Erikson, *Childhood and Society* (New York: W. W. Norton, 1963), pp. 105–6.

40. Balint, *Thrills and Regressions,* pp. 34, 68–69; Pirsig, *Zen and the Art of Motorcycle Maintenance.*

41. Machover, *Personality Projection in the Drawing of the Human Figure*, pp. 95–97; Witkin et al., *Psychological Differentiation*, pp. 2, 5, 10; Fisher and Cleveland, "Personality, Body Perception, and Body Image Boundary"; Fisher and Cleveland, *Body Image and Personality;* Seymour Fisher, *Body Experience in Fantasy and Behavior* (New York: Appleton-Century-Crofts, 1970).

42. D. W. Winnicott, "Transitional Objects and Transitional Phenomena," in *Playing and Reality* (London: Tavistock, 1971 [1953]), pp. 4, 14; D. W. Winnicott, "The Location of Cultural Experience," in *Playing and Reality*, pp. 96–97.

43. Richard A. Koenigsberg, *Symbiosis and Separation* (New York: Library of Art and Social Science, 1989), p. 49.

44. Berman, *Coming to Our Senses*, p. 50.

45. Desmond Morris, *Intimate Behavior* (New York: Random House, 1971), pp. 193–212.

46. See also Kegan, *The Evolving Self*, pp. 121–28.

47. Lloyd Silverman et al., *The Search for Oneness* (New York: International Universities Press, 1982); Koenigsberg, *Symbiosis and Separation*, pp. 25–31.

48. Koestler, *The Act of Creation*, p. 295.

49. Mihaly Csikszentmihalyi, *Beyond Freedom and Anxiety* (San Francisco: Jossey-Bass, 1975), pp. 36, 42, 85.

50. Paul Federn, "Some Variations in Ego Feeling," in *Ego Psychology and the Psychoses* (London: Imago Publishing Co., 1953 [1926]), pp. 30–31; Anton Ehrenzweig, *The Psychoanalysis of Artistic Vision and Hearing* (London: Sheldon, 1975 [1953]), p. 30; Ehrenzweig, *The Hidden Order of Art*, p. 87; Balint, *The Basic Fault*, pp. 49–50.

51. Marion Milner, *On Not Being Able to Paint* (Los Angeles: James P. Tarcher, 1957), p. 163; Milner, *The Suppressed Madness of Sane Men*, pp. 79–82, 231, 239–40.

52. See also Milner, *The Suppressed Madness of Sane Men*, p. 218.

53. Tulku, *Time, Space, and Knowledge*, pp. 4, 6, 11.

54. Ibid., pp. 13–16, 26–29.

55. Ibid., pp. 13, 15, 28–29, 36–37.

56. Ibid., p. 23; Watts, *The Book;* Capra, *The Tao of Physics*, p. 128. See also Scholem, *The Messianic Idea in Judaism*, p. 214.

57. Werner, *Comparative Psychology of Mental Development*, p. 461.

58. Zali D. Gurevitch, "The Embrace: On the Element of Nondistance in Human Relations," *Sociological Quarterly* 31 (1990): 187–201.

59. Ibid.; Schilder, *The Image and Appearance of the Human Body*, p. 210.

60. Searles, *Collected Papers on Schizophrenia and Related Subjects*, p. 430; Davis, *Smut*, pp. 96–124; Milner, *The Suppressed Madness of Sane Men*, p. 119.

61. Schilder, *The Image and Appearance of the Human Body*, pp. 235–36.

62. Scholem, *The Messianic Idea in Judaism*, pp. 203–27.

63. Genesis 2:24.

64. Freud, *Civilization and Its Discontents*, p. 13. See also Paul Federn, "On the Distinction between Healthy and Pathological Narcissism," in *Ego Psychology and the Psychoses* (London: Imago Publishing Co., 1953), p. 350; Modell, *Object Love and Reality*, pp. 61–62; Davis, *Intimate Relations*, pp. 169–205.

65. Koenigsberg, *Symbiosis and Separation*, p. 37. See also Erich Fromm, *The Art of Loving* (New York: Harper & Row, 1956), p. 19.

66. Davis, *Intimate Relations,* pp. 103–15; Altman and Taylor, *Social Penetration,* pp. 110, 112; Zerubavel, "Personal Information and Social Life," pp. 100–2.

67. Shell, "The Family Pet," p. 122.

68. See, for example, Kinsey et al., *Sexual Behavior in the Human Male,* pp. 459–64, 667–78.

69. Philip Roth, *Portnoy's Complaint* (New York: Random House, 1969), pp. 148–50.

70. See also Davis, *Smut,* pp. 134–60.

71. Turner, *The Ritual Process,* pp. 82, 115, 119; Victor Turner, "Pilgrimages as Social Processes," in *Dramas, Fields, and Metaphors* (Ithaca: Cornell University Press, 1975 [1973]), p. 202; Turner, "Metaphors of Anti-Structure," pp. 274, 284, 288, 293. See also Durkheim, *The Division of Labor in Society,* pp. 31–64.

72. See also Alfred Schutz, "Making Music Together: A Study in Social Relationship," *Social Research* 18 (1951):76–97.

73. Turner, "Betwixt and Between," pp. 98–99; Turner, *The Ritual Process,* pp. 89, 92–93; Victor Turner, "Passages, Margins, and Poverty: Religious Symbols of Communitas," in *Dramas, Fields, and Metaphors* (Ithaca: Cornell University Press, 1975 [1972]), pp. 247, 253; Turner, "Pilgrimages as Social Processes."

74. Victor Turner, "Variations on a Theme of Liminality," in Sally F. Moore and Barbara G. Myerhoff, eds., *Secular Ritual* (Amsterdam: Van Gorcum, 1977), p. 37.

75. See, for example, Aldona Jonaitis, *Art of the Northern Tlingit* (Seattle: University of Washington Press, 1986), p. 129. On masks, see also A. David Napier, *Masks, Transformation, and Paradox* (Berkeley: University of California Press, 1986), p. 17.

76. Van Gennep, *The Rites of Passage,* p. 173.

77. Turner, *The Ritual Process,* pp. 155–93; Robert B. Edgerton, *Rules, Exceptions, and Social Order* (Berkeley: University of California Press, 1985), pp. 95–107.

78. Bakhtin, *Rabelais and His World,* pp. 10, 40, 90, 264, 411.

79. Susan Stewart, *Nonsense* (Baltimore: Johns Hopkins University Press, 1979), p. 39.

80. Bouissac, "Circus Performance as Ritual," pp. 116–18; Peter Stallybrass and Allon White, *The Politics and Poetics of Transgression* (Ithaca: Cornell University Press, 1986), pp. 58–59.

81. Fiedler, *Freaks,* pp. 274–86.

82. Mark Lewisohn, *The Beatles—Recording Sessions* (New York: Harmony, 1988), p. 109.

83. Clark Kinnaird, ed., *Encyclopedia of Puzzles and Pastimes* (New York: Grosset & Dunlap, 1946), p. 250.

84. Stewart, *Nonsense,* p. 105.

85. Kinnaird, *Encyclopedia of Puzzles and Pastimes,* pp. 61–62, 231.

86. Stewart, *Nonsense,* p. 105.

87. Joseph Rosenbloom, *Doctor Knock-Knock's Official Knock-Knock Dictionary* (New York: Sterling, 1976), pp. 53, 58; Sam Schultz, *Make Me Laugh Again* (Los Angeles: Price/Stern/Sloan, 1984).

88. Ian Hamnett, "Ambiguity, Classification and Change: The Function of Riddles," *Man* 2 (1967):379–92; Elli Köngäs Maranda, "Theory and Practice in

Riddle Analysis," in Americo Paredes and Richard Bauman, eds., *Toward New Perspectives in Folklore* (Austin: University of Texas Press, 1972), p. 53.

89. See, for example, Wilden, *System and Structure,* p. 118.
90. Koestler, *The Act of Creation,* pp. 94–95.
91. Bakhtin, *Rabelais and His World,* pp. 462–63.
92. Ragnar Johnson, 1976. "Two Realms and a Joke: Bisociation Theories of Joking," *Semiotica* 16 (1976):195–221.
93. Personal communication from Deborah Wolfe.
94. Bateson et al., "Toward a Theory of Schizophrenia," p. 203; Fry, *Sweet Madness,* pp. 137–72.
95. Lewis Carroll, "Through the Looking Glass," in *Complete Works* (New York: Vintage, 1976 [1872]), pp. 189–90. See also p. 233.
96. Jonathan Gefen, "The Story About the Green Man," in *The Sixteenth Lamb* (Jerusalem: Dvir, 1983), p. 36.
97. Goffman, *Frame Analysis,* p. 412.
98. Ibid., pp. 392–93.
99. See also ibid., p. 395.
100. Rebecca Hicks, "What Is Going On Here?—An Analysis of the Stand-Up Comedy Show as Play Frame" (unpublished paper, 1988).
101. Bakhtin, *Rabelais and His World,* pp. 26, 42–44, 281, 317–18, 339.
102. Ibid., pp. 26, 317.
103. Ibid., p. 317; Paul Radin, *The Trickster* (New York: Schocken, 1972 [1956]), p. 140.
104. See also Radin, ibid., passim; William Willeford, *The Fool and His Scepter* (Evanston, Ill.: Northwestern University Press, 1969).
105. G. Legman, *Rationale of the Dirty Joke* (New York: Grove, 1968), p. 216.
106. Georg Simmel, "The Adventure," in Kurt H. Wolff, ed., *Georg Simmel, 1858–1918* (Columbus: Ohio State University Press, 1959 [1911]), pp. 243–44.
107. Nancy Friday, *My Secret Garden* (New York: Pocket Books, 1974), pp. 158–70; Nancy Friday, *Men in Love* (New York: Dell, 1981), pp. 151–75, 259–73.
108. Sandra Kornstein, "The Stranger in Our Midst: The Making of an American Superhero" (M.A. thesis, Rutgers University, 1989).
109. Helen Hutton, *The Technique of Collage* (London: B. T. Batsford, 1968), pp. 13–30, 106–10.
110. See also Roland Barthes, *Empire of Signs* (New York: Hill and Wang, 1982 [1970]), pp. 15–18 on the use of chopsticks.
111. Michael Kirby, ed., *Happenings* (New York: E. P. Dutton, 1965), pp. 31–32; Allan Kaprow, *Assemblage, Environments, and Happenings* (New York: Harry N. Abrams, 1966), p. 212.
112. Gerald Woods et al., eds., *Art Without Boundaries* (New York: Praeger, 1974 [1972]), p. 16. See also p. 13.
113. Some classic examples are the segues between the reprise of *Sgt. Pepper's Lonely Hearts Club Band* and *A Day in the Life* or *Polythene Pam* and *She Came in Through the Bathroom Window.* See also Lewisohn, *The Beatles—Recording Sessions,* pp. 107, 162, 183.
114. Köhler, *Gestalt Psychology,* p. 120. See also Alexander et al., *A Pattern Language,* pp. 518–22.
115. Koffka, *Principles of Gestalt Psychology,* pp. 184–86, 194–95, 208–9; Köhler,

ibid., pp. 106–20; Ehrenzweig, *The Psychoanalysis of Artistic Vision and Hearing,* pp. 26–27; Rudolf Arnheim, "The Perception of Maps," in *New Essays on the Psychology of Art* (Berkeley: University of California Press, 1986 [1976]), p. 199; Edwards, *Drawing on the Artist Within,* p. 152. See also Paul Klee, *Notebooks, vol. 1: The Thinking Eye* (London: Lund Humphries, 1961), pp. 50–52.

116. Ehrenzweig, ibid., p. 28; Ehrenzweig, *The Hidden Order of Art,* pp. 22–23; Edwards, ibid., pp. 155–65; Betty Edwards, *Drawing on the Right Side of the Brain* (Los Angeles: J. P. Tarcher, 1979), pp. 98–113.

117. Sandra G. Shuman, *Source Imagery* (New York: Doubleday, 1989), pp. 142–44, 153.

118. Arnheim, *Art and Visual Perception,* pp. 218–19; Milner, *The Suppressed Madness of Sane Men,* p. 118.

119. Maurits C. Escher, "How Did You as a Graphic Artist Come to Make Designs for Wall Decorations?" in *Escher on Escher* (New York: Harry N. Abrams, 1989 [1941]), pp. 83–84; Maurits C. Escher, "The Regular Division of the Plane," in *Escher on Escher,* pp. 93–94, 99; Maurits C. Escher, "The Regular Division of the Plane," in *Escher on Escher,* pp. 25–26, 29, 32, 35. See also Doris Schattschneider, *Visions of Symmetry* (New York: W. H. Freeman, 1990), pp. 116–234.

120. Some other spectacular examples are his *Study of Regular Division of the Plane with Human Figures* (1944), *Study of Regular Division of the Plane with Horsemen,* and *Circle Limit IV.*

121. Kepes, *Language of Vision,* p. 102.

122. Ehrenzweig, *The Psychoanalysis of Artistic Vision and Hearing,* pp. 41–43, 90; Leonard B. Meyer, *Emotion and Meaning in Music* (Chicago: University of Chicago Press, 1956), pp. 185–86; Ehrenzweig, *The Hidden Order of Art,* pp. 25–27, 71.

123. Ehrenzweig, *The Hidden Order of Art,* pp. 84–86.

124. Ehrenzweig, *The Psychoanalysis of Artistic Vision and Hearing,* pp. 156–57.

125. Ibid., pp. 34, 133, 143, 190; Ehrenzweig, *The Hidden Order of Art,* pp. 8, 21, 23, 31–46, 294–95.

126. Crockett Johnson, *Harold and the Purple Crayon* (New York: Harper & Row, 1955). See also David Grossman, *Itamar Walks on Walls* (Tel-Aviv: Am Oved, 1986).

127. David McPhail, *The Magical Drawings of Moony B. Finch* (Garden City, N.Y.: Doubleday, 1978).

128. See also Douglas R. Hofstadter, *Gödel, Escher, Bach* (New York: Vintage, 1980), pp. 15, 715–17.

129. Rousseau, "A Discourse on the Origin of Inequality"; Karl Marx and Friedrich Engels, "Manifesto of the Communist Party," in Robert C. Tucker, ed., *The Marx-Engels Reader* (New York: W. W. Norton, 1978 [1848]), pp. 484ff.

130. See, for example, Dalton Trumbo, *Johnny Got His Gun* (New York: Bantam, 1970 [1939]), p. 242.

131. Sambursky, *The Physical World of the Greeks,* pp. 132–57.

132. Epictetus, *The Discourses of Epictetus* (New York: Heritage Press, 1968), book 1, ch. 9. See also book 2, ch. 10.

133. Romans 10:12. See also 3:29–30.

134. Ephesians 2:14–15.

135. I Corinthians 7:12–14, 10:27; Wayne A. Meeks, *The First Urban Christians* (New Haven: Yale University Press, 1983), pp. 92, 97.

136. See also Shell, "The Family Pet," p. 130.

137. Albert Schweitzer, *Indian Thought and Its Development* (Boston: Beacon, 1957 [1936]), pp. 261–62.

138. Ibid., pp. 259–60. See also Singer, *Animal Liberation,* pp. xii, 21; Peter Singer, *The Expanding Circle* (New York: Farrar, Straus & Giroux, 1981), p. 120.

139. Charles R. Joy, ed., *Albert Schweitzer—An Anthology* (Boston: Beacon, 1956), p. 273.

140. Edward A. Armstrong, *Saint Francis: Nature Mystic* (Berkeley: University of California Press, 1973), p. 144.

141. Schweitzer, *Indian Thought and Its Development,* p. 10; Klaits and Klaits, *Animals and Man in Historical Perspective,* pp. 5–6; W. Norman Brown, "The Unity of Life in Indian Religion," in *Animals and Man in Historical Perspective,* pp. 56–57.

142. Brown, ibid., p. 57; Mrs. Sinclair Stevenson, *The Heart of Jainism* (London: Humphrey Milford, 1915), p. 295; Padmanabh S. Jaini, *The Jaina Path of Purification* (Berkeley: University of California Press, 1979), p. 108.

143. Stevenson, ibid., pp.116, 206–7, 234; Schweitzer, *Indian Thought and Its Development,* pp. 79–84; Jaini, ibid., pp. 172–73.

144. Stevenson, ibid., pp. 100, 146, 227, 234–35; Schweitzer, ibid., p. 82; Jaini, ibid., pp. 167–69, 242–45.

145. Joy, *Albert Schweitzer—An Anthology,* p. 273.

146. Aldo Leopold, "The Land Ethic," in *A Sand County Almanac* (New York: Oxford University Press, 1966 [1953]), pp. 219, 231–32; Stone, *Should Trees Have Standing?*

147. Kingsley Davis, "Intermarriage in Caste Societies," *American Anthropologist* 43 (1941):391–92; William Petersen, "The Classification of Subnations in Hawaii: An Essay in the Sociology of Knowledge," *American Sociological Review* 34 (1969): 863–77; Marvin Harris, "Referential Ambiguity in the Calculus of Brazilian Racial Identity," *Southwestern Journal of Anthropology* 26 (1970):1–14.

148. Hans-Dieter Evers, "The Culture of Malaysian Urbanization: Malay and Chinese Conceptions of Space," *Urban Anthropology* 6 (1977):205–16; Hall, *The Hidden Dimension,* pp. 132–36.

149. Donald N. Levine, *The Flight from Ambiguity* (Chicago: University of Chicago Press, 1985), pp. 21–28; Werner, *Comparative Psychology of Mental Development,* pp. 433–39; Tuan, *Segmented Worlds and Self,* pp. 14–17, 141–46.

150. Edmund Carpenter et al., *Eskimo* (Toronto: University of Toronto Press, 1959), W. E. Willmott, "The Flexibility of Eskimo Social Organization," in Victor F. Valentine and Frank G. Vallee, eds., *Eskimo of the Canadian Arctic* (Toronto: McClelland and Stewart, 1968 [1960]), pp. 151, 155; Heluiz C. Washburne, *Land of the Good Shadows* (New York: John Day, 1960).

151. Sollors, *Beyond Ethnicity,* pp. 66–101; Richard M. Merelman, *Making Something of Ourselves* (Berkeley: University of California Press, 1984), pp. 44–64; Liora Gvion-Rosenberg, "Culinary Pluralism or Culinary Hegemony: The Case of Ethnic Dishes, 1945–1987" (paper presented at the annual meeting of the American Sociological Association, Atlanta, August 1988). See also Daniel J. Boorstin, "The Fertile Verge: Creativity in the United States" (paper presented at

the Inaugural Meeting of the Council of Scholars of the Library of Congress, Washington, D.C., 1980), pp. 15–16.

152. W. W. Hill, "The Status of the Hermaphrodite and Transvestite in Navaho Culture," *American Anthropologist* 37 (1935):274–76; Donald N. Michael, "A Cross-Cultural Investigation of Closure," *Journal of Abnormal and Social Psychology* 48 (1953): 225–26; David F. Aberle, "Some Sources of Flexibility in Navaho Social Organization," *Southwestern Journal of Anthropology* 19 (1963): 1–8.

153. Mary Douglas, "Animals in Lele Religious Symbolism," *Africa* 27 (1957):46–58; Douglas, "Self-Evidence," pp. 297–302.

154. Bakhtin, *Rabelais and His World.*

155. See, for example, *The Millennium, The Temptation of Saint Anthony, As It Was in the Days of Noah,* and *Saint John on Patmos.*

156. See Levine, *The Flight from Ambiguity,* pp. 2–8 on the modern assault on ambiguity.

157. David P. Handlin, *The American Home* (Boston: Little, Brown, 1979), p. 349. See also Tatsuo Ishimoto and Kiyoko Ishimoto, *The Japanese House* (New York: Crown, 1963), p. 31; Kiyoyuki Nishihara, *Japanese Houses* (Tokyo: Japan Publications, 1968), p. 221; Teiji Itoh and Yukio Futagawa, *The Classic Tradition in Japanese Architecture* (New York: John Weatherhill, 1972), p. 190; Botond Bognar, *Contemporary Japanese Architecture* (New York: Van Nostrand Reinhold, 1985), p. 58; Kisho Kurokawa, *Rediscovering Japanese Space* (New York: Weatherhill, 1988), p. 54.

158. Sigfried Giedion, *Space, Time, and Architecture* (Cambridge: Harvard University Press, 1956), pp. 225, 237, 252, 264–68; Vincent Scully, *Modern Architecture* (New York: George Braziller, 1974 [1961]), p. 13; Christian Norberg-Schulz, *Meaning in Western Architecture* (New York: Rizzoli International Publications, 1980 [1974]), pp. 174, 178; Claude Mignot, *Architecture of the Nineteenth Century in Europe* (New York: Rizzoli International Publications, 1984), pp. 177, 180–86. 201–3, 238–46; Frances H. Steiner, *French Iron Architecture* (Ann Arbor: UMI Research Press, 1984), pp. 26, 53–56.

159. Kepes, *Language of Vision,* p. 32; Giedion, ibid., p. 265; Herb Greene, *Mind and Image* (Lexington: University Press of Kentucky, 1976), p. 203.

160. Pirsig, *Zen and the Art of Motorcycle Maintenance,* p. 4.

161. See also Oswald Spengler, *The Decline of the West* (New York: Alfred A. Knopf, 1926), vol. 1, pp. 183ff.

162. Frank L. Wright, *The Natural House* (New York: Horizon, 1954), pp. 19, 50; Scully, *Modern Architecture,* pp. 13–21; Merelman, *Making Something of Ourselves,* p. 49.

163. Wright, ibid., pp. 39–40. See also pp. 20, 45; Giedion, *Space, Time, and Architecture,* pp. 398, 543–44.

164. Walter Gropius, *The New Architecture and the Bauhaus* (New York: Museum of Modern Art, 1937), p. 210.

165. Wright, *The Natural House,* pp. 137, 165–66.

166. Ibid., pp. 38, 50.

167. Giedion, *Space, Time, and Architecture,* pp. 282, 432; Scully, *Modern Architecture,* p. 13; Kern, *The Culture of Time and Space 1880–1918,* p. 185.

168. Umberto Boccioni, "The Plastic Foundations of Futurist Sculpture and Paint-

ing," in Umbro Apollonio, ed., *Futurist Manifestos* (New York: Viking, 1973 [1913]), p. 89; Kern, ibid., pp. 153, 159–61.

169. Ehrenzweig, *The Psychoanalysis of Artistic Vision and Hearing,* p. 23; Giedion, *Space, Time, and Architecture,* pp. 433–34; Kern, ibid., pp. 195–96.

170. E. E. Cummings, *A Selection of Poems* (New York: Harvest, 1965), pp. 35–36. See also John Cage, *Empty Words* (Middletown, Conn.: Wesleyan University Press, 1979).

171. See, for example, Cummings, ibid., pp. 141, 148, 169.

172. James Joyce. *Ulysses* (New York: Random House, 1986 [1922]).

173. Goffman, *Frame Analysis,* p. 391n.

174. Cummings, *A Selection of Poems,* p. 140. See also Smith, *Poetic Closure,* pp. 237, 246–50.

175. Cone, *Musical Form and Musical Performance,* p. 19.

176. Luigi Pirandello, *Tonight We Improvise* (New York: Samuel French, 1960 [1932]), pp. 39–46.

177. Kirby, *Happenings;* Kaprow, *Assemblage, Environments, and Happenings,* pp. 185–87, 193, 210–341; Goffman, *Frame Analysis,* pp. 433–34n.

178. Kaprow, ibid., pp. 188–89; Harriet Janis and Rudi Blesh, *Collage* (Philadelphia: Chilton Book Co., 1967), pp. 17, 268.

179. See also Arnheim, *Art and Visual Perception,* p. 231; Teddy Brunius, "Inside and Outside the Frame of a Work of Art," in *Idea and Form* (Stockholm: Almqvist & Wiksell, 1959), pp. 15–16; Arnheim, *The Power of the Center,* pp. 58–59.

180. Michel Butor, "Mondrian: The Square and Its Inhabitant," in *Inventory* (New York: Simon & Schuster, 1968 [1965]), p. 239; Arnheim, *The Power of the Center,* pp. 150–51.

181. Umberto Boccioni, "Technical Manifesto of Futurist Sculpture," in Umbro Apollonio (ed.), *Futurist Manifestos* (New York: Viking, 1973 [1912]), p. 63; Schapiro, "On Some Problems in the Semiotics of Visual Art," p. 225.

182. Pirandello, *Tonight We Improvise,* pp. 8–10, 50; Richard Kostelanetz, *The Theater of Mixed Means* (New York: Dial Press, 1968), pp. 23–25; Schechner, *Environmental Theater,* pp. 4, 35–39; Uspensky, *A Poetics of Composition,* p. 139; Tuan, *Segmented Worlds and Self,* pp. 189–92.

183. Arnheim, *Art and Visual Perception,* p. 231.

184. Kirby, *Happenings,* p. 24; Kaprow, *Assemblage, Environments, and Happenings,* pp. 154, 160, 165.

185. Kirby, ibid., p. 22; Kaprow, ibid., pp. 154–57, 165; Janis and Blesh, *Collage,* pp. 15–24, 110–11, 130, 268; Uspensky, *A Poetics of Composition,* p. 139n.

186. Kaprow, ibid., p. 158; Janis and Blesh, ibid., pp. 55, 60, 88–89; Hutton, *The Technique of Collage,* pp. 14, 28, 70.

187. Kirby, *Happenings,* p. 29.

188. Janis and Blesh, *Collage,* pp. 284–88; Adrian Henri, *Total Art* (New York: Praeger, 1974), pp. 96–97, 114; Richard Schechner, *Between Theater and Anthropology* (Philadelphia: University of Pennsylvania Press, 1985), pp. 303–7.

189. Kern, *The Culture of Time and Space 1880–1918,* pp. 199–201; Michael Kirby and Victoria N. Kirby, *Futurist Performance* (New York: PAJ Publications, 1986), pp. 48, 69; Schechner, *Environmental Theater,* pp. 7, 49–53, 59.

190. Joseph Heller, *We Bombed in New Haven* (New York: Delta, 1967), pp. 26, 74–75. See also Pirandello, *Tonight We Improvise,* pp. 16–25, 63–64, 70–72, 75.

191. Goffman, *Frame Analysis,* p. 392. See also Cone, *Musical Form and Musical Performance,* p. 20.
192. John Barth, *Giles Goat-Boy, or The Revised New Syllabus* (Garden City, N.Y.: Doubleday, 1966).
193. Heller, *We Bombed in New Haven,* pp. 3–6. See also Pirandello, *Tonight We Improvise,* pp. 7–9.
194. Pirandello, ibid., pp. 20–21.
195. See also Merelman, *Making Something of Ourselves,* pp. 71–72.
196. Meyrowitz, *No Sense of Place,* pp. 77–79, 85–87, 222–25, 235–53, 309–12.
197. Ibid., p. 80; Merelman, *Making Something of Ourselves,* pp. 96–97.
198. Rosabeth M. Kanter, *The Change Masters* (New York: Touchstone, 1984).
199. Simon Dinitz and Nancy Beran, "Community Mental Health as a Boundary-less and Boundary-Busting System," *Journal of Health and Social Behavior* 12 (1971): 99–108.
200. Betty Roszak, "The Human Continuum," in Betty Roszak and Theodore Roszak, eds., *Masculine/Feminine* (New York: Harper Torchbooks, 1969), p. 304; Singer, *Androgyny,* pp. viii, 22.
201. See also James Clifford, *The Predicament of Culture* (Cambridge: Harvard University Press, 1988), pp. 13–17.
202. Merelman, *Making Something of Ourselves,* pp. 136, 142–45; Paul DiMaggio, "Classification in Art," *American Sociological Review* 52 (1987):450.
203. Mattei Dogan and Robert Pahre, *Creative Marginality* (Boulder, Colo.: Westview Press, 1990), pp. 85–113, 173.
204. Alexander Frazier, *Open Schools for Children* (Washington, D.C.: Association for Supervision and Curriculum Development, 1972).
205. DiMaggio, "Classification in Art," p. 452.
206. Clifford Geertz, "Blurred Genres: The Refiguration of Social Thought," in *Local Knowledge* (New York: Basic Books, 1983 [1980]), p. 20.
207. Ibid.

Chapter 6 *The Flexible Mind*

1. De Bono, *The Mechanism of Mind,* p. 205.
2. Indeed, in Hebrew, there is one word (*nituach*) for both *surgery* and *analysis*. See also James H. Bunn, *The Dimensionality of Signs, Tools, and Models* (Bloomington: Indiana University Press, 1981), p. 47.
3. Pirsig, *Zen and the Art of Motorcycle Maintenance,* p. 70. See also p. 66.
4. Elliot G. Mishler, "Meaning in Context: Is There Any Other Kind?" *Harvard Educational Review* 49 (1979):1–19.
5. See, for example, Witkin et al, *Psychological Differentiation,* pp. 214–15, 218.
6. Dale Spender, *Man Made Language* (London: Routledge & Kegan Paul, 1980), p. 165. See also Janice Haaken, "Field Dependence Research: A Historical Analysis of a Psychological Construct," *Signs* 13 (1988):312.
7. See also Haaken, ibid., pp. 325–27.
8. Lidz and Fleck, *Schizophrenia and the Family,* p. 431. Emphasis added. See also Frenkel-Brunswik, "Intolerance of Ambiguity as an Emotional and Perceptual Personality Variable"; Merleau-Ponty, "The Child's Relations with Others," p. 101.

9. Milner, *On Not Being Able to Paint*, pp. 16–17.

10. Witkin et al, *Psychological Differentiation*, p. 261.

11. Thomas, *Man and the Natural World*, p.135.

12. Richard Sennett, *The Uses of Disorder* (New York: Vintage, 1971), pp. 14–15.

13. Shepard, *Thinking Animals*, pp. 92, 94.

14. See also Donna Haraway, "A Manifesto for Cyborgs: Science, Technology, and Socialist Feminism in the 1980s," *Socialist Review* 80 (1985):69.

15. See also ibid., pp. 97–98.

16. See also Geertz, "Blurred Genres," p. 20; Kanter, *The Change Masters*, pp. 28–32, 160.

17. Salman Rushdie, "A Pen against the Sword: In Good Faith," *Newsweek*, Feb. 12, 1990, p. 52.

18. Henry Schaefer-Simmern, *The Unfolding of Artistic Activity* (Berkeley: University of California Press, 1961 [1948]), pp. 10–25; Arnheim, *Visual Thinking*, pp. 283–87.

19. Boorstin, "The Fertile Verge."

20. Koestler, *The Act of Creation*, pp. 105–44, 230–33.

21. See, for example, Bernstein, "On the Classification and Framing of Educational Knowledge."

22. Donald T. Campbell, "Ethnocentrism of Disciplines and the Fish-Scale Model of Omniscience," in Muzafer Sherif and Carolyn W. Sherif, eds., *Interdisciplinary Relationships in the Social Sciences* (Chicago: Aldine, 1969), pp. 328–48; Dogan and Pahre, *Creative Marginality*, pp. 65–68.

23. See also Ben-Yehuda, *Deviance and Moral Boundaries*, p. 7.

24. Listen, for example, to Antonio Carlos Jobim play his *Chega de Saudade* or *Insensatez*.

25. Liedloff, *The Continuum Concept*, pp. 58–66.

26. In Hebrew the words for both *discrete* and *lonely* indeed derive from the same root.

27. Emile Durkheim, *Suicide* (New York: Free Press, 1966 [1897]), pp. 152–216; Fromm, *The Art of Loving*, pp. 8–9; John Bowlby, *Separation* (New York: Basic Books, 1973), pp. xi–xiii; Liedloff, *The Continuum Concept*; Berman, *Coming to Our Senses*; Koenigsberg, *Symbiosis and Separation*, p. 35. See also Jacobson, *The Self and the Object World*, pp. 40–41, 69.

28. Wilber, *No Boundary*, p. 5; Anzieu, *The Skin Ego*, pp. 40, 89, 103. See also Machover, *Personality Projection in the Drawing of the Human Figure*, p. 137; Fisher, *Body Experience in Fantasy and Behavior*, pp. 312–15.

29. Schwartz, "The Social Psychology of Privacy," p. 750.

30. Tausk, "On the Origin of the 'Influencing Machine' in Schizophrenia," p. 67. See also Simmel, "The Secret and the Secret Society," pp. 334–35.

31. Kanter, *Commitment and Community*, p. 170.

32. Hunter, *Symbolic Communities*, pp. 67, 88; Pauline Boss, "A Clarification of the Concept of Psychological Father Presence in Families Experiencing Ambiguity of Boundary," *Journal of Marriage and the Family* 39 (1977):141–51.

33. Erikson, *Wayward Puritans*.

34. Alexander et al., *A Pattern Language*, pp. 76–79, 87–89.

35. Marvin Minsky, *The Society of Mind* (New York: Simon & Schuster, 1986), p. 134.

36. Köhler, *Gestalt Psychology*, pp. 84, 93.

37. See also Zerubavel, *Patterns of Time in Hospital Life*, pp. 18–20.

38. See also Darnton, *The Great Cat Massacre*, p. 193.

39. Kevin Lynch, *The Image of the City* (Cambridge: MIT Press, 1964 [1960]), pp. 62–66, 100.

40. See also Smith, *Poetic Closure*, pp. 33–36.

41. Henry Heydenryk, *The Art and History of Frames* (New York: James H. Heineman, 1963), p. 5.

42. Paul Zucker, *Town and Square* (New York: Columbia University Press, 1959), p. 9. See also Camillo Sitte, *The Art of Building Cities* (New York: Reinhold, 1945 [1889]), pp. 20–24, 97, 101, 109.

43. Durkheim, *Suicide*, pp. 247–50, 254–76; Emile Durkheim, *Moral Education* (New York: Free Press, 1973 [1925]), pp. 39–46.

44. Catherine J. Schmidt, "Tourism: Sacred Sites, Secular Seers," (Ph.D. diss., State University of New York at Stony Brook, 1984), pp. 125–26. See also p. 140.

45. Amos Rapoport and Robert E. Kantor, "Complexity and Ambiguity in Environmental Design," *Journal of the American Institute of Planners* 33 (1967):210–21; Greene, *Mind and Image*, pp. 56–57; Alexander et al., *A Pattern Language*, pp. 581–83.

46. Alexander et al., ibid., pp. 893–94. See also Henry James, *The American Scene* (New York: Harper, 1907), p. 161.

47. Zerubavel, *The Seven-Day Circle*, p.120.

48. Zerubavel, *Hidden Rhythms*, pp. 155–66.

49. Evelyn F. Keller, *Reflections on Gender and Science* (New Haven: Yale University Press, 1985), pp. 99–102; Koenigsberg, *Symbiosis and Separation*, pp. 8, 25–26, 33.

50. Witkin, "Psychological Differentiation and Forms of Pathology," pp. 325–26; Landis, *Ego Boundaries*, pp. 2–3; Shepard, *Thinking Animals*, pp. 70–71.

51. Durkheim, *Suicide*, pp. 152–240.

52. See also Alexander et al., *A Pattern Language*, pp. 519–22, 717–18, 893–95, 1103, 1125–27.

53. Edward S. Morse, *Japanese Homes and Their Surroundings* (Boston: Ticknor, 1886), p. 177; Tetsuro Yoshida, *The Japanese House and Garden* (New York: Frederick A. Praeger, 1955), pp. 72, 152–56; Ishimoto and Ishimoto, *The Japanese House*, pp. 25, 28, 90; Nishihara, *Japanese Houses*, p. 190; Itoh and Futagawa, *The Classic Tradition in Japanese Architecture*, pp. 21, 130, 154, 208; Bognar, *Contemporary Japanese Architecture*, pp. 58–60.

54. Simmel, "Brücke und Tür," p. 4.

55. Phyllis Greenacre, "The Family Romance of the Artist," *Psychoanalytic Study of the Child* 13 (1958): 34; Gilbert J. Rose, "Creative Imagination in Terms of Ego 'Core' and Boundaries," *International Journal of Psycho-Analysis* 45 (1964):75–77, 81–84; Fisher, *Body Experience in Fantasy and Behavior*, p. 316; Abraham H. Maslow, *The Farther Reaches of Human Nature* (Harmondsworth, England: Penguin, 1976 [1971]), pp. 68, 250–51; Shepard, *Thinking Animals*, p. 71.

56. See also Salvador Minuchin, *Families and Family Therapy* (Cambridge: Harvard University Press, 1974), pp. 54–60 on flexibility in family life.

57. Jerre Levy, "Psychological Implications of Bilateral Asymmetry," in Stuart J.

Dimond and J. Graham Beaumont, eds., *Hemisphere Function in the Human Brain* (New York: Halsted, 1974), pp. 167, 173; Edwards, *Drawing on the Right Side of the Brain,* p. 40; Sally P. Springer and George Deutsch, *Left Brain, Right Brain* (New York: W. H. Freeman, 1985), p. 49; Edwards, *Drawing on the Artist Within,* pp. 10–13.

58. Ornstein, *The Psychology of Consciousness,* pp. 58, 184.

59. See, for example, Ehrenzweig, *The Hidden Order of Art,* pp. 79, 87, 120.

60. C. M. Mooney, "A Factorial Study of Closure," *Canadian Journal of Psychology* 8 (1954):53; Richard M. Warren, "Illusory Changes of Distinct Speech upon Repetition: The Verbal Transformation Effect," *British Journal of Psychology* 52 (1961):254. See also Carol Pemberton, "The Closure Factors Related to Other Cognitive Processes," *Psychometrika* 17 (1952):269.

61. See also Frenkel-Brunswik, "Intolerance of Ambiguity as an Emotional and Perceptual Personality Variable," p. 121; Edwards, *Drawing on the Artist Within,* pp. 155–65.

62. See, for example, Goffman, *Behavior in Public Places.*

63. Bloomer, *Principles of Visual Perception,* p. 44.

64. See also Turner, "Variations on a Theme of Liminality," p. 38.

65. Whorf, "Language, Mind, and Reality," p. 258. See also p. 259.

66. Edwards, *Drawing on the Artist Within,* p. 175. See also pp. 172–74.

67. Susanne K. Langer, *Philosophy in a New Key* (Cambridge: Harvard University Press, 1957), pp. 75–76.

68. Rand J. Spiro et al., "Cognitive Flexibility and Transfer in Complex Content Domains," in Bruce K. Britton and Shawn M. Glynn, eds., *Executive Control Processes in Reading* (Hillsdale, N.J.: Lawrence Erlbaum Associates, 1987), pp. 181, 186–87; Rand J. Spiro et al., "Cognitive Flexibility Theory: Advanced Knowledge Acquisition in Ill-Structural Domains," in *Program of the Tenth Annual Conference of the Cognitive Science Society* (Hillsdale, N.J.: Lawrence Erlbaum Associates, 1988), pp. 381–82.

69. Werner, *Comparative Psychology of Mental Development,* p. 156; Leslie A. White, *The Science of Culture* (New York: Farrar, Straus & Giroux, 1949), p. 29.

70. Balint, *Thrills and Regressions,* p. 120.

71. Pirsig, *Zen and the Art of Motorcycle Maintenance,* pp. 46–47.

72. Jean L. Briggs, "Le Modèle Traditionnel d'Education chez les Inuit," *Recherches Amérindiennes au Quebec* 13 (1983):14.

73. For a discussion of a dynamic concept of selfhood that allows for both intimacy and autonomy, see also Keller, *Reflections on Gender and Science,* pp. 99–102.

Bibliography

Abbott, Andrew. *The System of Professions*. Chicago: University of Chicago Press, 1988.

Aberle, David F. "Some Sources of Flexibility in Navaho Social Organization."*Southwestern Journal of Anthropology* 19 (1963):1–8.

Acredolo, Linda P., and Lyn T. Boulter. "Effects of Hierarchical Organization on Children's Judgments of Distance and Direction." *Journal of Experimental Child Psychology* 37 (1988):409–25.

Adams, Ansel. *Camera and Lens*. Rev. ed. Hastings-on-Hudson, N.Y.: Morgan & Morgan, 1970.

Albert, Stuart, and William Jones. "The Temporal Transition from Being Together to Being Alone: The Significance and Structure of Children's Bedtime Stories." In Bernard S. Gorman and Alden E. Wessman, eds., *The Personal Experience of Time,* pp. 111–32. New York: Plenum, 1977.

Albert, Stuart, and Suzanne Kessler. "'Processes for Ending Social Encounters: The Conceptual Archaeology of a Temporal Place." *Journal for the Theory of Social Behavior* 6 (1976):147–70.

Alexander, Christopher, et al. *A Pattern Language*. New York: Oxford University Press, 1977.

Allen, Gary T. "A Developmental Perspective on the Effects of 'Subdividing' Macrospatial Experience." *Journal of Experimental Psychology:Human Learning and Memory* 7 (1981):120–32.

Altman, Irwin, and Dalmas A. Taylor. *Social Penetration*. New York: Holt, Rinehart and Winston, 1973.

Andersen, Elaine S. "Cups and Glasses: Learning That Boundaries Are Vague." *Journal of Child Language* 2 (1975):79–103.

Anzieu, Didier. *The Skin Ego*. New Haven: Yale University Press, 1989 (1985).

Aristotle. *The Complete Works*. Princeton: Princeton University Press (Bollingen Series 71. Revised Oxford translation, edited by Jonathan Barnes), 1984.

Armstrong, Edward A. *Saint Francis: Nature Mystic*. Berkeley: University of California Press, 1973.

Arnheim, Rudolf. *Art and Visual Perception*. Berkeley: University of California Press, 1967 (1954).

————. *Visual Thinking.* Berkeley: University of California Press, 1969.

————. "The Perception of Maps." In *New Essays on the Psychology of Art,* pp. 194–202. Berkeley: University of California Press, 1986 (1976).

————. *The Power of the Center.* Berkeley: University of California Press, 1982.

Arnold, Jack B. "A Multidimensional Scaling Study of Semantic Distance." *Journal of Experimental Psychology* 90 (1971):349–72.

Attneave, Fred. "Dimensions of Similarity." *American Journal of Psychology* 63 (1950): 516–56.

Auden, Wystan H. "Prologue: The Birth of Architecture." In *About the House,* pp. 3–4. New York: Random House, 1965.

Authorized Daily Prayer Book. Edited by Joseph H. Hertz. New York: Bloch, 1960.

Bachelard, Gaston. *The Poetics of Space.* Boston: Beacon, 1969 (1958).

Bakhtin, Mikhail. *Rabelais and His World.* Cambridge: MIT Press, 1968 (1965).

Balint, Michael. *Thrills and Regressions.* New York: International Universities Press, 1959.

————. *The Basic Fault.* London: Tavistock, 1968.

Barker, Roger G., ed. *The Stream of Behavior.* New York: Appleton-Century-Crofts, 1963.

Barker, Roger G., and Herbert F. Wright. *Midwest and Its Children.* Hamden, Conn.: Archon, 1971 (1955).

Barth, Fredrik. *Ethnic Groups and Boundaries.* Boston: Little, Brown, 1969.

Barth, John. *Giles Goat-Boy, or The Revised New Syllabus.* Garden City, N.Y.: Doubleday, 1966.

Barthes, Roland. *Empire of Signs.* New York: Hill and Wang, 1982 (1970).

Bates, Frederick L., and Walter G. Peacock. "Conceptualizing Social Structure: The Misuse of Classification in Structural Modeling." *American Sociological Review* 54 (1989):565–77.

Bateson, Gregory. "A Theory of Play and Fantasy." In *Steps to an Ecology of Mind,* pp. 177–93. New York: Ballantine, 1972 (1955).

————. *Mind and Nature.* New York: E. P. Dutton, 1979.

Bateson, Gregory, et al. "Toward a Theory of Schizophrenia." In *Steps to an Ecology of Mind,* pp. 201–27. (1956).

Beals, Richard, et al. "Foundations of Multidimensional Scaling." *Psychological Review* 75 (1968): 127–42.

Beare, William. *The Roman Stage.* 3rd ed. London: Methuen, 1964.

Ben-Yehuda, Nachman. *Deviance and Moral Boundaries.* Chicago: University of Chicago Press, 1985.

Berger, Kevin, and Todd Berger. *Zen Driving.* New York: Ballantine, 1988.

Berger, Peter L., and Thomas Luckmann. *The Social Construction of Reality.* Garden City, N.Y.: Anchor, 1967.

Bergesen, Albert J. "Political Witch Hunts: The Sacred and the Subversive in Cross-National Perspective." *American Sociological Review* 42 (1977):220–33.

Bergson, Henri. *Matter and Memory*. London: George Allen & Unwin, 1911 (1908).

Berlin, Brent, and Paul Kay. *Basic Color Terms*. Berkeley: University of California Press, 1969.

Berman. Morris. *Coming to Our Senses*. New York: Simon & Schuster, 1989.

Bernstein, Basil. "On the Classification and Framing of Educational Knowledge." In *Class, Codes, and Control*, pp. 202–29. London: Routledge & Kegan Paul, 1971.

Bettelheim, Bruno. *The Empty Fortress*. New York: Free Press, 1967.

Birdwhistell, Ray L. *Kinesics and Context*. Philadelphia: University of Pennsylvania Press, 1970.

Blatt, Sidney J., and Barry A. Ritzler."Thought Disorder and Boundary Disturbance in Psychosis." *Journal of Consulting and Clinical Psychology* 42 (1974):370–81.

Blau, Peter M., and Otis D. Duncan. *The American Occupational Structure*. New York: John Wiley, 1967.

Block, Jack, and Jeanne Block. "An Investigation of the Relationship between Intolerance of Ambiguity and Ethnocentrism." *Journal of Personality* 19 (1950–51):303–11.

Bloland, Harland G. "'Opportunities, Traps, and Sanctuaries: A Frame Analysis of Learned Societies." *Urban Life* 11 (1982):79–105.

Blom, Jan-Peter, and John J. Gumperz. "Social Meaning in Linguistic Structure: Code-Switching in Norway." In John J. Gumperz and Dell Hymes, eds., *Directions in Sociolinguistics*, pp. 407–34. New York: Holt, Rinehart and Winston, 1972.

Bloomer, Carolyn M. *Principles of Visual Perception*. New York: Van Nostrand Reinhold, 1976.

Bloor, David. "Polyhedra and the Abominations of Leviticus: Cognitive Styles in Mathematics." In Mary Douglas, ed., *Essays in the Sociology of Perception*, pp. 191–218. London: Routledge & Kegan Paul, 1982.

Boccioni, Umberto. "Technical Manifesto of Futurist Sculpture." In Umbro Apollonio, ed., *Futurist Manifestos*, pp. 51–65. New York: Viking, 1973 (1912).

————. "The Plastic Foundations of Futurist Sculpture and Painting." In *Futurist Manifestos*, pp. 88–90. (1913).

Bognar, Botond. *Contemporary Japanese Architecture*. New York: Van Nostrand Reinhold, 1985.

Bolinger, Dwight. *Aspects of Language*. New York: Harcourt, Brace & World, 1968.

Bolles, Marjorie, and Kurt Goidstein. "A Study of the Impairment of 'Abstract Behavior' in Schizophrenic Patients." *Psychiatric Quarterly* 12 (1938):42–65.

Bonner, R. E. "On Some Clustering Techniques." *IBM Journal of Research and Development* 8 (1964):22–32.

Boorstin, Daniel J. "'The Fertile Verge: Creativity in the United States." Paper presented at the Inaugural Meeting of the Council of Scholars of the Library of Congress, Washington, D.C., 1980.

Borges, Jorge Luis. "The Analytical Language of John Wilkins." In *Other Inquisitions, 1937–1952,* pp. 101–5. Austin: University of Texas Press, 1964 (1952).

Boss, Pauline, "A Clarification of the Concept of Psychological Father Presence in Families Experiencing Ambiguity of Boundary." *Journal of Marriage and the Family* 39 (1977):141–51.

Bouissac, Paul. "Circus Performance as Ritual: An Aspect of Animal Acts." In *Circus and Culture,* pp. 108–22. Bloomington: Indiana University Press, 1976.

Bourdieu, Pierre. "'The Berber House." In Mary Douglas, ed., *Rules and Meanings,* pp. 98–110. Harmondsworth, England: Penguin, 1973 (1971).

————. *Distinction.* Cambridge: Harvard University Press, 1984 (1979).

————. "The Social Space and the Genesis of Groups." *Theory and Society* 14 (1985):723–44.

Bowlby, John. *Separation.* New York: Basic Books, 1973.

Brandes, Stanley. *Forty.* Knoxville: University of Tennessee Press, 1985.

Braverman, Harry. *Labor and Monopoly Capital.* New York: Monthly Review Press, 1974.

Briggs, Jean L. "Le Modèle Traditionnel d'Education chez les Inuit." *Recherches Amérindiennes au Quebec* 13 (1983):13–25.

Brodsky, Jodi E. "Intellectual Snobbery: A Socio-Historical Perspective." Ph.D. diss., Columbia University, 1987.

Brown, Peter G., and Henry Shue, eds. *Boundaries.* Totowa, N.J.: Rowman and Littlefield, 1981.

Brown, W. Norman. "The Unity of Life in Indian Religion." In Joseph and Barrie Klaits, eds., *Animals and Man in Historical Perspective,* pp. 51–58. New York: Harper Torchbooks, 1974 (1966).

Bruner, Jerome S., et al. *A Study of Thinking.* New York: John Wiley, 1956.

Brunius, Teddy. "Inside and Outside the Frame of a Work of Art." In *Idea and Form* (Uppsala Studies in the History of Art, Figura Nova series, no. 1), pp. 1–23. Stockholm: Almqvist & Wiksell, 1959.

Bunn, James H. *The Dimensionality of Signs, Tools, and Models.* Bloomington: Indiana University Press, 1981.

Burke, Kenneth. *A Grammar of Motives.* Berkeley: University of California Press, 1969 (1945).

Burns, Elizabeth. *Theatricality.* New York: Harper Torchbooks, 1973.

Butor, Michel. "On Fairy Tales." In *Inventory,* pp. 211–23. New York: Simon & Schuster, 1968 (1960).

————. "Mondrian: The Square and Its Inhabitant." In *Inventory,* pp. 235–52. (1965).

————. "The Book as Object." In *Inventory,* pp. 39–56. (1968).

Bychowski, Gustav. *Psychotherapy of Psychosis.* New York: Grune & Stratton, 1952.

Cage, John. *Empty Words.* Middletown, Conn.: Wesleyan University Press, 1979.

Campbell, Donald T. "Enhancement of Contrast as Composite Habit." *Journal of Abnormal and Social Psychology* 53 (1956):350–55.

———. "Common Fate, Similarity, and Other Indices of the Status of Aggregates of Persons as Social Entities." *Behavioral Science* 3 (1958):14–25.

———. "Ethnocentrism of Disciplines and the Fish-Scale Model of Omniscience." In Muzafer Sherif and Carolyn W. Sherif, eds., *Interdisciplinary Relationships in the Social Sciences,* pp. 328–48. Chicago: Aldine, 1969.

Capra, Fritjof. *The Tao of Physics.* Rev. ed. New York: Bantam, 1984.

Caramazza, Alfonso, et al. "Subjective Structures and Operations in Semantic Memory."*Journal of Verbal Learning and Verbal Behavior* 15 (1976):103–17.

Carey, John."Temporal and Spatial Transitions in American Fiction Films." *Studies in the Anthropology of Visual Communication* 1 (1974):45–50.

Carpenter, Edmund, et al. *Eskimo.* Toronto: University of Toronto Press, 1959.

Carroll, J. Douglas, and Myron Wish. "Multidimensional Perceptual Models and Measurement Methods." In Edward C. Carterette and Morton P. Friedman, eds., *Handbook of Perception, vol.2: Psychophysical Judgment and Measurement,* pp. 391–447. New York: Academic Press, 1974.

Carroll, John B., and Joseph B. Casagrande. "The Functions of Language Classifications in Behavior." In Eleanor E. Maccoby et al. eds., *Readings in Social Psychology.* 3rd ed., pp. 18–31. New York: Holt, Rinehart and Winston, 1958.

Carroll, Lewis. "Through the Looking Glass." In *Complete Works,* pp. 135–271. New York: Vintage, 1976 (1872).

Cassirer, Ernst. *The Philosophy of Symbolic Forms, vol.2: Mythical Thought.* New Haven: Yale University Press, 1955 (1925).

Chambliss, Daniel F. "The Mundanity of Excellence: An Ethnographic Report on Stratification and Olympic Swimmers," *Sociological Theory* 7 (1989):70–86.

Chance, John K. *Race and Class in Colonial Oaxaca.* Stanford: Stanford University Press, 1978.

Chodorow, Nancy. *The Reproduction of Mothering.* Berkeley: University of California Press, 1978.

Choksy, Jamsheed K. *Purity and Pollution in Zoroastrianism.* Austin: University of Texas Press, 1989.

Cleveland, David. *The April Rabbits.* New York: Scholastic Books Services, 1978.

Clifford, James. *The Predicament of Culture.* Cambridge: Harvard University Press, 1988.

Code of Jewish Law. Edited by Solomon Ganzfried. New York: Hebrew Publishing Co., 1961.

Cohen, Yehudi A. "Social Boundary Systems." *Current Anthropology* 10 (1969):103–17.

Coleman, Linda, and Paul Kay. "Prototype Semantics: The English Word *Lie.*" *Language* 57 (1981):26–44.

Collins, Randall. *The Credential Society.* New York: Academic Press, 1979.

Cone, Edward T. *Musical Form and Musical Performance*. New York: W. W. Norton, 1968.

Cooley, Charles H. *Human Nature and the Social Order*. Rev. ed. New York: Schocken, 1964 (1922).

Coombs, Clyde H. "Psychological Scaling without a Unit of Measurement." *Psychological Review* 57 (1950):145–58.

Coser, Lewis A. *The Functions of Social Conflict*. New York: Free Press, 1964 (1956).

Csikszentmihalyi, Mihaly. *Beyond Freedom and Anxiety*. San Francisco: Jossey-Bass, 1975.

Cummings, Edward E. *A Selection of Poems*. New York: Harvest, 1965.

Danet, Brenda. " 'Baby' or 'Fetus'?: Language and the Construction of Reality in a Manslaughter Trial." *Semiotica* 32 (1980):187–219.

Darnton, Robert. *The Great Cat Massacre and Other Episodes in French Cultural History*. New York: Vintage, 1985.

Davies, Christie. "Sexual Taboos and Social Boundaries." *American Journal of Sociology* 87 (1982):1032–63.

Davis, Fred. "Decade Labeling: The Play of Collective Memory and Narrative Plot." *Symbolic Interaction* 7 (1984), no. 1:15–24.

Davis, Kingsley. "Intermarriage in Caste Societies." *American Anthropologist* 43 (1941):376–95.

Davis, Murray S. *Intimate Relations*. New York: Free Press, 1973.

———. *Smut*. Chicago: University of Chicago Press, 1983.

De Bono, Edward. *The Mechanism of Mind*. Harmondsworth, England: Penguin, 1971 (1969).

Deutsch, Karl W. "Autonomy and Boundaries according to Communications Theory." In Roy R. Grinker, ed., *Toward a Unified Theory of Human Behavior*, pp. 278–97. New York: Basic Books, 1956.

———. *Nationalism and Social Communication*. 2nd ed. Cambridge: MIT Press, 1966.

DiMaggio, Paul. "Cultural Entrepreneurship in Nineteenth-Century Boston: The Creation of an Organizational Base for High Culture in America." *Media, Culture and Society* 4 (1982):33–50.

———. "Cultural Entrepreneurship in Nineteenth-Century Boston, Part II: The Classification and Framing of American Art." *Media, Culture and Society* 4 (1982):303–22.

———. "Classification in Art." *American Sociological Review* 52 (1987):440–55.

Dinitz, Simon, and Nancy Beran. "Community Mental Health as a Boundaryless and Boundary-Busting System." *Journal of Health and Social Behavior* 12 (1971):99–108.

Dogan, Mattei, and Robert Pahre. *Creative Marginality*. Boulder, Colo.: Westview Press, 1990.

Domínguez, Virginia R. *White by Definition*. New Brunswick, N.J.: Rutgers University Press, 1986.

Douglas, Mary. "Animals in Lele Religious Symbolism." *Africa* 27 (1957):46–58.

———. *Purity and Danger*. New York: Praeger, 1966.

———. *Natural Symbols*. New York: Vintage, 1973 (1970).

———. "Deciphering a Meal." In *Implicit Meanings*, pp. 249–75. London: Routledge & Kegan Paul, 1978 (1972).

———. "Self Evidence." In *Implicit Meanings*, pp. 276–318. (1972).

Downs, Roger M., and David Stea. *Maps in Minds*. New York: Harper & Row, 1977.

Doyle, Bertram W. *The Etiquette of Race Relations in the South*. New York: Schocken, 1971 (1937).

DuBois, Page. *Centaurs and Amazons*. Ann Arbor: University of Michigan Press, 1982.

Duerr, Hans P. *Dreamtime*. London: Basil Blackwell, 1985 (1978).

Dundes, Alan. *Cracking Jokes*. Berkeley: Ten Speed, 1987.

Dürckheim, Karlfried G. *Zen and Us*. New York: E. P. Dutton, 1987 (1961).

Durkheim, Emile. *The Division of Labor in Society*. New York: Free Press, 1984 (1893).

———. *The Rules of Sociological Method*. New York: Free Press, 1982 (1895).

———. *Suicide*. New York: Free Press, 1966 (1897).

———. *The Elementary Forms of the Religious Life*. New York: Free Press, 1965 (1912).

———. "The Dualism of Human Nature and Its Social Conditions." In Robert N. Bellah, ed., *On Morality and Society*, pp. 149–63. Chicago: University of Chicago Press, 1973 (1914).

———. *Moral Education*. New York: Free Press, 1973 (1925).

Durkheim, Emile, and Marcel Mauss. *Primitive Classification*. Chicago: University of Chicago Press, 1963 (1903).

Dyk, Ruth B., and Herman A. Witkin. "Family Experiences related to the Development of Differentiation in Children." *Child Development* 36 (1965):21–55.

Eco, Umberto. *A Theory of Semiotics*. Bloomington: Indiana University Press, 1976.

Edgerton, Robert B. *Rules, Exceptions, and Social Order*. Berkeley: University of California Press, 1985.

Edwards, Betty. *Drawing on the Right Side of the Brain*. Los Angeles: J. P. Tarcher, 1979.

———. *Drawing on the Artist Within*. New York: Simon & Schuster, 1986.

Ehrenzweig, Anton. *The Psychoanalysis of Artistic Vision and Hearing*. 3rd ed. London: Sheldon, 1975 (1953).

———. *The Hidden Order of Art*. Berkeley: University of California Press, 1967.

Eichler, Margrit. "Sex Change Operations: The Last Bulwark of the Double Standard." In Laurel Richardson and Verta Taylor, eds., *Feminist Frontiers*, pp. 281–90. New York: Random House, 1989 (1980).

Elias, Norbert. *The Civilizing Process*. New York: Urizen, 1978 (1939).

Emerson, Joan P. "Behavior in Private Places: Sustaining Definitions of Reality in Gynecological Examinations." In Hans P. Dreitzel, ed., *Recent Sociology No.2*, pp. 74–97. London: Macmillan, 1970.

Epictetus. *The Discourses of Epictetus*. New York: Heritage Press, 1968.

Epstein, Cynthia F. *Deceptive Distinctions.* New Haven: Yale University Press, 1988.

Erasmus. "On Good Manners for Boys." In *Collected Works,* vol. 25, pp. 273–89. Toronto: University of Toronto Press, 1985.

Erikson, Erik H. *Childhood and Society.* 2nd ed. New York: W. W. Norton, 1963.

Erikson, Kai T. *Wayward Puritans.* New York: John Wiley, 1966.

Escher, Maurits C. "How Did You as a Graphic Artist Come to Make Designs for Wall Decorations?" In *Escher on Escher,* pp. 83–88. New York: Harry N. Abrams, 1989 (1941).

———. "The Regular Division of the Plane." In *Escher on Escher,* pp. 90–136. (1958).

———. "The Regular Division of the Plane." In *Escher on Escher,* pp. 25–53. (1964).

Evans, E. P. *The Criminal Prosecution and Capital Punishment of Animals.* London: William Heinemann, 1906.

Evans-Pritchard, E. E. *Nuer Religion.* London: Oxford University Press, 1956.

Evers, Hans-Dieter. "The Culture of Malaysian Urbanization: Malay and Chinese Conceptions of Space." *Urban Anthropology* 6 (1977):205–16.

Falk, Avner. "Border Symbolism." *The Psychoanalytic Quarterly* 43 (1974):650–60.

Fawcett, C. B. *Frontiers.* Oxford: Oxford University Press, 1918.

Federn, Paul. "Some Variations in Ego Feeling." In *Ego Psychology and the Psychoses,* pp. 25–37. London: Imago Publishing Co., 1953 (1926).

———. "The Ego as Subject and Object in Narcissism." In *Ego Psychology and the Psychoses,* pp. 283–322. (1928).

———. "The Ego in Schizophrenia." In *Ego Psychology and the Psychoses,* pp. 227–40. (1949).

———. "Ego Psychological Aspect of Schizophrenia." In *Ego Psychology and the Psychoses,* pp. 210–26. (1949).

———. "On the Distinction between Healthy and Pathological Narcissism." In *Ego Psychology and the Psychoses,* pp. 323–64. (1953).

Fenichel, Otto. *The Psychoanalytic Theory of Neurosis.* New York: W. W. Norton, 1945.

Ferguson, Charles A. "Diglossia." *Word* 15 (1959):325–40.

Fiedler, Leslie. *Freaks.* New York: Simon & Schuster, 1978.

Fillenbaum, Samuel, and Amnon Rapoport. *Structures in the Subjective Lexicon.* New York: Academic Press, 1971.

Fine, Gary A. *Shared Fantasy.* Chicago: University of Chicago Press, 1983.

Firth, Raymond. *Symbols—Public and Private.* Ithaca: Cornell University Press, 1973.

Fisher, Seymour. "Patterns of Personality Rigidity and Some of Their Determinants." *Psychological Monographs* 64 (1950):1–47.

———. *Body Experience in Fantasy and Behavior.* New York: Appleton-Century-Crofts, 1970.

Fisher, Seymour, and Sidney E. Cleveland. "Personality, Body Perception, and Body Image Boundary." In Seymour Wapner and Heinz Werner, eds., *The Body Percept,* pp. 48–67. New York: Random House, 1965.

———. *Body Image and Personality.* Rev. ed. New York: Dover, 1968.

Fleck, Ludwik. *Genesis and Development of a Scientific Fact.* Chicago: University of Chicago Press, 1981 (1935).

Foucault, Michel. *Madness and Civilization.* New York: Vintage, 1973 (1961).

———. *The Order of Things.* New York: Vintage, 1973 (1966).

Fraiberg, Selma H. *The Magic Years.* New York: Charles Scribner's Sons, 1959.

Frake, Charles O. "The Diagnosis of Disease among the Subanun of Mindanao." *American Anthropologist* 63 (1961): 113–32.

———. "The Ethnographic Study of Cognitive Systems." In Stephen A. Tyler, ed., *Cognitive Anthropology,* pp. 28–41. New York: Holt, Rinehart and Winston, 1969 (1962).

Franck, Kate, and Ephraim Rosen. "A Projective Test of Masculinity and Femininity." *Journal of Consulting Psychology* 13 (1949):247–56.

Frazer, James G. *Folk-Lore in the Old Testament.* London: Macmillan, 1918.

Frazier, Alexander. *Open Schools for Children.* Washington, D.C.: Association for Supervision and Curriculum Development, 1972.

Frede, Martha C., et al. "Relationships between Body Image Boundary and Interaction Patterns on the MAPS Test." *Journal of Consulting and Clinical Psychology* 32 (1968):575–78.

Freeman, Thomas, et al. *Studies on Psychosis.* New York: International Universities Press, 1966.

Frege, Gottlob. "Logic in Mathematics." In *Posthumous Writings,* pp. 203–50. Chicago: University of Chicago Press, 1979 (1914).

Freidson, Eliot. *Doctoring Together.* Chicago: University of Chicago Press, 1980 (1975).

Frenkel-Brunswik, Else. "Intolerance of Ambiguity as an Emotional and Perceptual Personality Variable." *Journal of Personality* 18 (1949):108–43.

———. "Dynamic and Cognitive Personality Organization as Seen through the Interviews." In T. W. Adorno et al., *The Authoritarian Personality,* pp. 442–67. New York: Harper, 1950.

———. "Comprehensive Scores and Summary of Interview Results." In *The Authoritarian Personality,* pp. 468–86.

Freud, Sigmund. "One of the Difficulties of Psycho-Analysis." In *Collected Papers,* vol. 4, pp. 347–56. London: Hogarth, 1925 (1917).

———. *The Ego and the Id.* New York: W. W. Norton, 1962 (1923).

———. *Civilization and Its Discontents.* New York: W. W. Norton, 1962 (1930).

Friday, Nancy. *My Secret Garden.* New York: Pocket Books, 1974.

———. *Men in Love.* New York: Dell, 1981.

Fromm, Erich. *The Art of Loving.* New York: Harper & Row, 1956.

Fry, William F. *Sweet Madness.* Palo Alto, Calif.: Pacific, 1968 (1963).

Garfinkel, Harold. "Common Sense Knowledge of Social Structures: The Documentary Method of Interpretation in Lay and Professional Fact

Finding." In *Studies in Ethnomethodology*, pp. 76–103. Englewood Cliffs, N.J.: Prentice-Hall, 1967 (1962).

———. "Passing and the Managed Achievement of Sex Status in an 'Intersexed' Person." In *Studies in Ethnomethodology*, pp. 116–85.

Geertz, Clifford. "Blurred Genres: The Refiguration of Social Thought." In *Local Knowledge*, pp. 19–35. New York: Basic Books, 1983 (1980).

Gefen, Jonathan. *The Sixteenth Lamb*. (In Hebrew.) Jerusalem: Dvir, 1983.

Gerson, Judith M., and Kathy Peiss. "Boundaries, Negotiation, Consciousness: Reconceptualizing Gender Relations." *Social Problems* 32 (1985):317–31.

Ghent, Lila. "Perception of Overlapping and Embedded Figures by Children of Different Ages." *American Journal of Psychology* 69 (1956):575–87.

Giedion, Sigfried. *Space, Time, and Architecture*. 3rd ed. Cambridge: Harvard University Press, 1956.

Gieryn, Thomas F. "Boundary-Work and the Demarcation of Science from Non-Science: Strains and Interests in Professional Ideologies of Scientists." *American Sociological Review* 48 (1983):781–95.

Giffin, Holly. "The Coordination of Meaning in the Creation of a Shared Make-Believe Reality." In Inge Bretherton, ed., *Symbolic Play*, pp. 73–100. Orlando, Fla.: Academic Press, 1984.

Gilligan, Carol. *In a Different Voice*. Cambridge: Harvard University Press, 1982.

Goffman, Erving. *The Presentation of Self in Everyday Life*. Garden City, N.Y.: Anchor, 1959.

———. *Encounters*. Indianapolis: Bobbs-Merrill, 1961.

———. *Behavior in Public Places*. New York: Free Press, 1963.

———. *Relations in Public*. New York: Harper Colophon, 1972.

———. *Frame Analysis*. New York: Harper Colophon, 1974.

———. *Forms of Talk*. Philadelphia: University of Pennsylvania Press, 1981.

Goldstein, Kurt. "Methodological Approach to the Study of Schizophrenic Thought Disorder." In J. S. Kasanin, ed., *Language and Thought in Schizophrenia*, pp. 17–39. Berkeley: University of California Press, 1944.

Goldstein, Kurt, and Martin Scheerer. "Abstract and Concrete Behavior: An Experimental Study with Special Tests." *Psychological Monographs* 53 (1941), no. 2:1–151.

Goodenough, Ward H. "Yankee Kinship Terminology: A Problem in Componential Analysis." In Stephen A. Tyler, ed., *Cognitive Anthropology*, pp. 255–88. New York: Holt, Rinehart and Winston, 1969 (1965).

Goody, Jack. *The Domestication of the Savage Mind*. Cambridge: Cambridge University Press, 1977.

Gould, Peter, and Rodney White. *Mental Maps*. Harmondsworth, England: Penguin, 1974.

Gould, Stephen J. "Human Equality Is a Contingent Fact of History." *Natural History* 93 (1984), no. 11:26–33.

————. "Taxonomy as Politics: The Harm of False Classification." *Dissent* (Winter 1990): 73–78.

Greef, Guillaume de. *La Structure Générale des Sociétés, vol.3: Théorie des Frontières et des Classes.* Brussels: Larcier, 1908.

Green, Richard. *Sexual Identity Conflict in Children and Adults.* New York: Basic Books, 1974.

Greenacre, Phyllis. "The Family Romance of the Artist." *Psychoanalytic Study of the Child* 13 (1958):9–36.

Greene, Herb. *Mind and Image.* Lexington: University Press of Kentucky, 1976.

Gricar, Julie M. "How Thick Is Blood? The Social Construction and Cultural Configuration of Kinship." Ph.D. diss., Columbia University, 1991.

————. "Strategies Children Use in the Cognitive Construction of Kinship." *Sociological Studies of Child Development* (forthcoming).

Gropius, Walter. *The New Architecture and the Bauhaus.* New York: Museum of Modern Art, 1937.

Grossman, David. *Itamar Walks on Walls.* (In Hebrew.) Tel-Aviv: Am Oved, 1986.

Gumperz, John J. *Discourse Strategies.* Cambridge: Cambridge University Press, 1982.

Gurevitch, Zali D. "The Embrace: On the Element of Nondistance in Human Relations." *Sociological Quarterly* 31 (1990):187–201.

Gvion-Rosenberg, Liora. "Culinary Pluralism or Culinary Hegemony: The Case of Ethnic Dishes, 1945–1987." Paper presented at the annual meeting of the American Sociological Association, Atlanta, August 1988.

Haaken, Janice. "Field Dependence Research: A Historical Analysis of a Psychological Construct." *Signs* 13 (1988):311–30.

Halbwachs, Maurice. *The Collective Memory.* New York: Harper Colophon, 1980 (1950).

Hall, Edward T. *The Hidden Dimension.* Garden City: Anchor, 1969 (1966).

Halley, M. Martin, and William F. Harvey. "Medical vs. Legal Definitions of Death." Journal of the American Medical Association 204 (May 6, 1968):423–25.

Hamnett, Ian. "Ambiguity, Classification and Change: The Function of Riddles." *Man* 2 (1967):379–92.

Handelman, Don. "The Ritual Clown: Attributes and Affinities." *Anthropos* 76 (1981): 321–70.

Handler, Richard. *Nationalism and the Politics of Culture in Quebec.* Madison: University of Wisconsin Press, 1988.

Handlin, David P. *The American Home.* Boston: Little, Brown, 1979.

Haraway, Donna. "A Manifesto for Cyborgs: Science, Technology, and Socialist Feminism in the 1980s." *Socialist Review* 80 (1985):65–107.

Harris, Janet. *The Prime of Ms. America.* New York: G. P. Putnam's Sons, 1975.

Harris, Marvin. "Referential Ambiguity in the Calculus of Brazilian Racial Identity." *Southwestern Journal of Anthropology* 26 (1970):1–14.

Heller, Joseph. *We Bombed in New Haven*. New York: Delta, 1967.

Helms, Mary W. *Ulysses' Sail*. Princeton: Princeton University Press, 1988.

Hemphill, John K. and Charles M. Westie. "The Measurement of Group Dimensions." *Journal of Psychology* 29 (1950):325–42.

Henningsen, Henning. *Crossing the Equator*. Copenhagen: Munksgaard, 1961.

Henri, Adrian. *Total Art*. New York: Praeger, 1974.

Hershfield, Harry. *Harry Hershfield Joke Book*. New York: Ballantine, 1964.

Hertz, Robert. "A Contribution to the Study of the Collective Representation of Death." In *Death and the Right Hand*, pp. 27–86. Aberdeen, Scotland: Cohen and West, 1960 (1907).

———. "The Pre-eminence of the Right Hand: A Study in Religious Polarity." In Rodney Needham, ed., *Right and Left*, p. 3–31. Chicago: University of Chicago Press, 1973 (1909).

Heydenryk, Henry. *The Art and History of Frames*. New York: James H. Heineman, 1963.

Hicks, Rebecca. "What is Going On Here? An Analysis of the Stand-up Comedy Show as Play Frame." Unpublished paper, 1988.

Hill, Reuben. *Families Under Stress*. Westport, Conn.: Greenwood, 1971 (1949).

Hill, W. W. "The Status of the Hermaphrodite and Transvestite in Navaho Culture." *American Anthropologist* 37 (1935):273–79.

Hinson, Sandra C. "How Feminist and Radical Books Are Classified: An Inter-Bookstore Comparison," Unpublished paper, 1986.

Hofstadter, Douglas R. *Gödel, Escher, Bach*. New York: Vintage, 1980.

Hogan, Richard. "The Frontier as Social Control." *Theory and Society* 14 (1985):35–51.

Holy Scriptures. Philadelphia: Jewish Publication Society of America, 1955.

Hozier, Ann. "On the Breakdown of the Sense of Reality: A Study of Spatial Perception in Schizophrenia." *Journal of Consulting Psychology* 23 (1959):185–94.

Hubert, Henri. "Etude Sommaire de la Représentation du Temps dans la Religion et al Magie." In Henri Hubert and Marcel Mauss, eds., *Mélanges d'Histoire des Religions*, pp. 189–229. Paris: Félix Alcan and Guillaumin, 1909 (1905).

Hunn, Eugene. "Toward a Perceptual Model of Folk Biological Classification." *American Ethnologist* 3 (1976):508–24.

Hunter, Albert. *Symbolic Communities*. Chicago: University of Chicago Press, 1982 (1974).

Hutton, Helen. *The Technique of Collage*. London: B. T. Batsford, 1968.

Hutton, J. H. *Caste In India*. 4th ed. Bombay: Oxford University Press, 1963.

Ichheiser, Gustav. *Appearances and Realities*. San Francisco: Jossey-Bass, 1970.

Inhelder, Bärbel, and Jean Piaget. *The Early Growth of Logic in the Child*. New York: Humanities Press, 1964.

Ishimoto, Tatsuo, and Kiyoko Ishimoto. *The Japanese House*. New York: Crown, 1963.

Itoh, Teiji, and Yukio Futagawa. *The Classic Tradition in Japanese Architecture*. New York: John Weatherhill, 1972.

Jacobson, Edith. *The Self and the Object World*. New York: International Universities Press, 1964.

Jaini, Padmanabh S. *The Jaina Path of Purification*. Berkeley: University of California Press, 1979.

Jakobson, Roman. *Six Lectures on Sound and Meaning*. Cambridge: MIT Press, 1978 (1942).

James, Henry. *The American Scene*. New York: Harper, 1907.

James, William. *The Principles of Psychology*. Cambridge: Harvard University Press, 1983 (1890).

Janis, Harriet, and Rudi Blesh. *Collage*. Rev. ed. Philadelphia: Chilton Book Co., 1967.

Johnson, Crockett. *Harold and the Purple Crayon*. New York: Harper & Row, 1955.

Johnson, Mark. *The Body in the Mind*. Chicago: University of Chicago Press, 1987.

Johnson, Ragnar. "Two Realms and a Joke: Bisociation Theories of Joking." *Semiotica* 16 (1976):195–221.

Johnson, Stephen C. "Hierarchical Clustering Systems." *Psychometrika* 32 (1967):241–54.

Jonaitis, Aldona. *Art of the Northern Tlingit*. Seattle: University of Washington Press, 1986.

Jordan, Winthrop D. *White over Black*. Chapel Hill: University of North Carolina Press, 1968.

Jortner, Sidney. "An Investigation of Certain Cognitive Aspects of Schizophrenia." *Journal of Projective Techniques and Personality Assessment* 30 (1966):559–68.

Jourard, Sidney M. "Some Lethal Aspects of the Male Role." *Journal of Existential Psychiatry* 7 (1962):333–44.

Joy, Charles R., ed. *Albert Schweitzer—An Anthology*. Boston: Beacon, 1956.

Joyce, James. *Ulysses*. New York: Random House, 1986 (1922).

Kanter, Rosabeth M. *Commitment and Community*. Cambridge: Harvard University Press, 1972.

———. *The Change Masters*. New York: Touchstone, 1984.

Kaplan, Louise J. *Oneness and Separateness*. New York: Touchstone, 1978.

Kaprow, Allan. *Assemblage, Environments, and Happenings*. New York: Harry N. Abrams, 1966.

Katz, Elihu and Daniel Dayan. "Contests, Conquests, Coronations: On Media Events and Their Heroes." In Carl F. Graumann and Serge Moscovici, eds., *Changing Conceptions of Leadership*, pp. 135–44. New York: Springer-Verlag, 1986.

Katz, Jacob. *Exclusiveness and Tolerance*. New York: Schocken, 1962.

Katzir, Yael. "Preservation of Jewish Ethnic Identity in Yemen: Segregation and Integration as Boundary Maintenance Mechanisms." *Comparative Studies in Society and History* 24 (1982):264–79.

Kay, Paul, and Chad K. McDaniel. "The Linguistic Significance of the Meanings of Basic Color Terms." *Language* 54 (1978):610:46.

Kearl, Michael C. *Endings*. New York: Oxford University Press, 1989.

Kegan, Robert. *The Evolving Self*. Cambridge: Harvard University Press, 1982.

Keller, Evelyn F. *Reflections on Gender and Science*. New Haven: Yale University Press, 1985.

Kepes, György. *Language of Vision*. Chicago: Paul Theobald, 1951 (1944).

Kerber, Linda K. "Separate Spheres, Female Worlds, Woman's Place: The Rhetoric of Women's History." *Journal of American History* 75 (1988):9–39.

Kern, Stephen. *The Culture of Time and Space 1880–1918*. Cambridge: Harvard University Press, 1983.

Kesey, Ken. *One Flew Over the Cuckoo's Nest*. New York: Viking, 1964.

Kessler, Suzanne J., and Wendy McKenna. *Gender*. New York: John Wiley, 1978.

Kidahashi, Miwako. "Dual Organization: A Study of a Japanese-Owned Firm in the United States." Ph.D. diss., Columbia University, 1987.

Kidd, Jeanne. "The Classification of Cars." Unpublished paper, 1988.

Kinnaird, Clark, ed. *Encyclopedia of Puzzles and Pastimes*. New York: Grosset & Dunlap, 1946.

Kinsey, Alfred C., et al. *Sexual Behavior in the Human Male*. Philadelphia: W. B. Saunders, 1948.

Kirby, Michael, ed. *Happenings*. New York: E. P. Dutton, 1965.

Kirby, Michael, and Victoria N. Kirby. *Futurist Performance*. New York: PAJ Publications, 1986.

Klaits, Joseph, and Barrie Klaits, eds. *Animals and Man in Historical Perspective*. New York: Harper Torchbooks, 1974.

Klee, Paul. *Notebooks, vol.1: The Thinking Eye*. London: Lund Humphries, 1961.

Koenigsberg, Richard A. *Symbiosis and Separation*. New York: Library of Art and Social Science, 1989.

Koestler, Arthur. *The Act of Creation*. New York: Macmillan, 1964.

Koffka, Kurt. *Principles of Gestalt Psychology*. New York: Harbinger, 1935.

Köhler, Wolfgang. *Gestalt Psychology*. New York: New American Library, 1947.

Köngäs Maranda, Elli. "Theory and Practice in Riddle Analysis." In Americo Paredes and Richard Bauman, eds., *Toward New Perspectives in Folklore,* pp. 51–61. Austin: University of Texas Press, 1972.

Koriat, Asher, et al. "An Inquiry into the Process of Temporal Orientation." *Acta Psychologica* 40 (1976):57–73.

Kornstein, Sandra. "The Stranger in Our Midst: The Making of an American Superhero." M.A. thesis, Rutgers University, 1989.

Kosslyn, Stephen M., et al. "Cognitive Maps in Children and Men." *Child Development* 45 (1974):707–16.

Kostelanetz, Richard. *The Theater of Mixed Means*. New York: Dial Press, 1968.

Krain, Mark. "A Definition of Dyadic Boundaries and an Empirical Study of Boundary Establishment in Courtship." *International Journal of Sociology of the Family* 7 (1977):107–23.

Kristeva, Julia. *Powers of Horror*. New York: Columbia University Press, 1982 (1980).

Kronus, Carol L. "The Evolution of Occupational Power: An Historical Study of Task Boundaries between Physicians and Pharmacists." *Sociology of Work and Occupations* 3 (1976):3–37.

Krumhansl, Carol L. "Concerning the Applicability of Geometric Models to Similarity Data: The Interrelationship between Similarity and Spatial Density." *Psychological Review* 85 (1978):445–63.

Kuhn, Thomas S. *The Structure of Scientific Revolutions*. 2nd ed. Chicago: University of Chicago Press, 1970 (1962).

Kurokawa, Kisho. *Rediscovering Japanese Space*. New York: Weatherhill, 1988.

Labov, William. "The Boundaries of Words and Their Meanings." In Charles-James N. Bailey and Roger W. Shuy, eds., *New Ways of Analyzing Variation in English,* pp. 340–73. Washington, D.C.: Georgetown University Press, 1973.

Lakatos, Imre. *Proofs and Refutations*. Cambridge, England: Cambridge University Press, 1976.

Lakoff, George. "Hedges: A Study in Meaning Criteria and the Logic of Fuzzy Concepts." *Journal of Philosophical Logic* 2 (1973):458–508.

———. *Women, Fire, and Dangerous Things*. Chicago: University of Chicago Press, 1987.

Lamarck, Jean-Baptiste. *Zoological Philosophy*. New York: Hafner, 1963 (1809).

Lamont, Michèle. "The Making of Inequality: Cultural and Moral Exclusion in the French and the American Middle Class." Paper presented at the meetings of the American Sociological Association, San Francisco, August 1989.

———. "The Power-Culture Link in a Comparative Perspective." *Comparative Social Research* 11 (1989):131–50.

Landecker, Werner S. "Class Boundaries." *American Sociological Review* 25 (1960): 868–77.

Landis, Bernard. *Ego Boundaries*. New York: International Universities Press (Monograph No. 24 [vol.6, no.4] in Psychological Issues series.), 1970.

Langer, Susanne K. *Philosophy in a New Key*. 3rd ed. Cambridge: Harvard University Press, 1957.

Lauderdale, Pat. "Deviance and Moral Boundaries." *American Sociological Review* 41 (1976):660–76.

Lavie, Esther. "Age as an Indicator for Reference in the Construction of Social Contexts." Ph.D. diss., Tel-Aviv University, 1987.

Leach, Edmund. "Two Essays Concerning the Symbolic Representation of Time." In *Rethinking Anthropology,* pp. 124–36. London: Athlone, 1961.

———. "Anthropological Aspects of Language: Animal Categories and Verbal Abuse." In Eric H. Lenneberg, ed., *New Directions in the Study of Language,* pp. 23–63. Cambridge: MIT Press, 1964.

———. "The Legitimacy of Solomon: Some Structural Aspects of Old Testament History." *European Journal of Sociology* 7 (1966):58–101.

———. *Culture and Communication.* Cambridge, England: Cambridge University Press, 1976.

Legman, G. *Rationale of the Dirty Joke.* New York: Grove, 1968.

Leopold, Aldo. "The Land Ethic." In *A Sand County Almanac,* pp. 217–41. New York: Oxford University Press, 1966 (1953).

Lévi-Strauss, Claude. *The Savage Mind.* Chicago: University of Chicago Press, 1966 (1962).

Levine, Donald N. *The Flight from Ambiguity.* Chicago: University of Chicago Press, 1985.

LeVine, Robert A., and Donald T. Campbell. *Ethnocentrism.* New York: John Wiley, 1972.

Levinson, Daniel J. "The Study of Ethnocentric Ideology." In T. W. Adorno et al., *The Authoritarian Personality,* pp. 102–50. New York: Harper, 1950.

Levy, Jerre. "Psychological Implications of Bilateral Asymmetry." In Stuart J. Dimond and J. Graham Beaumont, eds., *Hemisphere Function in the Human Brain,* pp.121–83. New York: Halsted, 1974.

Lévy-Bruhl, Lucien. *How Natives Think.* New York: Washington Square Press, 1966 (1910).

Lewin, Kurt. *Principles of Topological Psychology.* New York: McGraw-Hill, 1936.

———. "Some Social-Psychological Differences between the United States and Germany." In *Resolving Social Conflicts,* pp. 3–33. London: Souvenir, 1973 (1936).

Lewis, Helen B. *Psychic War in Men and Women.* New York: New York University Press, 1976.

Lewisohn, Mark. *The Beatles—Recording Sessions.* New York: Harmony, 1988.

Lidz, Theodore, and Stephen Fleck. *Schizophrenia and the Family.* 2nd ed. New York: International Universities Press, 1985.

Liedloff, Jean. *The Continuum Concept.* New York: Alfred A. Knopf, 1977.

Lincoln, Bruce. *Discourse and the Construction of Society.* New York: Oxford University Press, 1989.

Locke, John. *An Essay Concerning Human Understanding.* Oxford: Oxford University Press, 1975 (1690).

Lovejoy, Arthur O. *The Great Chain of Being.* Cambridge: Harvard University Press, 1964 (1936).

Lukács, Georg. *History and Class Consciousness.* Cambridge: MIT Press, 1971 (1923).

Lynch, Kevin. *The Image of the City.* Cambridge: MIT Press, 1964 (1960).

Maccoby, Eleanor E., and Carol N. Jacklin. *The Psychology of Sex Differences.* Stanford: Stanford University Press, 1974.

Machover, Karen. *Personality Projection in the Drawing of the Human Figure.* Springfield, Ill.: Charles C. Thomas, 1949.

Mac Low, Jackson. *Representative Works 1938–1985*. New York: Roof, 1986.

Mahler, Margaret S. "On Human Symbiosis and the Vicissitudes of Individuation." *Separation-Individuation,* pp. 77–97. New York: Jason Aronson, 1979 (1967).

———. "On the First Three Subphases of the Separation-Individuation Process." In *Separation-Individuation,* pp. 119–30. (1972).

Mahler, Margaret S., and Kitty La Perriere. "Mother-Child Interaction during Separation-Individuation." In *Separation-Individuation,* pp. 35–48. (1965).

Mahler, Margaret S., et al. *The Psychological Birth of the Human Infant*. New York: Basic Books, 1975.

Maki, Ruth H. "Why Do Categorization Effects Occur in Comparative Judgment Tasks?" *Memory and Cognition* 10 (1982):252–64.

Mallarmé, Stéphane. *A Tomb for Anatole*. San Francisco: North Point, 1983 (1961).

Mann, Jacob. "Genizah Fragments of the Palestinian Order of Service." *Hebrew Union College Annual* 2 (1925):269–328.

Mannheim, Karl. *Ideology and Utopia*. New York: Harvest, 1936.

Marx, Karl, and Friedrich Engels. "Manifesto of the Communist Party." In Robert C. Tucker, ed., *The Marx-Engels Reader*. 2nd ed. New York: W. W. Norton, 1978 (1848).

Maslow, Abraham H. *The Farther Reaches of Human Nature*. Harmondsworth, England: Penguin, 1976 (1971).

McCloskey, Michael E., and Sam Glucksberg. "Natural Categories: Well Defined or Fuzzy Sets?" *Memory and Cognition* 6 (1978):462–72.

McPhail, David. *The Magical Drawings of Moony B. Finch*. Garden City, N.Y.: Doubleday, 1978.

Mead, George H. *Mind, Self, and Society*. Chicago: University of Chicago Press, 1934.

Mead, Margaret. "Crossing Boundaries in Social Science Communications." *Social Science Information* 8 (1969):7–15.

Meeks, Wayne A. *The First Urban Christians*. New Haven: Yale University Press, 1983.

Merelman, Richard M. *Making Something of Ourselves*. Berkeley: University of California Press, 1984.

Merleau-Ponty, Maurice. "The Child's Relations with Others." In *The Primacy of Perception,* pp. 96–155. Evanston, Ill.: Northwestern University Press, 1964 (1960).

———. *Phenomenology of Perception*. New York: Humanities Press, 1962.

Merton, Robert K. "Intermarriage and the Social Structure: Fact and Theory." *Psychiatry* 4 (1941):361–74.

Messick, Samuel, and John W. French. "Dimensions of Cognitive Closure." *Multivariate Behavioral Research* 10 (1975):3–16.

Meyer, Leonard B. *Emotion and Meaning in Music*. Chicago: University of Chicago Press, 1956.

Meyrowitz, Joshua. *No Sense of Place*. New York: Oxford University Press, 1985.

Michael, Donald N. "A Cross-Cultural Investigation of Closure." *Journal of Abnormal and Social Psychology* 48 (1953):225–30.

Mignot, Claude. *Architecture of the Nineteenth Century in Europe*. New York: Rizzoli International Publications, 1984.

Miller, Carol. "American Rom and the Ideology of Defilement." In Farnham Rehfisch, ed., *Gypsies, Tinkers, and Other Travellers*, pp. 41–54. London: Academic Press, 1975.

Milner, Marion. *On Not Being Able to Paint*. Los Angeles: James P. Tarcher, 1957.

———. *The Suppressed Madness of Sane Men*. London: Tavistock, 1987.

Minsky, Marvin. *The Society of Mind*. New York: Simon & Schuster, 1986.

Minuchin, Salvador. *Families and Family Therapy*. Cambridge: Harvard University Press, 1974.

Mishler, Elliot G. "Meaning in Context: Is There Any Other Kind?" *Harvard Educational Review* 49 (1979):1–19.

Mishnah. Translated by Herbert Danby. Oxford: Oxford University Press, 1933.

Modell, Arnold H. *Object Love and Reality*. London: The Hogarth Press, 1969.

Moles, Abraham A. *Théorie des Objets*. Paris: Éditions Universitaires, 1972.

Mooney, C. M. "A Factorial Study of Closure." *Canadian Journal of Psychology* 8 (1954):51–60.

Morison, Robert A. "Death: Process or Event?" *Science* 173 (August 20, 1971):694–98.

Morris, Desmond. *Intimate Behavior*. New York: Random House, 1971.

Morse, Edward S. *Japanese Homes and Their Surroundings*. Boston: Ticknor, 1886.

Murphy, Raymond. *Social Closure*. Oxford: Oxford University Press, 1988.

Napier, A. David. *Masks, Transformation, and Paradox*. Berkeley: University of California Press, 1986.

Needham, Joseph. *The Grand Titration*. London: George Allen & Unwin, 1969.

Needham, Rodney. "Introduction" to Emile Durkheim and Marcel Mauss, *Primitive Classification*. Chicago: University of Chicago Press, 1963.

———. "Polythetic Classification: Convergence and Consequences." *Man* 10 (1975): 349–69.

Nelson, Cordner, and Roberto Quercetani. *The Milers*. Los Altos, Calif.: Tafnews, 1985.

Nippert-Eng, Christena. "Liminality in Everyday Life: Commuting and the Transition between Home and Work." Paper presented at the annual meeting of the American Sociological Association, Atlanta, August 1988.

Nishihara, Kiyoyuki. *Japanese Houses*. Tokyo: Japan Publications, 1968.

Norberg-Schulz, Christian. *Meaning in Western Architecture*. New York: Rizzoli International Publications, 1980 (1974).

Okely, Judith, *The Traveller-Gypsies*. Cambridge: Cambridge University Press, 1983.

Olesker, Wendy. "Cognition and the Separation-Individuation Process: A

Study of Three Boys at Nursery School." *Psychoanalysis and Contemporary Thought* 1 (1978): 237–67.

Ornstein, Robert E. *The Psychology of Consciousness*. San-Francisco: W. H. Freeman, 1972.

Orwell, George. *Nineteen Eighty Four*. New York: New American Library, 1961 (1949).

Osgood, Charles E., et al. *The Measurement of Meaning*. Urbana: University of Illinois Press, 1957.

Palombo, Stanley R., and Hilde Bruch. "Falling Apart: The Verbalization of Ego Failure." *Psychiatry* 27 (1964):248–58.

Papanek, Hanna, and Gail Minault, eds. *Separate Worlds*. Delhi: Chanakya, 1982.

Park, Robert E. "The Concept of Social Distance." *Journal of Applied Sociology* 8 (1924): 339–44.

―――. "Human Migration and the Marginal Man." *American Journal of Sociology* 33 (1928):881–93.

Parkin, Frank. *Marxism and Class Theory*. New York: Columbia University Press, 1979.

Parsons, Talcott. *The Social System*. New York: Free Press, 1964 (1951).

Patterson, Orlando. *Slavery and Social Death*. Cambridge, England: Cambridge University Press, 1982.

Pei, Mario. *Glossary of Linguistic Terminology*. New York: Columbia University Press, 1966.

Pemberton, Carol. "The Closure Factors Related to Other Cognitive Processes." *Psychometrika* 17 (1952):267–88.

Perin, Constance. *Belonging in America*. Madison: University of Wisconsin Press, 1988.

Petersen, William. "The Classification of Subnations in Hawaii: An Essay in the Sociology of Knowledge." *American Sociological Review* 34 (1969):863–77.

Piaget, Jean. *The Child's Conception of the World*. Totowa, N.J.: Helix, 1983 (1929).

―――. *The Construction of Reality in the Child*. New York: Basic Books, 1954.

Piaget, Jean, and Bärbel Inhelder. *The Child's Conception of Space*. New York: W. W. Norton, 1967 (1948).

Pike, Kenneth L. *Language in Relation to a Unified Theory of the Structure of Human Behavior*. The Hague: Mouton, 1967 (1954).

Pirandello, Luigi. *Tonight We Improvise*. New York: Samuel French, 1960 (1932).

Pirsig, Robert M. *Zen and the Art of Motorcycle Maintenance*. New York: Bantam New Age, 1981 (1974).

Plato, *Statesman*. Translated by J. B. Skemp. New Haven: Yale University Press, 1952.

Poole, Reginald L. "The Beginning of the Year in the Middle Ages." *Proceedings of the British Academy* 10 (1921–23):113–37.

Prelinger, Ernst. "Extension and Structure of the Self." *Journal of Psychology* 47 (1959): 13–23.

"Proselytes." *Encyclopaedia Judaica,* vol. 13, pp. 1182–93. Jerusalem: Keter, 1972.

Radcliffe-Brown, A. R. "The Study of Kinship Systems." In *Structure and Function in Primitive Society,* pp. 49–89. New York: Free Press, 1965 (1941).

Radin, Paul, *The Trickster.* New York: Schocken, 1972 (1956).

Rapoport, Amnon, and Samuel Fillenbaum. "An Experimental Study of Semantic Structures." In A. Kimball Romney, et al., eds., *Multidimensional Scaling,* vol. 2, pp. 93–131. New York: Seminar Press, 1972.

Rapoport, Amos, and Robert E. Kantor. "Complexity and Ambiguity in Environmental Design." *Journal of the American Institute of Planners* 33 (1967):210–21.

Rapoport, Anatol. "Statistical Boundaries." In Roy R. Grinker, ed., *Toward a Unified Theory of Human Behavior,* pp. 307–24. New York: Basic Books, 1956.

Raymond, Janice G. *The Transsexual Empire.* Boston: Beacon, 1979.

Reed, Stephen K. "Pattern Recognition and Categorization." *Cognitive Psychology* 3 (1972):382–407.

Rickers-Ovsiankina, Maria A. "Social Accessibility in Three Age Groups." *Psychological Reports* 2 (1956):283–94.

Rickers-Ovsiankina, Maria A., and Arnold A. Kusmin. "Individual Differences in Social Accessibility." *Psychological Reports* 4 (1958):391–406.

Rogin, Michael P. *Ronald Reagan, the Movie.* Berkeley: University of California Press, 1987.

Rokeach, Milton. *The Open and Closed Mind.* New York: Basic Books, 1960.

Rosch, Eleanor H. "On the Internal Structure of Perceptual and Semantic Categories." In Timothy E. Moore, ed., *Cognitive Development and the Acquisition of Language,* pp. 111–44. New York: Academic Press, 1973.

———. "Human Categorization." In Neil Warren, ed., *Studies in Cross-Cultural Psychology,* vol. 1, pp. 1–49. London: Academic Press, 1977.

———. "Principles of Categorization." In Eleanor Rosch and Barbara B. Lloyd, eds., *Cognition and Categorization,* pp. 27–48. Hillside, N.J.: Lawrence Erlbaum Associates, 1978.

Rose, Gilbert J. "Creative Imagination in Terms of Ego 'Core' and Boundaries." *International Journal of Psycho-Analysis* 45 (1964):75–84.

———. "Body Ego and Reality." *International Journal of Psycho-Analysis* 47 (1966):502–9.

Rosenberg, Harold. *Saul Steinberg.* New York: Alfred A. Knopf, 1978.

Rosenbloom, Joseph. *Doctor Knock-Knock's Official Knock-Knock Dictionary.* New York: Sterling, 1976.

Roszak, Betty. "The Human Continuum." In Betty Roszak and Theodore Roszak, eds., *Masculine/Feminine,* pp. 297–306. New York: Harper Torchbooks, 1969.

Roth, Philip. *Portnoy's Complaint.* New York: Random House, 1969.

Rousseau, Jean Jacques. "A Discourse on the Origin of Inequality." In *The Social Contract and Discourses,* pp. 176–282. New York: E. P. Dutton, 1950 (1754).

Rubin, Edgar. *Visuell wahrgenommene Figuren*. Copenhagen: Gyldendal, 1921 (1915).

Rubinstein, Amnon. *To Be a Free People*. (In Hebrew.) Tel-Aviv: Schocken, 1977.

Rushdie, Salman. "A Pen Against the Sword: In Good Faith." *Newsweek,* Feb. 12, 1990, pp. 52–57

Sahlins, Marshall. *Culture and Practical Reason*. Chicago: University of Chicago Press, 1976.

Sambursky, S. *The Physical World of the Greeks*. New York: Macmillan, 1956.

Sartre, Jean-Paul. *Existential Psychoanalysis*. Chicago: Henry Regnery, 1966 (1943).

Saussure, Ferdinand de. *Course in General Linguistics*. New York: Philosophical Library, 1959 (1915).

Scarlett, W. George, and Dennie Wolf. "When It's Only Make-Believe: The Construction of a Boundary between Fantasy and Reality in Storytelling." *New Directions for Child Development* 6 (1979):29–40.

Schaefer-Simmern, Henry. *The Unfolding of Artistic Activity*. Berkeley: University of California Press, 1961 (1948).

Schapiro, Meyer. "On Some Problems in the Semiotics of Visual Art: Field and Vehicle in Image-Signs." *Semiotica* 1 (1969):223–42.

Schattschneider, Doris. *Visions of Symmetry*. New York: W. H. Freeman, 1990.

Schechner, Richard. *Environmental Theater*. New York: Hawthorn, 1973.

———. *Between Theater and Anthropology*. Philadelphia: University of Pennsylvania Press, 1985.

Schegloff, Emanuel A., and Harvey Sacks. "Opening Up Closings." *Semiotica* 8 (1973):289–327.

Schilder, Paul. *The Image and Appearance of the Human Body*. New York: International Universities Press, 1950 (1935).

Schmidt, Catherine J. "Tourism: Sacred Sites, Secular Seers." Ph.D. diss., State University of New York at Stony Brook, 1984.

Schneider, David M. "American Kin Terms and Terms for Kinsmen: A Critique of Goodenough's Componential Analysis of Yankee Kinship Terminology." In Stephen A. Tyler, ed., *Cognitive Anthropology*, pp. 288–311. New York: Holt, Rinehart and Winston, 1969 (1965).

———. *American Kinship*. 2nd ed. Chicago: University of Chicago Press, 1980.

Scholem, Gershom. *The Messianic Idea in Judaism*. New York: Schocken, 1971.

Schultz, Sam. *Make Me Laugh Again*. Los Angeles: Price/Stern/Sloan, 1984.

Schutz, Alfred. "On Multiple Realities." *Collected Papers,* vol. 1, pp. 207–59. The Hague: Martinus Nijhoff, 1973 (1945).

———. "Making Music Together: A Study in Social Relationship." *Social Research* 18 (1951):76–97.

Schutz, Alfred, and Thomas Luckmann. *The Structures of the Life-World*. Evanston, Ill.: Northwestern University Press, 1973.

Schwartz, Barry. "The Social Psychology of Privacy." *American Journal of Sociology* 78 (1968):741–52.

————. *Vertical Classification*. Chicago: University of Chicago Press, 1981.

Schwartz, Hillel. *Century's End*. New York: Doubleday, 1990.

Schweitzer, Albert. *Indian Thought and Its Development*. Boston: Beacon, 1957 (1936).

Scully, Vincent. *Modern Architecture*. Rev. ed. New York: George Braziller, 1974 (1961).

Searles, Harold F. *The Nonhuman Environment*. New York: International Universities Press, 1960.

————. *Collected Papers on Schizophrenia and Related Subjects*. New York: International Universities Press, 1965.

Segal, Samuel M. *The Sabbath Book*. New York: Thomas Yoseloff, 1957.

Seligman, Paul. *The Apeiron of Anaximander*. London: Athlone Press, 1962.

Sennett, Richard. *The Uses of Disorder*. New York: Vintage, 1971.

Shell, Marc. "The Family Pet." *Representations* 15 (1986):121–53.

Shepard, Paul. *Thinking Animals*. New York: Viking, 1978.

Shepard, Roger N. "The Analysis of Proximities: Multidimensional Scaling with an Unknown Distance Function." *Psychometrika* 27 (1962):125–40, 219–46.

————. "Representation of Structure in Similarity Data: Problems and Prospects." *Psychometrika* 39 (1974):373–421.

Shepard, Roger N., and Phipps Arabie. "Additive Clustering: Representation of Similarities as Combinations of Discrete Overlapping Properties." *Psychological Review* 86 (1979): 87–123.

Sherman, Richard C., et al. "Movement and Structure as Determinants of Spatial Representation." *Journal of Nonverbal Behavior* 4 (1979):27–39.

Shuman, Sandra G. *Source Imagery*. New York: Doubleday, 1989.

Silverman, Carol. "Pollution and Power: Gypsy Women in America." In Matt T. Salo, ed., *The American Kalderaš*, pp. 55–70. Hackettstown, N.J.: Gypsy Lore Society North American Chapter Publications, 1981.

Silverman, Lloyd, et al. *The Search for Oneness*. New York: International Universities Press, 1982.

Simmel, Georg. "Quantitative Aspects of the Group." In Kurt H. Wolff, ed., *The Sociology of Georg Simmel*, pp. 87–177. New York: Free Press, 1950 (1908).

————. "The Secret and the Secret Society." In *The Sociology of Georg Simmel*, pp. 307–76. (1908).

————. "The Stranger." In *The Sociology of Georg Simmel*, pp. 402–8. (1908).

————. "Conflict." In *Conflict and the Web of Group Affiliations*, pp. 13–123. New York: Free Press, 1964 (1908).

————. "The Web of Group Affiliations." In *Conflict and the Web of Group Affiliations*, pp. 127–95. (1908).

————. "Brücke und Tür." In *Brücke und Tür*, pp. 1–7. Stuttgart: K. F. Koehler, 1957 (1909).

————. "The Adventure." In Kurt H. Wolff, ed., *Georg Simmel, 1858–1918*, pp. 243–58. Columbus: Ohio State University Press, 1959 (1911).

————. "The Handle." In *Georg Simmel, 1858–1918,* pp. 267–75. (1911).

————. "Sociability: An Example of Pure, or Formal Sociology." In *The Sociology of Georg Simmel,* pp. 40–57. (1917).

Simpson, George G. *Principles of Animal Taxonomy.* New York: Columbia University Press, 1961.

Singer, June. *Androgyny.* Garden City, N.Y.: Anchor, 1976.

Singer, Peter. *Animal Liberation.* New York: Discus, 1977.

————. *The Expanding Circle.* New York: Farrar, Straus & Giroux, 1981.

Sitte, Camillo. *The Art of Building Cities.* New York: Reinhold, 1945 (1889).

Smith, Barbara H. *Poetic Closure.* Chicago: University of Chicago Press, 1968.

Smith, Edward E., and Douglas L. Medin, *Categories and Concepts.* Cambridge: Harvard University Press, 1981.

Sneath, Peter H. A., and Robert R. Sokal. *Numerical Taxonomy.* San Francisco: W. H. Freeman, 1973.

Snow, C. P. *The Two Cultures and A Second Look.* London: Cambridge University Press, 1969 (1959).

Snyder, Louis L. ed. *Hitler's Third Reich.* Chicago: Nelson-Hall, 1981.

Sokal, Robert R. "Classification: Purposes, Principles, Progress, Prospects." *Science* 185 (1974):1115–23.

————. "Clustering and Classification: Background and Current Directions." In J. Van Ryzin, ed., *Classification and Clustering,* pp. 1–15. New York: Academic Press, 1977.

Sollors, Werner. *Beyond Ethnicity.* New York: Oxford University Press, 1986.

Sommer, Robert. *Personal Space.* Englewood Cliffs, N.J.: Prentice-Hall, 1969.

Sorabji, Richard. *Time, Creation, and the Continuum.* Ithaca: Cornell University Press, 1983.

Sorokin, Pitirim A. *Social and Cultural Mobility.* New York: Free Press, 1964 (1927).

————. *Sociocultural Causality, Space, Time.* New York: Russell & Russell, 1964 (1943).

Spender, Dale. *Man Made Language.* London: Routledge & Kegan Paul, 1980.

Spengler, Oswald. *The Decline of the West.* New York: Alfred A. Knopf, 1926.

Spiro, Rand J., et al. "Cognitive Flexibility and Transfer in Complex Content Domains." In Bruce K. Britton and Shawn M. Glynn, eds., *Executive Control Processes in Reading,* pp. 177–99. Hillsdale, N.J.: Lawrence Erlbaum Associates, 1987.

————. "Cognitive Flexibility Theory: Advanced Knowledge Acquisition in Ill-Structured Domains." In *Program of the Tenth Annual Conference of the Cognitive Science Society,* pp. 375–83. Hillsdale, N.J.: Lawrence Erlbaum Associates, 1988.

Springer, Sally P., and George Deutsch. *Left Brain, Right Brain.* Rev. ed. New York: W. H. Freeman, 1985.

Stack, Carol B. *All Our Kin.* New York: Harper & Row, 1974.

Stallybrass, Peter, and Allon White. *The Politics and Poetics of Transgression.* Ithaca: Cornell University Press, 1986.

Starr, Paul. "Social Categories and Claims in the Liberal State." In Mary Douglas, ed., *How Classification Works.* Edinburgh: Edinburgh University Press, forthcoming.

Stein, Howard F. *Developmental Time, Cultural Space.* Norman: University of Oklahoma Press, 1987.

Steiner, Frances H. *French Iron Architecture.* Ann Arbor: UMI Research Press, 1984.

Stephenson, Gilbert T. *Race Distinctions in American Law.* New York: D. Appleton, 1910.

Stevenson, Mrs. Sinclair. *The Heart of Jainism.* London: Humphrey Milford, 1915.

Stewart, Susan. *Nonsense.* Baltimore: Johns Hopkins University Press, 1979.

———. *On Longing.* Baltimore: Johns Hopkins University Press, 1984.

Stone, Christopher D. *Should Trees Have Standing?* Los Altos, Calif.: William Kaufmann, 1974.

Stonequist, Everett V. *The Marginal Man.* New York: Charles Scribner's Sons, 1937.

Sumner, William G. *Folkways.* New York: New American Library, 1960 (1906).

Sutherland, Anne. *Gypsies.* London: Tavistock, 1975.

Suttles, Gerald D. *The Social Order of the Slum.* Chicago: University of Chicago Press, 1968.

Tagore, Rabindranath. *The Home and the World.* London: Macmillan, 1971 (1919).

Tajfel, Henri. *Human Groups and Social Categories.* Cambridge, England: Cambridge University Press, 1981.

Tambiah, Stanley J. "Animals Are Good to Think and Good to Prohibit." *Ethnology* 8 (1969):423–59.

Tausk, Victor. "On the Origin of the 'Influencing Machine' in Schizophrenia." In Robert Fliess, ed., *The Psychoanalytic Reader,* vol. 1, pp. 52–85. New York: International Universities Press, 1948 (1919).

Tedlock, Dennis. *Finding the Center.* New York: Dial Press, 1972.

Teodorsson, Sven-Tage. *Anaxagoras' Theory of Matter.* Goteborg, Sweden: Acta Universitatis Gothoburgensis, 1982.

Tertullian. "On the Soul." In *The Fathers of the Church,* vol. 10, pp. 165–309. Washington, D.C.: Catholic University of American Press, 1950.

Theweleit, Klaus. *Male Fantasies.* Minneapolis: University of Minnesota Press, 1987 (1977).

Thomas, Keith. *Man and the Natural World.* New York: Pantheon, 1983.

Thompson, Jane. "The Ability of Children of Different Grade Levels to Generalize on Sorting Tests." *Journal of Psychology* 11 (1941):119–26.

Thompson, Michael. *Rubbish Theory.* Oxford: Oxford University Press, 1979.

Thorndyke, Perry W. "Distance Estimation from Cognitive Maps." *Cognitive Psychology* 13 (1981):526–50.

Torgerson, Warren S. *Theory and Methods of Scaling.* New York: John Wiley, 1958.

———. "Multidimensional Scaling of Similarity" *Psychometrika* 30 (1965):379–93.

Trumbo, Dalton. *Johnny Got His Gun.* New York: Bantam, 1970 (1939).

Trumbull, H. Clay. *The Threshold Covenant.* New York: Charles Scribner's Sons, 1906.

Tryon, Robert C. *Identification of Social Areas by Cluster Analysis.* Berkeley: University of California Press (University of California Publications in Psychology series, vol. 8, pp. 1–99), 1955.

Tuan, Yi-Fu. *Segmented Worlds and Self.* Minneapolis: University of Minnesota Press, 1982.

Tulku, Tarthang. *Time, Space, and Knowledge.* Berkeley: Dharma, 1977.

Turner, Roy. "Some Formal Properties of Therapy Talk." In David Sudnow, ed., *Studies in Social Interaction,* pp. 367–96. New York: Free Press, 1972.

Turner, Terence S. "Transformation, Hierarchy and Transcendence: A Reformulation of Van Gennep's Model of the Structure of Rites of Passage."In Sally F. Moore and Barbara G. Myerhoff, eds., *Secular Ritual,* pp. 53–70. Amsterdam: Van Gorcum, 1977.

Turner, Victor. "Betwixt and Between: The Liminal Period in *Rites de Passage.*" In *The Forest of Symbols,* pp. 93–111. Ithaca: Cornell University Press, 1970 (1964).

———. *The Ritual Process.* Harmondsworth, England: Penguin, 1974 (1969).

———. "Passages, Margins, and Poverty: Religious Symbols of Communitas." In *Dramas, Fields, and Metaphors,* pp. 231–71. Ithaca: Cornell University Press, 1975 (1972).

———. "Pilgrimages as Social Processes." In *Dramas, Fields, and Metaphors,* pp. 166–230. (1973).

———. "Metaphors of Anti-Structure in Religious Culture." In *Dramas, Fields, and Metaphors,* pp. 272–99. (1974).

———. "Variations on a Theme of Liminality." In Sally F. Moore and Barbara G. Myerhoff, eds., *Secular Ritual,* pp. 36–52. Amsterdam: Van Gorcum, 1977.

Tversky, Amos. "Features of Similarity." *Psychological Review* 84 (1977):327–52.

Uspensky, Boris. *A Poetics of Composition.* Berkeley: University of California Press, 1973.

Van Gennep, Arnold. *The Rites of Passage.* Chicago: University of Chicago Press, 1960 (1908).

Veblen, Thorstein. *The Theory of the Leisure Class.* New York: Macmillan, 1899.

Vinitzky-Seroussi, Vered. "Classification of Special Days and Specific People." Paper presented at the annual meeting of the Midwest Modern Language Association, Kansas City, November 1990.

Von Senden, M. *Space and Sight.* London: Methuen, 1960 (1932).

Von Wiese, Leopold, and Howard Becker. *Systematic Sociology.* New York: John Wiley, 1932.

Wallace, Anthony F., and John Atkins. "The Meaning of Kinship Terms." *American Anthropologist* 62 (1960):58–80.

Wallis, Roy, ed. *On the Margins of Science.* Keele: University of Keele (Sociological Review Monograph No. 27), 1979.

Warren, Richard M. "Illusory Changes of Distinct Speech upon Repetition: The Verbal Transformation Effect." *British Journal of Psychology* 52 (1961):249–58.

Washburne, Heluiz C. *Land of the Good Shadows.* New York: John Day, 1940.

Watts, Alan. *The Book.* New York: Vintage, 1972 (1966).

Weber, Max. *Economy and Society.* Berkeley: University of California Press, 1978 (1925).

Weiner, Joan. "The Philosopher Behind the Last Logicist." In Crispin Wright, ed., *Frege—Tradition and Influence,* pp. 57–79. Oxford: Basil Blackwell, 1984.

Weitman, Sasha R. "Intimacies: Notes toward a Theory of Social Inclusion and Exclusion." *Archives Européennes de Sociologie* 11 (1970):348–67.

Werner, Heinz. *Comparative Psychology of Mental Development.* Rev. ed. New York: International Universities Press, 1957 (1940).

Wertheimer, Max. "Untersuchungen zur Lehre von der Gestalt." *Psycholo. Forsch.* 4 (1923):301–50.

White, Leslie A. *The Science of Culture.* New York: Farrar, Straus & Giroux, 1949.

Whorf, Benjamin L. "Science and Linguistics." In *Language, Thought, and Reality,* pp. 207–19. Cambridge: MIT Press, 1956 (1940).

———. "Language, Mind, and Reality." In *Language, Thought, and Reality,* pp. 246–70. (1942).

Wilber, Ken. *No Boundary.* Boston: New Science Library, 1981 (1979).

Wilden, Anthony. *System and Structure.* London: Tavistock, 1972.

———. *The Rules Are No Game.* London: Routledge & Kegan Paul, 1987.

Willeford, William. *The Fool and His Scepter.* Evanston, Ill.: Northwestern University Press, 1969.

Williams, Richard. *Hierarchical Structures and Social Value.* Cambridge, England: Cambridge University Press, 1990.

Williamson, Joel. *New People.* New York: Free Press, 1980.

Willmott, W. E. "The Flexibility of Eskimo Social Organization." In Victor F. Valentine and Frank G. Vallee, eds., *Eskimo of the Canadian Arctic,* pp. 149–59. Toronto: McClelland and Stewart, 1968 (1960).

Wilson, Edward O. *Biophilia.* Cambridge: Harvard University Press, 1984.

Winnicott, D. W. "Transitional Objects and Transitional Phenomena." In *Playing and Reality,* pp. 1–25. London: Tavistock, 1971 (1953).

———. "The Location of Cultural Experience." In *Playing and Reality,* pp. 95–103. (1967).

Witherspoon, Gary. *Language and Art in the Navajo Universe.* Ann Arbor: University of Michigan Press, 1977.

Witkin, Herman A. "Psychological Differentiation and Forms of Pathology." *Journal of Abnormal Psychology* 70 (1965):317–36.

Witkin, Herman A., et al. *Psychological Differentiation*. Potomac, Md.: Lawrence Erlbaum Associates, 1974 (1962).

Wittgenstein, Ludwig, *Philosophical Investigations*. 3rd ed. New York: Macmillan, 1958 (1953).

Woods, Gerald, et al., eds. *Art Without Boundaries*. New York: Praeger, 1974 (1972).

Woolf, Virginia. *A Room of One's Own*. San Diego: Harcourt Brace Jovanovich, 1957 (1929).

World Sports International Athletics Annual—1966. London: World Sports, 1966.

Wright, Frank L. *The Natural House*. New York: Horizon, 1954.

Wright, Lawrence. *Clockwork Man*. London: Elek, 1968.

Yoshida, Tetsuro. *The Japanese House and Garden*. New York: Frederick A. Praeger, 1955.

Zadeh, Lotfi A. "Fuzzy Sets." *Information and Control* 8 (1965):338–53.

———. "A Fuzzy-Set-Theoretic Interpretation of Linguistic Hedges." *Journal of Cybernetics* 2 (1972), No. 3:4–34.

Zelizer, Viviana A. *Pricing the Priceless Child*. New York: Basic Books, 1985.

Zerubavel, Eviatar. *Patterns of Time in Hospital Life*. Chicago: University of Chicago Press, 1979.

———. *Hidden Rhythms*. Chicago: University of Chicago Press, 1981.

———. "Easter and Passover: On Calendars and Group Identity." *American Sociological Review* 47 (1982):284–89.

———. "Personal Information and Social Life." *Symbolic Interaction* 5 (1982), no. 1:97–109.

———. "The Standardization of Time: A Sociohistorical Perspective." *American Journal of Sociology* 88 (1982):1–23.

———. *The Seven-Day Circle*. New York: Free Press, 1985.

———. "The Language of Time: Toward a Semiotics of Temporality." *Sociological Quarterly* 28 (1987):343–56.

Zerubavel, Yael. "The Last Stand: On the Transformation of Symbols in Modern Israeli Culture." Ph.D. diss., University of Pennsylvania, 1980.

———. "Collective Memory and Historical Metaphors: Masada and the Holocaust as National Israeli Symbols." Paper presented at the meetings of the Association for Jewish Studies, Boston, December 1987.

Zucker, Luise J. *Ego Structure in Paranoid Schizophrenia*. Springfield, Ill.: Charles C. Thomas, 1958.

———. "Evaluating Psychopathology of the Self." *Annals of the New York Academy of Sciences* 96 (1962):844–52.

Zucker, Paul. *Town and Square*. New York: Columbia University Press, 1959.

Zussman, Robert. *Intensive Care*. Chicago: University of Chicago Press, forthcoming.

Author Index

Subject Index

199